T0371186

WHY WE'RE GETTING POORER

WHY WE'RE GETTING POORER

A REALIST'S GUIDE TO THE ECONOMY AND HOW WE CAN FIX IT

CAHAL MORAN

WILLIAM
COLLINS

William Collins
An imprint of HarperCollins*Publishers*
1 London Bridge Street
London SE1 9GF

WilliamCollinsBooks.com

HarperCollins*Publishers*
Macken House,
39/40 Mayor Street Upper,
Dublin 1, D01 C9W8, Ireland

First published in Great Britain in 2025 by William Collins

1

A catalogue record for this book is available from the British Library

ISBN 978–0–00–863795–8 (Hardback)
ISBN 978–0–00–863796–5 (Trade paperback)

Typeset in 11.8/17pt Sabon LT Pro by Jouve (UK), Milton Keynes

Printed and bound in Great Britain by CPI Group (UK) Ltd, Croydon

This book contains FSC™ certified paper and other controlled
sources to ensure responsible forest management.

For more information visit: www.harpercollins.co.uk/green

For Chaya

CONTENTS

INTRODUCTION

A GOOD TIME TO STUDY ECONOMICS

The course of my adult life has been defined by economic crisis. The 2007–9 global financial crisis hit just as I first began studying economics at high school. My economics tutor at the time commented that the recession was horrible, but the silver lining was that it was 'a good time to study economics'. Unfortunately for everyone, the subsequent decade and a half has proved to be a very good time to study economics. That recession was the largest in 70 years at the time, and saw massive spikes in unemployment, declines in living standards and the shutting down of countless businesses, including my stepfather's. Many people across the globe found their access to basic necessities like food threatened. But even those difficult events would seem mild compared to what was to come.

THE END OF HISTORY?

Since the 1990s, the prevailing mentality has been one of the 'end of history'. The Cold War had ended and with it Western, capitalist, liberal democratic countries had triumphed over Communism. It was believed that this template would be the aspiration, at least, for all countries, and hoped that it would be their eventual destination. Throughout the 1990s and 2000s, the UK and others seemed to be doing well with a 'third way': capitalist, but with a safety net to protect against the system's harsh edges. Growing up in the 2000s, I was always aware that things weren't perfect but believed we could work it out gradually rather than throwing it all out and starting again. In some cases, countries escaping poverty would just be a matter of time as growth took hold and they joined the ranks of the wealthy nations. A rising tide lifts all boats.

However, the crisis had exposed deep-seated problems with the economy that were temporarily hidden by an unsustainable boom. Throughout the 2000s, banks in the USA and the UK had lent mortgages to people who could not pay them back, inflating a bubble in house prices in the process. While this alone may well have led to recession and hardship, it was magnified by the complex web of financial instruments across the world that banks had created based on these mortgages. In simple terms, these were effectively bets on the repayment capacity of homeowners, often gambled on many such mortgages at once. When the bubble burst, the ripples were felt throughout the financial system, as this web of obligations proved impossible to make sense of and large financial institutions felt the rug pulled out from under them. Famously, Lehman Brothers was allowed to go bankrupt early on in the crisis, which proved so catastrophic that the only feasible option was funnelling public money into the banks to keep them afloat.

Following the financial crisis, many governments across the Western world pursued austerity policies, hoping to balance the government budget. This was a case of misdiagnosis and misdirection: the crisis had led to the collapse of tax revenues and rise in unemployment benefits that accompanies any recession, which explained the budget imbalance. In the UK, a solid recovery was on the way and borrowing was actually falling before the cuts to spending began in 2010. Besides, austerity did not even achieve its stated aim of balancing the budget: it was promised that we'd be in the black by 2015, but as that year rolled around, we were still borrowing 4.4 per cent of GDP.[1] In 2010, the Chancellor George Osborne urged us to 'fix the roof while the sun was shining', but his cuts to schools resulted not only in stunted growth among schoolchildren[2] but also led to the collapse of an actual roof in a school in Kent.[3] The effects of austerity are still being felt as the UK seems to be stuck in a 'doom loop', where poor economic performance means there is less money to go around, which in turn means more cuts to public services.[4]

The Eurozone experienced its own sovereign debt crisis at around the same time: the now defunct acronym PIGS referred to the southern countries Portugal, Italy, Greece and Spain, all of whom were experiencing low growth and high debt. Owing to economic imbalances across the continent, sharing one currency gave these countries little room to manoeuvre following the 2007–9 crash. The Euro was like a straitjacket, stopping each country from pursuing its own policies. It was therefore deemed that austerity measures even harsher than those in the UK were necessary. The result was a gutting of public services, falls in living standards and riots in Greece. When they eviscerated their social safety net, their debt promptly rose rather than fell, contrary to expectations.[5] Athens literally had to burn to prove that austerity was both tragic and ineffective. The authorities eventually admitted that these measures weren't working, so more flexibility was warranted. Though some of the PIGS – most notably Spain – have been doing much better recently, the effects of the Eurozone crisis will last for decades.[6]

These catastrophes were compounded by the fact that many towns and cities in the West had experienced relative decline since the 'golden age' of 1945–73, as industry disappeared over the 1980s and local economies flatlined. Wrexham in the UK suffered from the disappearance of its coal mines; Detroit in the USA suffered from the dwindling of its famous car industry; the North of France saw its garment manufacturing industry moved elsewhere. This problem was not confined to the rich world, either: the entire country of Brazil moved away from exporting industrial machinery and towards exporting commodities like iron and oil. India saw its main growth in precarious forms of employment: low-paid service-sector jobs, epitomised by the pedicabs that transport tourists through Delhi.[7] While these trends were counterbalanced by notable growth elsewhere, epitomised especially by the rise of China, they made a big impact in other places as opportunity dried up and communities struggled.

In 2016, the communities that had been left behind made their voices heard. In the UK we voted to leave the EU, the biggest trading bloc in the world; in the USA they voted in Donald Trump, who promised to put America first; two years later Brazilians voted in Jair Bolsonaro (the 'tropical Trump'). Countries across Europe felt similar jitters, with Hungary's Victor Orban having been elected in 2010 and the far-right continuing to rise across Europe to this day, including in stereotypically progressive countries such as Sweden and the Netherlands.[8] In 2024, the UK and France moved to the left, but the far right remain a considerable presence in both countries.

These shifts in the political landscape – which usually came as shocks to their respective metropolitan elites – were, in my view, the political fallout of failed economies. Although each case has its individual complexities, all are noticeable for signalling a move away from globalisation to prioritise people in the home nation. At the time of writing, the past two US presidents have been Joe Biden and Donald Trump. Despite their obvious differences, both have actively pursued policies that put America first, not least of which are tariffs on goods from China.[9] It seems that the old era of globalisation and free trade has passed.

The decline of the old industrial hubs was merely one face of rising inequality. Peter Mandelson of New Labour stated in 1998 that he was 'intensely relaxed about people getting filthy rich as long as they pay their taxes'. The number of billionaires in the world increased twenty-fold between 1987 and 2024, with their total wealth increasing forty-fold, from $295 billion to $14.2 trillion. This wealth allowed a select few to dominate our economy: Elon Musk, the (at the time) richest man in the world, was able to purchase the globe's most important social media platform, seemingly on a whim, and run it according to his own interest and beliefs. This stood in stark contrast to the many people of my generation who may never be able to afford a home. Inequality has had visible effects on our world that are clear to anyone who has been paying attention – including Mandelson himself, who has since repented.[10]

The uncomfortable truth is that inequality and poverty have been persistent features of the world since I was born: by any reasonable measure, most of the world is living in poverty. Only a handful of countries, most of them in Southeast Asia, have truly managed to attain the status of 'rich' over the past few decades. Many Latin American countries, though they have experienced some overall growth, seem trapped at a middling stage of economic development and still contain a solid proportion of the world's poverty. Despite some progress, countries in Sub-Saharan Africa like Rwanda still struggle with widespread malnutrition. Like most, I had learned to see this poverty as a harsh but unchangeable backdrop of existence. I now see it as an active failure of our global economy.

The convulsions of the 2007–9 crisis, the failed response to them and the political reaction to these problems are what began to shake me out of my complacency. Events showed that there were deep-seated issues that had been temporarily hidden by steady economic growth and a narrative of triumphalism in the West. Was the stability I had experienced just a temporary calm in the storm that is the global economy? Were others – both across the globe and in my own country – struggling while the rich world's middle class celebrated their prosperity? Perhaps if the response to the global financial crisis had shifted us towards preventing future crises while making the present-day economy work for everyone, I'd have continued to believe in the narrative of progress. As it stood, it seemed we were doubling down on failed ideas.

PERPETUAL CRISIS

The English historian G. M. Young once said that to understand a person, you have to look at what was happening in the world when they were twenty. So many transformative events have occurred in my life that I feel like I'm perpetually twenty. The early experience of the financial crisis pushed me to study economics at university, where I met like-minded students who had experienced the same thing. We formed a student group called the Post-Crash Economics Society (PCES), which openly wondered why we were not taught anything about the crash that had shaped our lives. We produced a report into the state of our education at the University of Manchester in 2014, charging that our degree was too focused on abstract mathematical theory, detached from the real world and failing to equip students with the critical thinking skills they rightly expected from a university education.[11]

Outside the classroom, my curiosity had led me to numerous authors who laid the blame for the crisis not just (reasonably) at the feet of bankers, but at the feet of economists themselves.[12] This blame was partially overstated but partially earned, given the know-it-all public face that the discipline of economics liked to project. Books like the bestselling *Freakonomics* had argued that economics could reveal 'the hidden side of everything', applying economists' ideas to crime, schools and racism. Apparently, economics was a great set of tools that had 'a serious shortage of interesting questions', presumably having answered the important questions within its domain.[13] In a telling twist of fate, *Freakonomics* was released in 2006. It contained not so much as a whiff of what was going on in the financial sector just as it was about to blow up. The hidden side of everything indeed.

Despite (or maybe because of) my complaints, I decided to stay at Manchester to pursue a career in economics. Following in the footsteps of the authors I admired, we turned the PCES report into a book, released in 2016. *The Econocracy* investigated the curricula at multiple universities, arguing that the state of economics education mattered to everyone. We inhabited a society that was obsessed with the economy and how it was doing, with discussions about economic success occupying a central role in political debate. More than this, ideas from the economics discipline itself were influential as economic experts occupied powerful positions. Events like 2007–9 could, to an extent, be traced back to the same ideas we were taught about how the economy could be managed.

Much has changed since then, not least that the economics profession has had a bit of a reckoning with its shortcomings. But the sad truth is that students around the world still feel let down by their education. In 2024, PCES Manchester released a report to mark the ten-year anniversary of our original one, a move that I'm convinced was intended to make me feel old. The report found that not enough had changed: still overly abstract, still overly narrow, still omitting the many crises we face.[14] One purpose of this book is to offer a realistic and grounded explainer of economics for these students, the type I wish I'd had all those years ago. After all, explaining our ailing economy is a perpetual challenge – an ongoing joke that emerged at the post-crash society was 'which crash?'.

THE WORST IS YET TO COME

It's easy to forget that the news cycle at the start of 2020 was consumed by talk of massive wildfires in Australia, which have repeated across the world every year since. As average global temperatures have risen, deaths related to heat mortality have been increasing across the world. As the global climate shifts and lurches, extreme weather events are becoming more common: floods, hurricanes and extreme temperatures in both directions look to be the likely outcome. As sea levels rise, countless coastal cities will experience flooding, and many Pacific islands may disappear altogether. Humanity will struggle with food production, disease, massive migration and even warfare. Naturally, this will all result in huge economic costs, impeding growth and disrupting livelihoods across the world.[15]

When Covid-19 swept across the globe in 2020, the virus was new and mysterious, but it was clearly contagious and could also be deadly. In the absence of vaccines or even a real understanding of the coronavirus, the world went into unprecedented lockdowns, shutting off half of its economies and ordering residents to stay indoors for months. Approximately 93 per cent of global workers were living in countries that implemented lockdowns.[16] This all meant huge restrictions on our freedom, a death toll reaching into the millions, untold fear and anxiety and trillions of dollars of lost economic output. The effects of the pandemic were magnified for the countries with lax social safety nets, the most sizable of these being India,[17] while North Africa and the Middle East had begun to experience an unprecedented rise in poverty even before the pandemic.[18]

Once the world came out of lockdown, owing to both the widespread availability of vaccines and a growing sense of political impatience, some thought we might be headed for a roaring return, not unlike the 'Roaring 20s' which followed the 1918 Spanish Flu. Yet turning our irredeemably complex global economy off and on again created more issues than anticipated, with supply chains seizing up and bottlenecks emerging across the globe. As with the votes for Trump and Brexit, this had revealed deep-seated problems with how we had chosen to organise our global economy. These bottlenecks in how our goods are produced and shipped had been hidden for years because things had seemed to be working, but the fault lines were exposed once subjected to a serious test. In a narrative that was starting to become familiar, the workers who we had depended upon to keep these systems running had not been given their due.

In hindsight, I can see that ideas about the end of history always required rose-tinted glasses. Another formative moment for me was the 2003 invasion of Iraq, which was deeply unpopular at the time and is now widely regarded as a failure. Today, Russia's invasion of Ukraine in 2022 has reminded people in the West that our world is not one of peace and harmony. To see this as the return of war itself would be a biased view: Syria, the Congo and Myanmar are among the countries who have experienced severe and protracted conflict over the past few decades. Nevertheless, the renewed potential for wars between great powers, including nuclear fallout, is a harrowing thought that has been buttressed by the continued escalation of the 'New Cold War' between the USA and China. The further invasion of Gaza by Israel, which threatens to escalate tensions in the Middle East and beyond, has only added to this sense of dread.

War disrupts ideas of prosperity beyond the immediate and sizable harms done by the conflicts themselves. Given that the global economy has relied so much on stability in the regions surrounding Russia and China, the implications of these conflicts will be felt far and wide. Europe has suffered from the sanctions on Russia, as supplies of the oil and gas we had depended on for so long dried up. Energy prices increased several times in some cases, buttressing the so-called cost-of-living crisis. Ukraine is also a major grower of wheat, and grain prices increased too – with the harshest impact on the nearby Middle East and Northern Africa.[19] Even when it does not disrupt our material standard of living, war forces us to ask questions about what such prosperity depends on. For example, the war in the Congo is vicious, having killed millions and displaced more, but the country still provides us with the raw minerals for iPhones.[20] We might ask why it makes fewer headlines than the others.

It's easy to see each crisis as self-contained and, like an engineer, to adopt a problem-solving mentality. One thing I've learned is that these things are usually linked – for example, climate change and inequality are far from separate issues. It is a sad historical injustice that the countries who are historically responsible for the most emissions will tend to lose out the least from climate change. Meanwhile, the poorest countries, who do not and have not emitted a large proportion of greenhouse gases, will suffer the most.[21] Even within individual countries, the richest emit far more than the poorest.[22] Luxury yachts, private flights, exotic goods, multiple homes and generally higher levels of consumption are just some of the ways the rich are more responsible for emissions than the poor. Any solution to climate change must by necessity tackle inequality for this reason alone.

The threats I've just detailed are so many that they might seem to be cause for despair: financial crisis, political crisis, pandemics, inequality, inflation, war, climate change. My point is not to make you despair. It is to be frank about these problems, to understand them better and hopefully to solve them. There are also many positive things about the world we live in: progress has been made in global poverty, health and education. Infant mortality had been high throughout human history; today, most parents around the globe can reasonably expect their children to make it past childhood.[23] In the end, change is always multifaceted and complex and it is up to us to scrutinise this complexity in the hope of retaining the good while vanquishing the bad. This requires realism, rather than either optimism or pessimism.

WHY WE'RE GETTING POORER

What exactly do I mean by 'getting poorer'? The answer is that across the global economy, people are much poorer than they *could* be and than they reasonably *should* be. Time and time again, the perverse dynamics of the global economy have led to situations where there is 'money on the table': situations that could be improved drastically if our economy were better designed. Over my lifetime, I've become curious about uncovering flaws in the way our economies are designed and how these have a material, negative impact on the everyday citizen. Throughout this book, I want to show you how our uneven and dysfunctional global economy has made the average person worse off for no justifiable reason. Many people are feeling the pinch: as life seems to get harder rather than easier, long-held expectations about progress are dashed and people start to question whether the dominant economic indicators matter any more.[24]

Our economy is *uneven* because there are massive inequalities between people which manifest in numerous, harmful ways. Many of our most essential workers are not properly valued when compared to those who perform functions that we know in our bones are not as important. We allow our economy to be dominated by wealthy individuals and huge corporations, despite the negative impact this has on the rest of us. People face countless economic barriers due to factors outside of their control, such as class, race and gender. Finally, across the global economy most people remain in poverty and we have not done enough to address this. All the problems with the uneven economy can be tackled by reining in the rich and powerful while boosting the poor and disadvantaged, though there is room for reasonable disagreement about how exactly to do this.

As well as uneven, our economy is *dysfunctional*. The housing market barely seems to be working for anybody, creating unacceptable living conditions for so many of our fellow citizens. Our money system is not well understood and this lack of transparency has resulted in poor policy choices. We do not have the correct systems in place to anticipate and manage massive inflation, as the cost-of-living crisis of 2023–24 taught us so dearly. Finally, our global trade system is brittle, stretched and underpinned by exploitation, making it prone to breakdown. These issues affect us all and as such the solutions are more specific than redistribution of money and power. They promise to benefit everyone, rich and poor alike.

An illustrative example of how we are getting poorer comes from the pursuit of austerity in my own country. Since the pandemic, the UK has seen a record number of people with long-term sickness as many have dropped out of the labour force. This means they are no longer looking for jobs, so technically they no longer even count as unemployed. There are now two and a half million of these long-term sick individuals, or 1 for every 13 workers.[25] This has been chalked up to various causes, such as mental health, long Covid and back pain from working at home. Regardless of the causes, what many of these conditions share is that they require medical treatment, and our health system has not been equipped to deliver it.

Investment in healthcare has obvious positive benefits for those receiving it directly: it can help people with serious illnesses; it can help people with mild illnesses; and it can provide everyone with the assurance that they will get help if they need it. Beyond these goals, healthcare illustrates a crucial truth that

I want you to keep in mind through this book, which is that the economy and human aims are not opposed. Too often, 'economics' is synonymous with 'tough love' and 'making difficult choices', as if what is good for the economy cannot be good for the people. For instance, in 2017 Dominic Raab, then the UK First Secretary of State, responded to a woman who criticised cuts to disabled benefits by saying: 'I can think of lots of things that I would like to avoid making difficult decisions on and lots of areas like the health service or schools that I want to put even more money in. But unless you've got a strong economy creating the revenue, it's just a childish wishlist.'[26]

The truth is that cutting spending on health and schools amounts to shooting oneself in the foot economically, while unnecessarily making the lives of sick people and children much worse in the process. One report found that ill health was costing the UK population around £2,200 in annual earnings because of leaving jobs, working fewer hours and health costs.[27] For context, this is around 7 per cent of average income in the UK, a pay rise that is nothing to be sniffed at. Even if your aim is having a 'strong economy creating the revenue', in Raab's terminology, low income and unemployment mean more spent on benefits and less taken in taxes as people languish in either poorly paid jobs or no jobs at all.

Skimping on health can also amplify costs down the line: you fail to treat an infection, then end up having a limb removed. Evidence shows that as preventative care has been cut in the UK, spending on crisis care has risen. Spending actively to reduce smoking and alcoholism, promote safe sex and increase breast-feeding tends to reduce the healthcare people need in the long term, and according to the World Health Organization (WHO), spending more on mental health, too, should return the investment fourfold over time.[28] Yet because of underfunding, doctors and nurses are stuck removing metaphorical limbs down the line. This is why every £200 million in cuts to NHS spending ends up costing £1 billion later on.[29]

These realities are not confined to rich countries like the UK. Rwanda, for example, suffered from one of the worst genocides in recorded history in 1994, with one million people losing their lives. The long-term consequences of this included a spread of sexually transmitted infections (STIs) from widespread rape during the war, as well as an outbreak of deadly diseases such as cholera. Following this tragedy, Rwanda decided to invest heavily in healthcare, with the prevalence of deadly diseases like HIV dropping dramatically while the economy also boomed, and they paid off their public debt.[30] Even – or perhaps especially – in unimaginably horrible circumstances, investing in basic human needs is the best path forward.

REIMAGINING THE ECONOMY

Wrongheaded ideas about economics have been costing us dearly for far too long. Owing partially to ideas within the discipline and buoyed by political actors, there is a widespread perception that hard times are inevitable. In 2023, Bank of England economist Huw Pill claimed that Britons need to 'accept they are poorer'.[31] Since I first became interested in economics, my aim has been to pull the rug out from under these arguments. In many cases, you can trace their roots to ideas and theories that just don't stand up to scrutiny. The overarching question I want to ask in this book is whether the present structure of the economy enables people not just to survive, but to thrive.

There are some who would regard this question as nonsense: according to them the economy just *is*, as it were, and what happens, happens. Economics is often defined as the study of 'the allocation of scarce resources', implying that there is little we can do about this inherent scarcity, at least in the short term. The economy itself, then, is just the generalisation of countless individual decisions given their resources, so messing with those decisions means messing with reality, which never ends well.[32] Although this is an extreme view, pessimism about our ability to improve the economy significantly is widespread. Plenty may broadly agree with my aims and would like to see some changes, such as commonsense reforms to education, health and housing. Nevertheless, they are also reluctant to rock the boat too much, lest we endanger the material gains made by the world over the past few hundred years.

Both of these opinions – pushing either non-interference or mild interference into the economy – are equally mistaken and frankly verge on mysticism. A thorough investigation of how the economy works reveals a complex web of practices, laws and powerful institutions which shape it in deliberate and changeable ways. Reifying these existing institutions as natural or inevitable is indefensible. We can understand how they are constructed and learn how to change them. Myriad examples throughout history illustrate the kinds of economic transformations that can be achieved that improve people's lives without posing significant danger to the undoubted merits of our existing society. There is no better way to begin to understand this than to look at how the economy itself emerged.

PART I

THE UNEVEN ECONOMY

CHAPTER 1

WHO IS ESSENTIAL TO THE ECONOMY?

How Wealth is Created and to Whom it Goes

'All right, I will buy it.
It will be good for the economy.'
Marge Simpson

Today, we have become used to thinking of 'the economy' as a separate sphere. We hear about the economy on the news: it may be growing, shrinking, booming, busting, stagnating or sick. There is a sense that the economy is autonomous – for better or for worse, it runs according to its own logic. When we hear that the economy is doing poorly, we understand that it affects us personally: we may lose our jobs, house prices may rise just out of reach, or public services may face cuts. We search for someone to blame when things go wrong, but ultimately the day-to-day movements and machinations of the economy remain inexplicable to most people. In fact, they are inexplicable even to most experts, who still aren't entirely sure what causes recessions – and much less how to stop them. The modern economy is not only separate, it is complex and mysterious, and how exactly income is apportioned between people is hard to understand. If people often yearn for a simpler time, perhaps it's because back then it was much easier to pinpoint who was ripping you off.

Thinking about the economy this way is historically unprecedented. Most settled civilisations did not believe there was a separate economic sphere. What is more, from the earliest Middle Eastern civilisations to the might of Imperial Rome, your economic fortune was openly and hopelessly intertwined with your political status: whoever was explicitly in charge would get the lion's share, while those below them had to fork it over. In the modern world we may still have a sense that someone, somewhere, is taking advantage of us, but it's not always obvious who that person is. In the past, it was plain for all to see.

A PRE-HISTORY OF 'THE ECONOMY'

'Some work with their minds, others with their bodies. Those who work with their minds rule, while those who work with their bodies are ruled. Those who are ruled produce foods; those who rule are fed.'

Ancient Chinese Saying[1]

Under Feudalism in Europe, the lord of the manor possessed a great deal of explicit power over his serfs. The serfs would work hard on the fields to produce food, generally grain, then be compelled to part ways with some of it. Lords were of high social status, they had authority over what happened on their land and they were licensed to take grain from the peasants. Were the peasants to refuse, the lord typically had his own armies and enforcement mechanisms to extract the grain himself. He might even have his own courts and trials. There was basically no distinction between being a boss, being a ruler and being wealthy. The lords did them all at once.[2]

Something similar could be said for the emperors, kings and sultans of ancient empires, who sat at the top of their respective civilisations. By virtue of their authority, grain and other goods – including exotic luxuries from around the world – flowed to them. Those who toiled on the fields, who travelled far and wide to trade, or who threaded garments produced everything used by the rulers. These rulers enjoyed a high standard of living because they were entitled to a share of the produce from their lands, whether through taxes or through direct appropriation. A clear ruling class maintained its position through force and standing armies. Ideas such as religious beliefs and the 'divine right of kings' also worked to justify their authority in the minds of the masses.[3]

This dynamic was not limited to those at the top extracting money from those at the bottom. In ancient times, professions such as writers, clerics and rulers could pursue activities not immediately related to survival full-time.[4] They would be funded, effectively, by the work of those who were below them in the pecking order. Although they may not have enjoyed quite the status or lavish lifestyles of the rulers, they were still better off, more independent and didn't have to get their hands dirty. For thousands of years, civilisation meant a large number of impoverished farmers producing for their own needs but also producing for a privileged minority of the population. This necessarily entailed the former being forced to hand over some of what they produced to the latter.

It's not that every worker other than the farmers was unnecessary. As settled agriculture spread around the globe – estimated to be approximately 10,000 years ago – this entailed the production of massive quantities of wheat, rice or barley, depending on where you were in the world. Writing and accounting were invented precisely to keep track of this grain so it could be produced, stored and distributed to the population. The resultant information and logistics were indispensable for keeping the economy functioning. Yet the ocean of bureaucrats, clerics and rulers could surely have stopped working much more readily than those directly producing the food, without the same catastrophic results. The most important workers at this time were always the farmers providing the crucial food that everyone else directly depended upon.

A standout feature of the old world is that it was relatively transparent in its exploitation of the most important members of society. Those who were not engaged in agriculture, as well as other essential work, were able to live off the produce of those who were, by taking that produce directly from them. In other words, early civilisations saw a transparent divide between how essential people were and how those same people were compensated and socially valued. Those who were the furthest from the farms and from the wars often enjoyed the most lavish lifestyles. Although force and ideology ensured the power of the rulers, it was plain to see that they were extracting the basics from the rest of society. Economic and political authority were one and the same, but this would all change with the emergence of the economy.

THE RISE OF THE ECONOMY

In Guy Ritchie's 2024 series *The Gentlemen,* wealthy American drug dealer Stanley Johnston states that he loves the British aristocracy because 'they're the original gangsters. The reason they own 75 per cent of this country is because they stole it'. This dates back to the invasion of William the Conqueror in the eleventh century, after which England became more unified than most other European countries. Norman rule concentrated ownership so that relatively few lords had all the land, a feature of the country that still persists today – seemingly in line with William's intentions. In addition, he began to separate economic and political power: the lords relied on the monarchy to enforce the rules instead of doing it themselves.

Now, you may be thinking that the political idiosyncrasies of one small country, 500 years ago, are unimportant, but over the long term these dynamics would give birth to what we now call capitalism.[5] When envisioning the emergence of capitalism, most people imagine smoky nineteenth-century factories as a symbol of the Industrial Revolution in Britain. While these factories marked a significant shift in the nature of the economy, historian Ellen Meiksins Wood has argued that capitalism began centuries earlier, in the English countryside. Owing to the legacy of the Normans, the centralised government would protect the lords' property, but unlike other feudal lords in Europe they couldn't just wade onto the land and demand extra grain payments one year. As of the sixteenth century, lords were increasingly realising that their incentive was to increase the productivity of the land instead. The unusually large plots of land also seemed to further incentivise this, since landlords could experiment and benefit from economies of scale.[6]

Owing to the strange features of the relationship between English landlords and peasants, something akin to a modern landlord-tenant relationship developed. Just like ordinary home-renters today, tenants would rent out the land at market value, and if the market value of the land increased, the landlord could charge more. As land became increasingly bought and sold tenants themselves also needed to become more productive to sell greater quantities of food so they could afford the rent. Much like a job today, peasants began to rely on their income from the market to survive. In this sense, the landlords' and the tenants' interests seemed to coincide, both of them aligning to push higher agricultural productivity, higher incomes and higher rents.[7]

To understand this better, contrast it with French feudalism at around the same time, which retained the older system: many smaller lords who each took grain from the peasants themselves. Peasants owned the land, they did not lease it, so they didn't have to worry about becoming more productive to afford rent – they could always grow their own food, knowing that the land would never be sold. What they did worry about was the lord who, if he desired more grain, would unilaterally up the required payment. In contrast, if the English landlords wanted more grain, they'd pressure tenants to be more productive so they could raise the rent over time, but they were not licensed by the central government to squeeze them directly as French landlords were. In other words, French landlords made a profit by upping their overt exploitation of their peasants; English landlords made a profit by upping the productivity of their tenants.[8]

In case the English experience of increasing productivity coupled with less exploitative lords sounds rosy compared to elsewhere, we must remind ourselves that it was anything but. As land was increasingly up for sale, many peasants began to find themselves, for the first time, completely landless. They would roam the roadsides searching for some kind, any kind, of work that would earn them the money to get by.[9] In the worst cases, direct efforts by the authorities forbade the kind of self-sufficient production most peasants across the world were engaged in. The famous enclosures sometimes seized land directly from peasants so that it could be used to turn a profit. The Black Acts of 1722 imposed excoriating penalties for poaching game, further reducing the ability of people to subsist without earning, buying and selling in the economy.[10] It was therefore our most basic need, food, which was the first to be subjected to the whims of the market.

THE RISE OF MARKETS

The term 'market' conjures up images of people buying and selling in physical locations such as a farmers' market, an auction of old antiques, or the stock market. These physical locations are easy to understand as places where people trade things with one another. Nowadays, though, 'the market' has come to mean something much broader: almost any time when a buyer and a seller interact. Market relationships extend to every facet of our lives: we buy food, clothing, shelter, jewellery, holidays, cars and much more. We rely on markets to get the income we need, to buy the things we need, which we in turn purchase through other markets. The term 'market' is really synonymous with the term 'economy' and whenever markets have spread, the idea of the economy has not been far behind.

Broadly speaking, markets have existed for as long as civilisation, but they have changed significantly in scale and scope in the modern world. Earlier civilisations had street markets where people would barter and haggle for the things they wanted, epitomised by the Arabic street markets which date back long before the turn of the first millennium. Early civilisations also featured trade between nations, epitomised by Marco Polo's famous thirteenth-century trip across Asia for silks and spices. The Mongolian Empire through which he travelled has actually been marked out as one of the first eras of globalisation, enabling mass trade within its borders.[11] Anthropologist David Graeber has detailed that even hunter-gatherer tribes traded with each other, though this trading was usually direct barter without money. It was also infrequent and marked by celebration, sex and violence – sometimes all at the same time.[12]

Over time, the process set in motion in the English countryside culminated in the emergence of what Polish historian Karl Polanyi called 'the market economy'.[13] Polanyi highlighted what he saw as three fundamental changes from earlier varieties of trade which gave rise to the new market economy: the buying and selling of land, labour and money. Previously, none of these three things were traded on any notable scale. Land was largely inherited: the lord would not dream of selling his land, which was a symbol of his status and wealth, but would instead pass it down to his heirs. Peasants themselves would likely be tied to one lord and therefore one land for generations. Yet as market value took over as a measure of the value of land, it was increasingly not only acceptable but necessary to sell land on the open market.

As peasants (and even lords) were increasingly dispossessed by land changing hands, they began to seek employment in something resembling a modern job. No longer able to subsist by growing their own food, they were now dependent on markets for income. What Polanyi called a 'market for labour' began to develop, with people being paid to work so that they could afford what they needed to survive. The idea of much of the population being compelled to sell their labour was actually quite novel: working for wages was previously rare, confined to temporary arrangements like master–apprentice relationships. Think of a blacksmith: the apprentice would work for a wage when young to accrue the skills needed to become a blacksmith once they were older. Over a period of centuries, working for wages gradually moved from the exception to the rule for most of the population for most of their lives, and it remains so today.[14]

Polanyi's other crucial commodity, money, naturally rose in prominence at the same time as land and labour because it was the only way of facilitating such exchanges. Being paid at one time and place, then being able to use that same payment to buy something completely different, at some unknown point in the future, required a consistent token which kept its value. Money had been used in earlier markets, but it was nowhere near as widespread. With the rise of the market economy, money has become a universal 'measuring stick', used to value commodities from food to fashion, and it continues to reach new corners of our lives today. For example, one recent development is that with the rise of working from home, you can pay for a new subscription service that puts you in a meeting with others who are also working to make you more productive. Markets are now so embedded that people are not just working hard to get paid; they are paying to work harder.[15]

The exact date, place and causes of the emergence of the market economy are still debated, as are its merits and drawbacks. One thing is for sure, though: once it started, there really was no stopping it. This was the point at which the economy emerged as a separate sphere with its own rules. Ancient civilisations saw great wonders, including the Pyramids and great cities such as Athens, but despite some key technological developments, their standard of living remained roughly the same throughout their history. The Roman Empire lasted for a thousand years, but the technologies and incomes its citizens enjoyed near the beginning were not dissimilar to those they enjoyed just before its downfall. As the modern economy took off, it changed everything, producing a massive increase in material living standards for the average person but also massive convulsions and considerable hardship for many.

With the emergence of the capitalist economy, it also became much harder to pinpoint exactly who was being exploited. People depended on farmers for food in Ancient Rome and they depend on them for food today. However, the market economy adds a layer of complexity compared to the past. Farmers now produce food to sell, while we work in our own jobs to be able to afford it. Unlike the French peasant and their lord there is no direct, forcible extraction of resources from ruled to ruler. After all, if we work enough to be able to afford the food, are we really exploiting the farmers any more than they are exploiting us? To understand this complexity, we have to move from thinking about simple stores of grain to thinking about the wealth of the economy as a whole.

THE CREATION OF WEALTH

When economists ask how wealth is created in a modern economy, the go-to answer is that it is some combination of labour, capital (machines and raw materials), plus an elusive unknown entity that could be summarised as 'knowledge'. Think about baking a cake: you need yourself (labour), the ingredients and cooking equipment (capital) and the recipe or know-how (knowledge). 'Labour' and 'capital' are relatively easy to grasp because we can see them. On the other hand, the 'knowledge' part is always a little mysterious, which is why your grandma's cake always tastes better than yours. In statistical breakdowns it is generally found that labour, capital and knowledge each contribute a roughly equal amount to economic growth.[16]

Delving into each of these categories is a good way to unravel contentious debates that have animated economists for centuries. As early as the fourteenth century, the Arabic scholar Ibn Khaldun noted that 'what is obtained through the co-operation of a group of human beings satisfies the need of a number many times greater than themselves'.[17] The basic insight was that of specialisation: by splitting up a task into different components, people could produce more than they could if they had worked separately, carrying out every part of the job alone. As Khaldun argued, no-one alone can grow and harvest all the wheat that they need, but several people – some ploughing the soil, others harvesting, others making tools – could collectively produce far and above what they needed. Khaldun therefore recognised early on the importance of the 'labour' part of our equation for wealth creation.

In the eighteenth century, the Scottish economist Adam Smith presented a similar, albeit refined version of Khaldun's insights about specialisation. Observing the emergence of industrial capitalism in Britain, Smith argued that there were several reasons why what he called 'the division of labour' was so effective.[18] The first was learning by doing: workers would become more adept at a specific task if they were doing it over and over again.

Anyone who can compare their first shift pulling pints at a bar to how they do it a year later will understand this (though if you're as bad at it as I was, you weren't called back after the first shift). Smith's second reason was the difficulty of switching tasks: even if workers were adept at multiple tasks, going from pulling pints to delivering the barrels to doing the books to cleaning to managing the bar would be a massive burden compared to splitting up at least some of those tasks.

The third factor, the presence of the equipment that enabled the division of labour, has proved the most important. This brings us to the 'capital' part of our equation for wealth creation. What exactly is meant by 'capital' is another controversial topic in economics, but for now, it is fine just to think of it as stuff: tools and equipment, raw materials, machines and buildings, and the like. Several pioneering inventions – new types of capital – were made during the eighteenth-century early industrial period, which transformed how workers worked, increasing their productivity massively. For example, in 1765 the Spinning Jenny allowed spinners to work eight spindles at a time, each spindle spinning its own length of unspun cotton into thread – and the number of spindles only increased later on.[19] Having workers with the access and ability to operate these machines on a permanent basis meant previously unimaginable productivity gains and a corresponding massive increase in the wealth available to humanity. The fact that the Jenny allowed workers to sit down probably didn't hurt, either.

As England went from farm to factory, capital became increasingly important. The industrialists who owned the capital would employ workers to produce commodities to sell on the market. For instance, the cotton industrialists would pay people to produce cloth for sale in Britain and beyond. They could pocket the difference between the cloth sales and the costs they had to pay, including the wages, equipment like the Spinning Jenny, the factory itself, rent for the land and the cotton or wool used up in the process. If this difference was positive, then they'd made a profit. Many industrialists became increasingly rich off the back of this process and landlords (many of them former feudal lords) were able to make money from renting the land – all while labourers often endured dangerous, mind-numbingly repetitive and poorly paid work.

The famous economist Karl Marx made one of the most important observations about what made capitalism, well, capitalism. He pointed to the fact that industrialists tended to reinvest their profits to expand their operations and make even more money down the line. Marx called this the M-C-M' circuit, where M was the initial amount of money invested in the business, C was the commodities produced for sale, and M' was a (hopefully) larger amount of money than M, which was made from selling the commodities.[20] In many ways, M-C-M' is just a fancy way of describing making a profit, but the idea of making a profit, then continually reinvesting that to make more, is a historically unique phenomenon. The relentless expansion created by capitalists and the M-C-M' circuit is one thing that sets the market economy apart from previous eras. It put what had previously been roughly stagnant material standards of living on an upward trajectory as they began to increase relentlessly, year on year.

These early economists were asking what exactly led to the massive increase in wealth stimulated by the market economy. Both Smith and Marx came to the same, natural conclusion (albeit 150 years apart): it was the workers. Just like the peasants of old, they were the ones toiling day after day to produce the goods everyone else relied upon. When Marx's collaborator Friedrich Engels visited Manchester in the UK in the nineteenth century, he was so appalled that he made the comparison himself in *The Condition of the Working Class*. It seemed that the industrial capitalists, who often did nothing more than own the factories, were making out like bandits from their clear exploitation of the workers:[21]

> In truth, the [peasants] were not human beings; they were merely toiling machines in the service of the few aristocrats who had guided history down to that time. The industrial revolution has simply carried this out to its logical end by making the workers machines pure and simple, taking from them the last trace of independent activity, and so forcing them to think and demand a position worthy of men.

The question of where (or who) wealth comes from has generated endless debates in economics. Marx, Smith and Engels thought it was the workers; critics charged that capitalists can create wealth, too.[22] It is clear even from Marx's M–C–M' circuit that capitalists serve a purpose, which is one of effecting economic development. As Marx and Engels put it, the capitalist class 'accomplished wonders far surpassing Egyptian pyramids, Roman aqueducts, and Gothic cathedrals'.[23] It also dismantled old hierarchies: the central storyline of *The Gentlemen* shows the landed upper class being forced to adapt to the market economy and make their land productive, albeit through nefarious means. Similar pressures befall the characters of *Downton Abbey* and *Bridgerton*, respectively set 100 and 200 years earlier than *The Gentlemen*, who are also forced to stop sitting on their substantial estates in order to keep things running.

At the same time, it *can* seem like capitalists are parasitic, sucking out the wealth created by everyone else like a gigantic vacuum at the top of the economy. When passive investment funds like Blackrock and Vanguard seem to cream money off the rest of the economy and send it to private shareholders, people fairly get suspicious. The question is then whether the income accruing to the capitalist class is necessary if we are to sustain and expand these wonders. Are those who earn a lot of money necessary engines of investment and wealth creation, or are they extracting their wealth from the rest of us?

THE INBETWEENERS THEORY OF EXPLOITATION

In the British comedy *The Inbetweeners,* teenager Simon is arguing with his friend Jay about who should organise a party. Simon calls Jay out:

'I've known you for ten years, and I've never seen you organise a party.'

'Bollocks. What about my birthday party last year?' says Jay.

'Your mum organised that.'

'Yeah. Under my supervision.'

You can probably count on one hand the number of people in the world who watched this scene and ended up thinking about income distribution in a capitalist economy. For me, Jay's comment captures something that we can all appreciate about the role of supervisors, bosses and owners, which is that they often take credit for things they didn't do. This credit could just be kudos; or they could use it as a justification for getting other roles, as does Jay; or it could amount to the income or wealth they get in their role as 'supervisor'. While Jay's status existed only in his head, modern economies grant explicit privileges to a select few, to the extent that we can reasonably charge that they are extracting money from everyone else.

The clearest way to demonstrate this is through the example of land. Land was not produced by anybody: depending on your predispositions, you could call it a gift from God or one from Mother Nature. Humans need land to live, to farm and to engage in whatever occupation or pursuit they wish to – pirates and spaceships aside, it is literally impossible to do anything without existing on land. Back when the economy was still agricultural, the prevailing idea was that value came from the land itself. And despite playing no role in producing the land they own, landlords cordoned off parts of the world and determined who could reside on them, including how much those people would have to pay for the privilege. As the philosopher Jean-Jacques Rousseau put it in 1755:[24]

> The first person who, having enclosed a plot of land, took it into his head to say this is mine and found people simple enough to believe him was the true founder of civil society. What crimes, wars, murders, what miseries and horrors would the human race have been spared, had someone pulled up the stakes or filled in the ditch and cried out to his fellow men: 'Do not listen to this imposter. You are lost if you forget that the fruits of the earth belong to all and the earth to nobody!'

From Ancient times to feudal lords to modern capitalism, ownership of land has been a key to securing income and power. Economists throughout history have agreed on this unique feature of land, with Adam Smith remarking that 'landlords . . . love to reap what they never sowed'.[25] Smith's successor David Ricardo also highlighted the problems created by landlords, who (Ricardo predicted) would demand increasing rents, squeezing both the workers and the industrial capitalists.[26] Henry George, who wrote in the late nineteenth century, thought that land ownership was the crucial problem with capitalism, which, if unaddressed, would see the poor placed in continual poverty.[27] In other words, landlords are the equivalent of Jay from *The Inbetweeners*: claiming credit for 'supervision' while doing nothing.

As the economy evolved from one that was dominated by landed aristocrats to one that was dominated by industry, the game changed. Many landlords are still powerful and wealthy, but these days land is far from the only thing that is marked by strong legal protections to secure income for its owners. Legal scholar Katharina Pistor has documented that the creation of capitalism first entailed legally defining and protecting what counted as 'capital'. In a telling historical evolution, the laws that previously applied to land have been readily transferred to ownership of factories, offices and these days even to financial assets and ideas. It's easy to see the unfolding of capitalism and the market economy that we outlined earlier as natural and inevitable, but it was a product of quite deliberate decisions.[28]

Maybe capital isn't just 'stuff' – maybe it's also the laws and rules we create that give people control over that stuff. This may sound abstract, but, to illustrate it in everyday terms, Pistor uses the example of a freelancer who realises that they can now classify themselves as a corporation. By becoming an owner of a corporation, they receive their income in the form of dividends instead of wages. They are now a shareholder in their one-person business which means that, in most countries, they become subject to lower taxes.[29] The actual work the freelancer is doing has not changed at all: they will still be taking photos, writing books or making YouTube videos. Yet their legal classification and therefore the amount of income flowing to them has changed completely. Being a capitalist often confers new privileges upon it, and this is not the only one.

Sometimes the privileges granted to capitalists can be more subtle. Adam Smith's division of labour is one reason that humans learned to produce more, accompanied by a number of path-breaking technological innovations like the Spinning Jenny. But in some cases, specialisation may have benefited capitalists rather than the population as a whole. Like Khaldun before him, Smith tended to assume that the division of labour was pursued for reasons of technical efficiency. People somehow realised that through specialisation they could produce more output with fewer inputs, and this specialisation resulted in greater skills and new technologies. People would gradually coalesce into companies where they all had different roles because this would benefit them individually: they'd be producing more, so they'd get paid more. According to this argument, specialisation would have the happy side-effect of benefiting the rest of us by generating wealth.

In a famous paper entitled 'What Do Bosses Do?', American economist Stephen Marglin took issue with Adam Smith's account of the division of labour because it missed the role of the capitalist in organisation. Marglin pointed out that there were many examples where the methods used in independent cottage industries were at least as productive as the methods used in early factories. For this reason, early capitalism was filled with all sorts of legal restrictions on production that pushed workers into factories, including restrictions on how many looms could be held in a home. Rather than increasing efficiency, capitalist firms aimed to increase the total work done by labourers and therefore total profits. As capitalists had ownership of what was produced and could sell it in ever-expanding markets, they were able to reinvest their profits and expand production further.[30]

In other words, it was the control over the production process and over large numbers of workers that characterised capitalism, rather than just increased technical efficiency. Nor did the privileges end there. As capitalism changed, the nature of companies changed and in the nineteenth century limited liability laws became more widespread, which put restrictions on how much lenders could claim back should a business fail. It may seem strange now, but previously a failing capitalist might have their home repossessed and even found themselves in a debtor's prison. Nowadays, Pistor's freelancer-turned-corporation will likely experience the reverse fortune: they will be better able to borrow due to their newfound status as a company, with more access to credit and with new legal protections against creditors knocking down their door.[31]

Economist Ha-Joon Chang has noted the historical irony that Karl Marx, the great critic of capitalism, was in favour of limited liability laws, which he saw as 'capitalist production in its highest development'. There is no doubt that protecting capitalists from serious downsides meant that they were more willing to invest and take on risk, which fuelled the engine of wealth creation. On the other hand, Adam Smith, who is often cited as one of capitalism's greatest admirers, was against limited liability because he felt that managers would take too many risks, gambling with other people's money.[32] You can't help but feel there is a truth to this, too, as many modern corporations like Goldman Sachs have been reckless at times under the assurance of limited liability and other protections.

The truth is that the original limited liability corporation was a vehicle for actively dispossessing people across the world and extracting wealth from them. The English and Dutch East India companies were some of the first major limited liability companies and their privileges were granted directly by the crown. Colonialism was itself pioneered by these private companies in the early days, licensed by the governments of their home countries. These companies took control of land in countries like Indonesia and India and repurposed economies to produce largely for their benefit. They made locals work in conditions that, even when they weren't outright slavery, certainly approached it.[33] The host countries generally experienced economic declines and humanitarian tragedies over the colonial period.[34]

Greek economist and former politician Yanis Varoufakis has drawn a direct parallel between these older forms of wealth extraction and modern computing companies. He argues that ownership over the 'cloud' conferred upon companies like Amazon means that, much like the landlords of old, everyone has to pay fealties to them to participate. If you want to sell your product these days then you generally need an online presence; if you need an online presence you must generally use Google, Amazon and social media sites; if you use them you have to agree to their terms and pay them fees.[35] As with land, the ownership of a resource that everyone has to use means that the owner of that resource has power to extract wealth and to determine how the rest of the economy is structured.

The point is not to draw a moral equivalence between slavery, feudal landlords, colonialism and modern forms of ownership under capitalism. As Pistor herself states, 'the legal coding of capital is an ingenious process without which the world would have never attained the level of wealth that exists today; yet the process itself has been largely hidden from view'. It is this exact fact that the rules of the game are hidden that leads to a 'fish don't know they're wet' situation. We are all so used to these rules that we don't see how historically unique they are. We think capital is just 'stuff' when it's actually much more.

Economist Suresh Naidu has highlighted that modern economies are filled with innumerable, jealously guarded legal protections: how we define ownership of companies; of housing and land; intellectual property like copyright and patents; financial assets; and countless rules that tilt the economic playing-field in favour of certain groups. In contrast, there are plenty of arrangements that tend to reduce the claims that more wealthy individuals have on our economic output. Examples most people will recognise are labour unions, state control over industry, and progressive taxes.[36] This flexibility in who gets what and why, is a key lesson that I want you to keep in mind throughout this book. It naturally raises the question: can we do it better?

HARRY MAGUIRE AND THE MARKET ECONOMY

In late 2022, Ghanian MP Isaac Adongo was not particularly happy with his country's economic performance. In a speech in parliament, he singled out the country's vice-president at the time, Mahamudu Bawumia, who had also been deputy governor of the Ghanaian central bank. Africa is known for its rich history of oral storytelling, and in typical style Adongo took a creative argumentative turn: he compared Bawumia to English footballer Harry Maguire. If you do not know much about football, then know that Maguire is so prone to defensive calamity that he is labelled with the mantra 'respected by his opponents, feared by his teammates'. Adongo charged that 'if the opponents failed to score, Maguire would score for them', and called Bawumia the country's 'economic Maguire'.[37]

Football (or soccer, if you must) is one of the best ways of illustrating how pay can get out of whack with performance. It is obvious to anyone paying attention that top footballers' pay has increased at a remarkable rate over the past few decades, as have the fees that clubs pay to acquire them. When I was growing up, the world record price for a footballer was made in 2001 when Real Madrid paid an astonishing £47 million for legend Zinedine Zidane. This record was broken eight years later when Manchester United paid £80 million for the almost as legendary Cristiano Ronaldo; then Madrid broke the record again in 2013, buying the not quite as legendary Gareth Bale for £86 million. Since then, things seem to have gone haywire: the current record holder is Neymar, who went to Paris Saint-Germain (PSG) for almost £200 million in 2017. We now regularly see transfers over £100 million and it's only a matter of time before Neymar's record is broken. Maguire himself broke the world record for a defender when he went from Leicester City to Manchester United for £80 million in 2019.

Has this huge increase in transfer fees, not to mention the accompanying salaries paid to the footballers, been accompanied by a rise in quality? Nobody can dispute that players like Neymar, Ronaldo and especially Lionel Messi – who actually went to PSG on a *free* transfer in 2021, though he was still paid £1 million a week while there – are incredible athletes. It is also difficult to compare quality because different players have different strengths and weaknesses, play in different positions and compete in different teams or leagues. This difficulty is multiplied when players are playing in different eras, since the game has changed so much since I was young. It's hard to know exactly how someone like Zidane would fit into today's game – he'd still be amazing, no doubt, but would he slot easily into a team like Manchester City? Nevertheless, the fact that Zidane, a player who is widely regarded as one of the all-time greats, went for £33 million less than Harry Maguire, may be illustrative of a mismatch between skill and pay.*

A watershed moment for money in the football market was when Russian oligarch Roman Abramovic purchased UK football club Chelsea FC in 2003. As a billionaire, Abramovic was able to plough enormous sums into the club, attracting both players and managers. This took Chelsea from a pretty good side who had never consistently competed for the top spot, to a team which has since repeatedly won the Premier League and every other competition to boot. In the process Chelsea have spent money frivolously, which has netted them some great players but also – and increasingly in recent years – plenty of Maguire-esque duds. In the top transfer fees of all time, Chelsea are joint top with Real Madrid. Each of them have seven out of the top fifty and each have spent roughly £530 million, or £75 million per player, on these seven. Are any of Chelsea's seven £75 million players really better than the £47-million Zidane?[38]

We can contrast the situation in countries like the UK, Spain and Italy with football in Germany, who have pursued a

---

* Maguire has improved recently and Adongo even issued an apology to him, saying that he was now a 'key player' for Manchester United.

different model. German football is internationally recognised
as top quality and their national team are regularly serious con-
tenders for the World Cup and European Championships. The
German League, the Bundesliga, has produced top talents and
remains one of the best leagues in the world, even if it's not
quite up there with the English or Spanish leagues. Germany
also stands out in the top transfer market – by not standing
out. They have one player who has appeared in the top fifty
transfers of all time. This is the same number of players as
Wales, Hungary or Algeria, none of which are usually considered top footballing countries.

Why is German football so different? Because German clubs
are not owned by billionaires, but by fans. In Germany, the clubs
abide by the so-called '50+1 Rule', where the fans have to own at
least 50 per cent of the shares in the club, plus one, giving them a
majority stake. In 2016, the CEO of Borussia Dortmund stated
that 'the German spectator traditionally has close ties with his
club. And if he gets the feeling that he's no longer regarded as a
fan but instead as a customer, we'll have a problem.'[39] This has
reoriented the priorities towards the fans, the club and the communities instead of ever-escalating pay for superstars (not that
the top German players still don't earn quite a bit, mind).

This philosophy could not be more different from the one in
the English Premier League. The Bundesliga boasts the lowest
ticket prices and highest attendances in the world, with a positive and lively fan culture (albeit cult-like at times).[40] In contrast,
Premier League ticket prices have grown out of reach for the
working-class communities who have traditionally supported
their clubs, with more and more space going to expensive facilities, middle-class ticket holders and executive boxes. Attendance
is down and the culture has waned with it. While the Premier

League is one of the best in the world, it illustrates the uncomfortable trade-off of the market economy: success along one dimension, for one group, often comes at a cost to other things and other groups.

What German football illustrates is that there are different ways of organising the industries that matter to us. We can all see that teams in the Bundesliga and in other European leagues play the same game at comparable levels of quality. But in one of these cases, the clubs are owned by people who prioritise throwing money at the best players, charging as much as they can for tickets and neglecting the communities that built the clubs. In the other case, the majority fan ownership ensures a completely different philosophy which nurtures players and rewards fans, resulting in a much better atmosphere – and still boasting excellent football.

WHY THE GERMANS DO IT BETTER

You may be wondering if this detour through modern football is just a random example that has little bearing on the rest of the economy, but I picked it for a reason: the German economy generally illustrates how things can be different. Germany is a case study in how we can reconfigure the way our economy works to benefit more of the population, without endangering the wealth creation process. The country has achieved remarkable growth since World War II and today it is the fourth largest economy in the world, boasting high levels of income, low hours worked, low unemployment and fewer low-wage workers when compared to the USA. Observers often puzzle over Germany's ability to 'do it better' and many countries would like to emulate it.[41]

Germany has a world-famous manufacturing sector boasting household names such as VW, Siemens and BMW. Many
of these industries are spread across the country, providing reliable employment for the entire population and driving the
economy. German businesses acknowledge their social obligations and are unwilling to step on workers or local communities.
One business owner speaks of 'stomach cramps' and being
labelled a 'coward' when he is asked if he would ever sell up
and cash out.[42] Although Germany's manufacturing sector has
regularly been buffeted by global slowdowns, including at the
time of writing, companies still do everything they can to retain
workers over the long term. Workers are in turn willing to
make short-term sacrifices such as shorter hours or pay freezes
to weather the storm. There is a pact between workers, owners
and the country as a whole.

Along with other countries in Northern Europe, German
businesses are known for their generally labour-friendly atmos-
pheres and cooperation between businesses and unions.
Companies are required to have workers' councils who participate in day-to-day decision making around things like pay and
management of the firm. Workers are guaranteed representation on corporate boards in the biggest companies, so they
regularly participate in major decisions. You can contrast this
with companies in the UK or USA, where shareholders make
the vast majority of decisions and workers do not have a direct
say. More of German national income goes to workers than
most other countries and inequality is low by international
standards.[43]

As with labour, Germany has quite a different approach to
its financial sector. Most banks are local rather than mega-
corporations like Goldman Sachs and many of these are owned

by the customers themselves. This is the so-called 'credit cooperative' model of banking and it relies on maintaining longstanding relationships with communities, which facilitates lending to businesses and to households. Exactly zero credit cooperatives *in the world* required bailing out during the 2007–9 financial crisis and their lending is much less volatile than 'normal' banks, making them a more reliable engine of growth. Their presence has been associated with reduced regional inequality, a feature of Germany which the citizens of the geographically unequal UK and USA may look upon with envy.[44] While disparities and resentments between the East and West exist, the country has done remarkably well at balancing its regional economy considering its seismic reunification is still in living memory for many people.

Of course, Germany has its fair share of problems. Although Germans are internationally regarded as punctual, their patchy train system does not reflect that (not that it's worse than my own country's). As in countries across the world, inequality has risen as insecure employment has become a pressing concern. There is some evidence that Germany's labour-friendly policies are being eroded over time, and even in previous years its minority representation of workers on boards was criticised for being too little, with shareholders and management able to override the decisions of workers through their majority stake.[45] Finally, the generally commendable banking system didn't stop major German banks like Deutsche Bank from being significant players in the global financial crisis.[46]

Nevertheless, the successes of the German model are a clear illustration of how we can change the way things work instead of considering the outcomes of existing market economies as natural or inevitable. While we may celebrate both the material progress of capitalism and the fact that its most brutal forms seem to be behind us, we face the pressing question of whether we can continue to improve the human condition while maintaining a high material standard of living. Hopefully, the example of Germany has persuaded you that the answer to this question is an unequivocal 'yes'. Too often, we lack creativity and imagination when it comes to the economy. We come to accept the current arrangements, with all their pain and absurdity. The Germans' own unwillingness to rest on their laurels in this way – themselves eager to point out their country's problems – is likely one reason the country perseveres.[47]

If economic arrangements are malleable, we can return to the question of who really counts and whether they are rewarded as such under current arrangements. In ancient civilisations, farmers and adjacent occupations seemed to form the crucial foundation of the economy, producing the things everyone else depended upon. When ancient kings and feudal lords directly took a portion of grain from peasants in exchange for very little, it was difficult to see it as anything other than exploitation. These were almost mafia-esque protection rackets, with commonfolk squeezed in exchange for some degree of security. But our modern economy seems much more complex than that – can we pinpoint who everyone else depends upon?

WHO REALLY MAKES AN ECONOMY?

During the coronavirus pandemic in the UK, people would get together every Thursday night at 8 p.m. and 'clap for the NHS'. This was meant to signal our appreciation for the doctors and nurses who were working exhausting shifts to fight Covid-19, back when it was still an unknown quantity. The workers at the NHS would brave the contagious and deadly virus, often dangerously underequipped and overworked, to save those who were suffering from it. The clapping was eventually extended to care workers, who were in a similar situation, as well as to signal our appreciation for all so-called essential workers across the country.

The term 'essential worker' has become a bit of an obsession for me. For decades, we have had to endure questionable arguments about what and who is most vital to our economy. The most widespread of these treats each person's economic standing as a simple outcome of how much they contribute to society. According to this logic, those who earn more deserve it: the fact that they're paid that much is itself evidence that they are worth it. You could call it the 'just desserts' view of income distribution. In 2009, the CEO of Goldman Sachs, Lloyd Blankfein, channelled this view when he responded to accusations that his employees were overpaid:[48]

I often hear references to higher compensation at Goldman. What people fail to mention is that the net income generated per head is a multiple of our peer average. The people of Goldman Sachs are among the most productive in the world.

Owing to this simple equation, there was little to no room for debates about pay at Goldman, since the issue had resolved itself. If you wanted to know how productive their employees were, you could simply look at their revenues and the resultant pay as evidence of high productivity. Markets had themselves signalled their worth.

The fact that Goldman Sachs had been bailed out by the US Government during the financial crisis, receiving $125 billion of public money not long before Blankfein's statements, did not seem to register. Banks like theirs were directly implicated in this crisis and Goldman was fined $550 million for irresponsible behaviour. They were among those who had taken loans made to borrowers who could not pay them back, then repackaged those loans in a complex web of semi-fraudulent financial instruments that few people understood. When it all imploded, it cost the world untold trillions in lost economic output. You would think that this information should have entered into Blankfein's calculations about how productive the company and its employees were.[49]

It's not that everybody believes Blankfein's arguments, of course. Bankers themselves are known for attracting public criticism, consistently ranking among the least trusted professions in surveys across the world – while doctors and nurses are typically among the most trusted.[50] Opinions about the rich have been shifting, with many feeling that the wealthiest among us are overpaid and do not pay their fair share in taxes.[51] Nevertheless, when push comes to shove, we have allowed these narratives to persist. Goldman Sachs may play a role in the economy, but to cast that role as the most productive requires a leap of faith. As we have seen, market incomes are a reflection of countless historical, legal and political forces. Even more so, the work that we judge as the most important to humanity is usually far from the best paid.

One of the incredible things about the coronavirus pandemic was how quickly everyone understood that workers like those at Goldman Sachs and other investment banks were not 'essential', whereas those in the health system were. The question of who an essential worker is comes down to who delivers the goods and services we need to survive and function. Most people can rattle off a list of ten or so basic goods and services that humans require to maintain acceptable levels of physical and psychological health. We do not rely on investment banks to deliver any of our physical human needs: healthcare, food, shelter, clothing, transportation. We do not even rely on them to deliver psychological needs: entertainment, social interaction, education, a sense of purpose. For those, we go elsewhere.

There is room for disagreement along the margins of who counts as an essential worker, and it varies across time and place. There is an argument that Netflix workers, for example, are essential even though the platform is relatively new and, to some, more of an indulgence than a necessity. I expect most people were grateful for the continued running of Netflix and platforms like it during the pandemic. Early on, teachers and schoolchildren were told to stay at home, but going into the second wave of lockdowns people were keen for the students not to have too long off school. People can reasonably disagree over these designations in a way they would not disagree over, say, farmers.

While there may be some ambiguities, Goldman Sachs employees sat clearly on one side of the essential worker divide. We can contrast the basic functions of banking and transactions with investment banking, which is responsible for work behind the scenes, investing and allocating money to different businesses and assets. We were able to access the things we needed even without this part of the financial sector running – it's fair to say that people notice train strikes in a way they wouldn't notice an investment banker strike. This is not to dismiss the entire investment banking industry as unnecessary; it's just to highlight that we may not have our priorities straight.

In fact, our priorities may be outright inverted: we reward the areas of the economy which are non-essential, while starving the areas which are. A review of essential workers in the USA found that the ones on the frontline – that is, those who physically had to travel to work – were generally paid a good 15 per cent less than the average worker.[52] These jobs include doctors and nurses, warehouse workers, bus drivers, food preparation and shop workers, builders and farmers. These individuals faced a much higher risk of contracting Covid-19 long before we had the vaccine. They were more likely to be non-white, immigrants and less educated. They were also more likely to be male – though it is worth noting that the review focused on paid work, which ignores the disproportionate amount of unpaid care work done by women during the pandemic.[53]

The modern world would not have functioned had all these people sat at home and watched every Marvel film multiple times, gone to play football in the park every day, and become unreasonably good at Mario Kart.* Our food would not have been grown or supplied to us, with catastrophic implications. Our entertainment and home gyms would not have been delivered, which would have meant we struggled to occupy and fulfil ourselves. Our health systems would have fallen apart, leading to a great deal more illness and death. Ultimately, the economy and society depend on these professions in a way that makes them necessary even under circumstances where everyone else must stop working, and even when the people working in them are being subjected to massive dangers.

There is no doubt that there was a lot of concern about the economy as a whole over the period where many non-essential

* Source: entirely hypothetical.

workers were furloughed, and many more were, ahem, 'working' from home. GDP declined by double digits in most countries and people were wondering if there would be a long-term economic fallout as industries shrivelled up and workers forgot what they knew. Surely, at some point virtually everybody has to get back to work – but it's strange that we can easily recognise those whose labour we literally cannot live without, then continue to pay them poorly and treat them badly. Meanwhile, we seem to reward those who can go on holiday for a couple of months without it directly impacting us. During the pandemic, the parallels between the rulers and ruled of ancient times became impossible to ignore.

THE COMPLEX ECONOMY

As we saw from Dominic Raab's comments in the introduction, socially valuable activities like healthcare are often sidelined in contemporary discussions about 'the economy', as if they are luxuries we may not be able to afford. In contrast, classical economists like Adam Smith long emphasised that the workers on which we all depend should be paid a decent wage so that they can thrive. This was not simply a matter of fairness or justice: it was itself an economic imperative. Workers who are well paid, well fed and well clothed are likely to be more productive as well as better off themselves. In Smith's time, higher wages allowed families to provide for their children, which would have long-term positive effects when the children grew up to be productive citizens. This is crucial for activities such as health, education and care which often lie outside the market economy but still provide the crucial foundation on which it depends.[54]

In contemporary Britain, our doctors and nurses are almost entirely paid through public spending, which naturally raises questions over whether and how much we as taxpayers should pay for them. There is no doubt that public expenditures deserve serious democratic scrutiny wherever they may fall, but once again I find that the disproportionate attention given to public pay misses crucial parts of the wealth creation puzzle. While people who are paid with public money are often thought of as uniquely benefiting from the taxes paid by the rest of us, they are not unique at all. We all benefit from public health and education, publicly funded roads and transport to get us to school or work, and a largely peaceful existence thanks to institutions like the judiciary and court system. This applies whether you are a doctor, a builder, or a financier.

What I am emphatically *not* saying is that only essential workers like doctors are the ones who should have a place in the economy. In truth, the economy is so interlinked, with all the different people, organisations and technologies in it depending on each other, that it becomes impossible to disentangle one part from another. When we look at someone's pay – whether they are a Goldman Sachs employee, a member of a German automotive union, or a nurse in the NHS – what we are seeing is an inexplicable reflection of multiple economic forces, past and present. Our sustained rise in living standards has been a collective effort; equivalently, so have the massive hardships we have visited on so many.

It follows that the parallels between ancient and modern essential workers can only take us so far. Doctors and nurses work incredibly hard to keep us alive, and this effort was maximal during the pandemic. Yet they also rely on advanced and expensive medical technologies which are produced by specialist engineers in countries across the world. The hospitals they operate in were built by construction workers, using an entirely different set of equipment and raw materials. So too are they dependent on each other: a doctor who does not have nurses to support them will not be able to treat anywhere near as many patients, and both depend on the administrative staff that keep hospitals running. Without all of these factors operating at some level, the system would struggle and possibly even fail entirely.

The mysterious 'knowledge' component of growth that we discussed earlier raises further issues. Medicine is the perfect example of an area dominated by past inventions by people who are long dead and so cannot claim their due. Antibiotics are one of the most significant inventions in the history of medicine, and before they existed even minor infections regularly killed people. When Alexander Fleming accidentally discovered penicillin, the key ingredient in antibiotics, he saved countless lives and limbs, and we still use his discovery to this day. The contributions of someone like Fleming – or Edward Jenner, who invented the first vaccine for smallpox in 1796 – are immeasurable, and they are not even alive to claim them.

When all is said and done, we may not truly know what creates wealth: the emergence of the economy remains something of a mystery. What we do know is that wealth creation is complex and changeable, yet it remains unevenly distributed. Wealth creation should be understood as a collective process which is not set in stone, and the fruits of which everyone is entitled to. The great tragedy is that we tend not to reward those who carry out the essential functions in our economy, especially when compared to those who have been shown to be non-essential. Ignoring the role of services like health only serves to make us all poorer.

If our economies can be defined in any number of ways, then in recent years they have been reconfigured to be dominated by extremely wealthy individuals and large corporations. These have not only controlled a disproportionate share of resources but seem to have infiltrated every aspect of our lives. In other words, globally we seem to be pursuing something like the polar opposite of the German model. In the next chapter, I want to take a tour through the commanding heights of the modern global economy, while bearing in mind the crucial lesson from this chapter: wealth is created by everyone and things could always be done differently, according to our chosen values.

CHAPTER 2

WHY ARE THERE SO MANY BILLIONAIRES?

How the Mega-rich Impact the Rest of Us

Growing up in England in the 1990s and 2000s, the idea of being a millionaire seemed radically out of reach for most people. Though I was from a middle-class background and had more affluent friends, none of those friends' parents earned anything like enough to put them into the millionaire category. They were all on around £30,000 to £50,000 a year and their most valuable houses were worth around £500,000, with a sizable mortgage always attached. No-one knew any millionaires, and those who had brushed shoulders with one would consider it worth talking about. It was quite difficult to imagine ever having a million pounds, but it was also an aspiration. Like most children at the time, I wanted to be rich when I grew up.

I haven't managed to make my millions, but even if I had, nowadays it would be no big deal. The number of millionaires has grown extremely fast: between 2000 and 2022 the number of millionaires in the world quadrupled to 62.5 million and their wealth grew from $41 trillion to $222 trillion, far faster than inflation. These days, millionaires are rarely mentioned because their numbers have grown – but also because they are now comparatively low on the economic ladder. Being a millionaire, though most people would welcome it, is not much of a landmark anymore. The economic landscape is instead dominated by billionaires and the companies that they own.

When I was born, the number of billionaires in the world was 273 and they were collectively worth $582 billion. By 2024, there were 2,781 billionaires, collectively worth $14.2 trillion.[1] If the worth of billionaires had simply increased with general inflation, today it would be over ten times less.[2] As you might expect, the USA hosts the most billionaires with 813, with China next on the list with 406, then India, Germany and Russia, each of whom contain over 100 billionaires. Billionaires are overrepresented in the West, though Brazil comes in at number seven and there are still plenty in Southeast Asia and the Middle East. Numbers in the latter countries will only grow with time.[3]

You can see the shift in focus from millionaires to billionaires in popular culture. In the 1990s, during the early years of *The Simpsons*, the town of Springfield's richest resident, Mr Burns, was regularly referred to as a 'millionaire'. He was certainly a multi-millionaire, and in one of the best-known episodes he bets exactly one million dollars on a baseball game with a fellow member of the 'millionaires' club'. It was only after the turn of the millennium that Burns started to be referred to as a billionaire, and by 2008 he was attending a 'billionaires' camp', which included figures like Mark Zuckerberg, Bill Gates and Richard Branson. In a telling illustration of the shift, at the end of the episode Burns' net worth drops slightly below one billion dollars, and he is punished by being sent to the millionaires' camp, exclaiming 'just kill me now'.

The difference between millionaires and billionaires is not well understood. This is perhaps partly owing to the general

human inability to comprehend large numbers, because historically we've not had to deal with millions, let alone billions, in
our everyday lives. It is also perhaps partly owing to the simple
fact that in most languages the two words are pretty similar, so
we assume the magnitudes are similar, too. Yet the magnitudes
are astonishingly different. If you were to count out loud to one
million, it would take you just over a week. If you were instead
to count to one billion, it would take you 31 years. Being a millionaire means a comfortable and privileged lifestyle, but being
a billionaire means you have more power and influence than
most countries, effectively inhabiting a different reality to the
rest of us.

It is common for people to misunderstand what being a billionaire means. These people do not have their net worth readily
available in their bank accounts. Instead, the figure is arrived at
through some combination of the value of their companies,
their investments and property, as well as their own personal
wealth. Valuing property and companies is always fraught with
difficulties, not least because the value can change day-to-day
or even hour-to-hour on the stock market: Jeff Bezos' wealth
once jumped $13 billion in a single day.[4] Were your average
billionaire to sell up and try to convert all their money into
cash, it would be a long and painful process. They may eventually find themselves with far less money than they were assigned
on the *Forbes* rich list. This is why such values are sometimes
called 'unrealised gains': they are estimated and so are less concrete than the money in your bank account.

This is not to play down the reality of being so rich. Your
typical billionaire will likely have access to everything they
want, including quick personal transportation to anywhere in
the world, multiple residences wherever they go, gourmet food

and other quality amenities, access to other rich and powerful people, as well as an army of employees ready to help them with whatever thing they need at any given moment. This last one is perhaps the most significant factor that separates a millionaire from a billionaire. Should the latter choose, they can marshal effectively unlimited resources to pursue whatever project they decide – whether business-oriented, philanthropic, or just a personal whimsy – and make it happen.

It is in these cases that unrealised gains are revealed to be a bit more realised than is sometimes made out. When Elon Musk elected to buy Twitter for $44 billion, he was able to use his wealth as collateral to borrow the money. His assets and companies were guarantees that enabled Wall Street to lend him this unimaginable amount. As the comedian Trevor Noah commented at the time, it is funny that when the authorities threaten to tax billionaires, they say their wealth is unrealised and they don't have it. But when they want to spend billions of dollars on whatever idea takes their fancy, suddenly it seems 'you do have it'.[5] It is this aspect of being a billionaire, rather than their lavish lifestyles, that I would like to focus on the most, because its impact on you and I is difficult to overstate.

The rise of billionaires is one of the most striking features of our modern economy. Whether it is Jeff Bezos and Amazon, Bill Gates and Microsoft, or Elon Musk and his numerous projects, billionaires and their enormous companies have become an integral part of our economies. We use their products every day, generally giving them money in the process, and we are all witness to their various schemes to revolutionise global health, take charge of media and social media outlets, or send humanity into outer space. It seems like not only our economies but our everyday lives are increasingly governed by the whims of relatively few people. We simply have to ask: is this is a good thing?

ARE BILLIONAIRES BAD?

You've likely never heard of Bernard Arnault. Having amassed a fortune approaching $200 billion, he is regularly estimated to be the richest man in the world. Arnault is head of the famous Louis Vuitton fashion empire, and the conglomerate LVMH owns 75 brands in total, including household names such as Dior, Stella McCartney and Tiffany & Co. LVMH has spent $50 billion on acquiring dozens of brands since Arnault took over in the 1980s and its revenues have increased 24 times, with Arnault's personal wealth following in step. LVMH is about five times as large as Mercedes, Germany's most successful car manufacturer.[6] Arnault has been nicknamed the 'wolf in cashmere' because of his aggressive business style, specialising in hostile takeovers after which he lays off thousands of workers.

The French documentary *Merci Padron!* (Thanks Boss!) follows some workers in northern France who were laid off and their campaign to seek compensation to avoid having their homes repossessed. There were suicides following their plant's closure and it is difficult not to be moved by quite how desolate the area now seems; how hopeless the former workers are. Early on in the documentary, an unemployed couple comment that they 'don't eat' though they managed 'sandwiches at Christmas'. In the past, they had stable jobs producing relatively affordable clothing under the LVMH brand. As the numbers of the global rich have grown, Arnault has shifted the focus to luxury items, increasing prices while shipping jobs overseas. The new workers in Bulgaria were producing jackets that sold at $1,000, even though those workers were only being paid around $30 per jacket.

In one sense, Arnault's profile stands in stark contrast to someone like Elon Musk, who is more overtly controversial. In France, Arnault is well known, but considering he regularly trades the top spot with Musk on the *Forbes* rich list, his fame is quite contained. Musk is known for his wacky schemes: travelling into space, drilling tunnels under Las Vegas, buying up Twitter – to name a few. Relative to Musk, Arnault seems to stay in his lane and keep his head down. In many ways, his story just reads like the standard playbook of a modern mega-corporation: taking over other businesses, stripping them down to make a profit, and squeezing workers and consumers in the process. Even if the 'wolf in cashmere' takes these practices to another level, nothing about his and LVMH's story is exactly shocking.

Yet Arnault and Musk are more similar than it may first seem. For while we often think of billionaires in terms of their money and companies in terms of their size, I would encourage you to think about both in terms of *control*. The incomprehensibly large numbers you see on the *Forbes* rich list are really a means to an end. Billionaires want to be able to corner their own markets and beyond to build what amount to economic empires. This gives them control over not just their companies and their workers, but entire industries and beyond. And their quest for control inevitably ends up as a quest for power, which affects all of us.

It is easy to see that billionaires seek control and power because they start with their own companies. Anyone who has seen the film *The Social Network* knows that Mark Zuckerberg's co-founder and 'friend' Eduardo Saverin saw the worth of his Facebook shares go down as new stock was issued, while the share Zuckerberg and others had in the company was maintained. Saverin was tricked into buying watered-down stock that would see his previously substantial stake in the company whither as Zuckerberg and others took control.

Although other billionaires aren't always quite this conniving, most got to where they are through behaviour many of us would regard as impolite, to say the least. In 1984, Bernard Arnault teamed up with fellow executive Henri Racamier to oust the head of LVMH Alain Chevalier, who had himself co-founded the company. By 1990, Arnault had managed to depose his former ally Racamier too, following a lengthy and bitter court battle, and assumed his position as head of the entire company. He has been in charge for over three decades and appears to be grooming his children to take charge after he retires, a real-life version of *Succession*.[7]

Like Arnault, Musk is Machiavellian in his private manoeuvring and prefers to be the one in control. In 1999, Musk owned a company called X.com and merged it with Confinity, run by fellow billionaire Peter Thiel. Thiel had already created PayPal at the time of the merger and they decided to use that name for the new company, in part because consumers reasonably assumed that X.com was a porn website (good thing Musk learned his lesson there). Musk insisted on being CEO even though the board was unhappy with his performance. He was eventually forced to stand down as CEO in what has been described as a 'nasty coup'. However, he retained a substantial stake in the company and walked away with $180 million when PayPal was sold to eBay in 2002, which helped him to purchase Tesla.[8]

So, Musk did not actually found the electric car company Tesla but bought into it as an investor at a later date. Tesla Motors was co-founded by Martin Eberhard and Marc Tarpenning in 2003 and the duo have spoken out against Musk's insistence that he was the founder.[9] Learning from his lesson at PayPal, Musk had surrounded himself with people who knew and supported him before trying to take control of the company.[10] Tarpenning eventually sued Musk for his ousting of the original founders and they reached an out of court settlement, with the strange stipulation that Musk could now legally call himself the co-founder, in an outright example of rewriting history.[11] The point is not that Musk has no achievements or contributions; it's that he is clearly obsessed with rising to the top and having absolute control over his endeavours.

CONTROLLING COMPETITION

Taking control of a company is only the first step. After control of a company is established, it is expanded relentlessly. Multinationals have increasingly grown not just in size but in scope, taking on numerous companies and operations until they have control over entire industries. As Peter Thiel himself put it, 'competition is for losers'. On their respective marches to the top, Facebook famously acquired Instagram and WhatsApp; Google acquired YouTube and Android; and Microsoft bought Skype and LinkedIn. Nor is this confined to tech: Arnault's LVMH is the largest luxury goods conglomerate in the world, accounting for almost a quarter of the entire globe's luxury market in 2023. It also stands out for the sheer diversity of its products, which include perfumes, clothing, bags, jewellery, makeup and wine. They own 100 per cent of their distribution and have 100 per cent control over the prices that are charged for their products.[12]

Since the 1980s, laws regarding how companies can merge with and acquire others have been relaxed, with the result that empires like Arnault's have become more commonplace.[13] The 1990 film *Pretty Woman* depicted the clash between the old type of family capitalist, played by Ralph Bellamy, who seemed to believe in building a better future through his shipbuilding business, and the new type of financial capitalist, played by Richard Gere, who just wanted to be rich and was willing to buy up as many businesses as possible in the process to make that happen – often with little regard for their history or what they produced. As one union representative said of Arnault in *Merci Padron!*, 'all he wants to do is dismantle and break up his companies'.

Anti-trust laws were created to prohibit monopolies from becoming too large or abusing their power. For most of the twentieth century, these laws had been focused on markets as a whole, investigating whether certain companies were too big or were exerting power over their competitors. The basic idea was a simple one: if there are too many big fish in the pond, they will dominate, to the detriment of smaller fish (i.e. you and me), and possibly to the ultimate detriment of the pond itself. Ensuring a healthy economic system, as with ensuring a healthy ecosystem, should mean not letting any one player dominate. For large companies, domination could mean making sure that most transactions in the market go through you, extracting fees and squeezing smaller businesses, gouging consumers with high prices, and exploiting workers.

US Senator John Sherman was the pioneer of the original anti-trust laws back in the late nineteenth century. Sherman's biggest targets back then were oil and railroad companies. The discovery of oil had led to great achievements in lighting, solvents and engines. At the same time, it had given its owners like John D. Rockefeller enormous wealth and power. He had exclusive deals with the railroad companies, obtaining special prices to transport large quantities of oil on their trains at a steep discount. In what became known as the Cleveland Massacre, he bought up most of the refineries in that city. The end result was that he had control over a quarter of oil production in the country.[14]

Rockefeller's Standard Oil had engaged in several secretive abusive practices, including price fixing and spying on competitors. Under the Sherman Act, the company was broken up into 34 subsidiary companies for the crime of establishing a monopoly by engaging in anti-competitive behaviour.[15] Arguably, though, the big question at stake was less the specific wrongs that Standard Oil had wrought (substantial though these were) and more the dominance it had over the market in the first place. In 1890, Sherman summed up his position by questioning the power and control of monopolists:

> If we will not endure a king as a political power, we should not endure a king over the production, transportation, and sale of any of the necessities of life. If we would not submit to an emperor, we should not submit to an autocrat of trade, with power to prevent competition and to fix the price of any commodity.

This philosophy persisted in the regulation of monopolies for most of the twentieth century. However, over the past few decades, the logic of anti-trust laws has changed entirely.[16]

Regulators are now less concerned with whether certain companies are dominating an industry than with whether customers are facing low enough prices. The idea is that anti-competitive practices would be reflected in prices that were way above costs, ripping off the customer. Competition forces companies to lower prices, so high prices would demonstrate that a company is not being exposed to the forces of competition. It follows that if companies are not increasing prices, then there is nothing to worry about; competition is alive and well.

The result of this laser-like focus on consumer prices has been a neglect of the broader market ecosystem. Arguably the starkest example of the trend towards market dominance has been Amazon, which now has an unprecedented degree of control over multiple, interconnected industries. Jeff Bezos started selling books online in the 1990s and there are famous pictures of him surrounded by books in his makeshift 1997 warehouse.

This is often used as a reminder that even titans come from humble beginnings and that hard work can achieve anything. Whatever the truth in this statement – or in Bezos' undoubted efforts and acumen – Amazon has clearly developed into something far beyond this folksy picture.

Legal expert Lina M. Khan summarised Amazon's growth strategy by saying, 'it is as if Bezos charted the company's growth by first drawing a map of anti-trust laws, and then devising routes to smoothly bypass them'. [17] After expanding quickly in the early 2000s, Amazon started selling electronics, toys and tools. These days it sells almost any product you can think of and manufactures plenty of them too, including publishing books itself. And that's not to mention its streaming service, credit-lending facilities and unparalleled delivery and logistics network. As with LVMH, some of these capabilities have been developed by Amazon, but many of them have come through acquiring other companies.

Bezos' early choice of books is instructive for how he wanted Amazon to operate. It did not stem from his love of books but because, in his words, 'there are more items in the book category than in any other category, by far'.[18] The largest libraries in the world could hold maybe 150,000 or so books – but an internet bookshop could hold millions in warehouses. Bezos saw the internet was growing at an enormously fast pace, which, together with the volume of books in the world, made the growth potential of an online book shop virtually unlimited. Since its birth in 1997, Bezos' vision of a complete library has basically been fulfilled, as Amazon has maintained growth rates that have exceeded 20 per cent per year, a truly extraordinary figure.

Amazon's business model is a curious one because despite its growth, for a long time the company made either meagre profits or no profit at all. While I'm no expert in running a business, I can tell you this is traditionally not how a successful business works. For a long time, Wall Street analysts agreed and thought that Bezos was building a house of cards – yet investors kept pouring in money. It was only in the second half of the 2010s that Amazon's profits started to consistently hit tens of billions of dollars. This was also around the time Jeff Bezos started to top the rich list, with his personal wealth regularly exceeding $100 billion. When the world locked down in 2020, online shopping became the only option for many of us and Amazon's profits soared – though they have since dipped back to more 'regular' levels.

An illustrative example of the grip Amazon has on the market comes from the now-defunct website Diapers.com, which was growing fast as a provider of baby care in 2008. Amazon offered to buy the corporation Quidsi, which owned Diapers.com alongside other websites focused on household essentials. When Quidsi declined, Amazon created algorithms that would follow the products on Diapers.com and automatically cut prices below theirs – up to 30 per cent lower in some cases. They also launched 'Amazon Mom', offering discounts for repeated purchases and free Prime membership. Quidsi eventually relented to the pressure this placed on them and accepted a bid to buy them from Amazon, who promptly raised prices again and all but ended the Amazon Mom scheme. Quidsi itself was eventually closed, too.[19]

We can see how Bezos' approach of growing the company in size and scope plays out. Potential competition is acquired or pushed out of business so that Amazon remains dominant in every market, from books to diapers to toy figurines. Many companies that attempt to compete with Amazon – for instance, by selling toys online – may at some point have to use some of Amazon's other infrastructure, relying on them to advertise or ship their goods. Early Amazon employees recognised that

Bezos' 'underlying goals were not to build an online bookstore or an online retailer, but rather a "utility" that would become essential to commerce'. Investors continued to bet on Amazon even as it made close to no profit for over a decade, precisely because they thought this strategy would eventually be rewarded.

There is no doubt that much of the infrastructure created by Amazon is something of a marvel. Same-day delivery of almost any good under the sun was unthinkable 20 years ago, as was the ability to stream such a wide variety of films and TV shows, not to mention the fact that all of this is integrated with Amazon's own manufacturing capabilities. Yet the original Sherman anti-trust laws were designed at a time when rail and oil barons had created remarkable infrastructure, too, and were responsible for industries which helped people and the economy enormously. As Sherman himself pointed out, this hardly justified the power and control the barons had. Bezos' idea of a 'utility' is especially instructive in this regard, since utilities are typically thought to be too important to allow unfettered private control over them.

Amazon may have kept prices down and offered consumers a wide variety of products, in line with what modern anti-trust laws require. While we can marvel at Amazon's services, what we do not see are the thousands of potential innovations that might have come from companies like Quidsi, which were acquired aggressively and will never be allowed a chance to develop of their own accord. Nor do we see the progression of outright rivals to Amazon like Jet.com, who were eventually bought up by the retail giant Walmart. It's possible that the economic landscape of the future is one where only huge incumbents can compete – although it is worth emphasising that even Walmart's online business was unable to make a siz-able dent in Amazon's online market position.

There is a notable difference between the anti-trust approaches taken in the USA and the European Union, and the latter's relative strictness has been a source of disquiet for many of the big tech companies. The year 2023 saw the passing of the Digital Markets Act, which has forced companies like Apple, Google and Amazon to stop favouring their own software on their platforms, from apps to payment software to search engines. EU anti-trust chief Margrethe Vestager has called for 'fair' digital markets and stated that these laws will prevent 'large gatekeeper platforms' from reducing competition.[20] Lina Khan has herself spearheaded initiatives in the USA to enact similar measures.[21]

TAMING THE INTERNET

In an infamous open letter to the computing community in 1976, Bill Gates, the founder of the then-fledgling company Microsoft, complained that he and his colleagues were not being paid enough for their creations: by his calculations, their wage reached a paltry $2 an hour. They had built a widely used coding language called BASIC, and while they were able to sell it to some, others were immediately able to copy and use it for free. He called those who used it without paying 'hobbyists' and explicitly accused them of stealing.[22] Since then, Gates has been so successful in making software into a profitable enterprise that he was the richest man in the world 18 out of 24 years before 2018, when Jeff Bezos overtook him. How exactly he did this reveals a lot about how our economies, especially the digital sector, have been reconfigured over the past few decades.

The USA's anti-trust laws may have become relatively toothless since the philosophy behind them was changed, but there have still been a few major cases against big players. One of the most famous modern anti-trust cases revolved around Bill Gates and Microsoft. Much like the newer tech giants today, Microsoft in the 1990s was accused of favouring its own software on its operating system. Specifically, Internet Explorer – a famously bad web browser which Microsoft has since abandoned – was automatically installed as the default browser, which was difficult to change. Its much-loved rival at the time, Netscape (of *Firefox* fame), was repeatedly frozen out and other companies reported Microsoft pressuring them to drop it. The ruling was made to split Microsoft into two companies, though this never happened because it was reversed under George W. Bush's presidency.

The tech sector is a revealing case study for understanding modern monopolies and the billionaires who own them – the oil barons of our age. This is not just because the sector is important but because of its history and its unique mechanics. The internet was initially created by the US Government in the 1960s so that academics and researchers could share data. It was inaccessible for most people, but it was largely a free content-sharing platform created by public money. It was established for a specific purpose, which was to facilitate the exchange of knowledge and information among people who were working to improve the human condition.

Part of the potential freedom of the virtual world stems from the fact that software has what economists call 'zero marginal cost'. The 'marginal' cost of building something is the cost of building one extra unit of it. Building a computer, for example, will inevitably involve physical parts and labour, so one more computer will always cost more money. While building software requires an initial investment of labour and a computer to work on, once the basic software is out it can be copied an unlimited number of times at essentially zero cost – much like copying and pasting a file. You can add to this that many communities will happily maintain and update the software of their own volition, something that still happens to this day with many freely developed and maintained programs that anyone can download.*

It may not surprise you to know that the academics who originally used the internet were not especially keen on sharing it with the riff raff. As computers became more widespread, enthusiastic amateurs worked relentlessly to create software that would work for everyone. The period from the 1970s to the 1990s was what many nerds regard as a golden age of the internet: people freely sharing code, data, files and software. All of this was 'open source': open and transparent to everyone and therefore easy to tweak and modify for whoever wanted to. It could be unclear who exactly was responsible for a given program and virtually everything was free to access for anyone with a computer. The internet, as well as other software, was a collectively produced and maintained resource, a bit like a digital watering hole. You had to have a relatively high level of computer skills given it was such a new technology, but the overarching philosophy was one of the internet being a community where money played little to no role.

One person who did not think this was a golden age was Bill Gates, which was why he wrote his testy open letter. Naturally, the letter was rebuffed by the community, who said that he was understating the money he had made, pointed out that the free sharing of BASIC had put him on the map, and highlighted that

---

* If you think I'm going to name these just so that they can be shut down then you've got another thing coming, buster.

he had created his software on a computer funded by the US Government. Having said that, my point is not that the Bill Gates of 1976 did not deserve to be remunerated for his efforts. The issue is what Gates signalled with his letter and what he would later put into practice. He has since been belligerent about implementing restrictions which ensure Microsoft gets to control who uses what, and crucially, when they have to pay for it.

INTELLECTUAL PROPERTY: THE ROOT OF ALL EVIL?

As the economist Dean Baker has pointed out, if we were in anything like the open source heyday of the internet, Microsoft and its various derivative programs would be possible to copy and share for free. It is inconceivable that Gates would be as rich as he is if this were the case, which is why he has worked so hard to prevent people from doing so. Without laws that can be used to fine or even imprison those who reproduce the software without paying for it, Gates would not have the legal power to control the market that he does. While Gates seems uniquely jealous in his protection of his software, something similar applies to the late Steve Jobs with Apple, as well as to Larry Page and Sergey Brin with Google.[23]

These restrictions are known as Intellectual Property (IP). The two main types of IP are copyrights and patents. Copyrights, as the name implies, prevent people from directly copying others and they are mostly used in the world of art. Ed Sheeran landed in hot water when his chart-topping 'Singing Out Loud' was compared to Marvin Gaye's 'Let's Get It On', an unexpected example of the two singers being mentioned in the same breath that should never be repeated. Although the two songs had some similarities, it was ruled that Sheeran was not guilty of direct copying since so many other songs use similar chords.[24] Since copyright laws have to prove one person copied another, they are often difficult to enforce.

Patents are a little different. They were created to protect physical inventions so that an engineer who came up with, say, a particular shape of car exhaust, could not have their design emulated. The key distinction from copyright laws is that with a patent, nobody has to prove that the copying was deliberate; you simply cannot use the same shape of exhaust pipe once the patent has been filed. This makes them easier to enforce than copyright laws, and patents have become a mainstay of business empires. They have also been extended to the design of software, which is one of the ways Gates has managed to extract money from the venture. Both types of IP apply for a set number of years, which can range from one decade to one century, and the average lengths of both have been continually expanded since the idea of patents took off in the nineteenth century.[25]

It is completely reasonable to look at IP laws as good and necessary. After all, shouldn't someone who creates a unique invention, or works hard on a praiseworthy piece of art, get reimbursed? The problem is that while, in theory, IP should protect the little guy from the big guy, in practice it is usually the opposite. Ironically, it was Disney who managed to achieve peak cartoon villain through intellectual property laws when they denied a grieving father the right to put an image of Spiderman, his four-year-old son's favourite superhero, on the child's grave. Their reasoning was that putting the image on a grave would not preserve the 'innocence' and 'magic' of the character.[26] Although Disney eventually relented after a massive public backlash, there are hundreds of equally restrictive

cases out there which favour these corporations over ordinary people.

Gates himself is a major investor in a company called Intellectual Ventures (IV). Microsoft, for all its flaws, actually does
produce things. IV, on the other hand, specialises in buying up
patent rights from others and charging companies for using them.
In their own words, they do not make products but invest in
'ideas themselves'. This could be mistaken for traditional investment, making funds available to inventors and innovators, but it
is not the same thing. IV is simply a company which buys the
legal permission to create technologies and either sells or rents
that permission to other companies.[27] Harassing companies with
legal claims over their ideas has been dubbed 'patent trolling' and
IV are not the only ones. Cases in the USA have involved companies being charged billions for using technologies. Often, the
companies who are doing the suing are not even the ones who
came up with the technology, nor do they use it themselves.[28]

One of the interesting things about software is that it is actually *more* difficult to charge money for it. This is why the
original version of the internet was *organically* free: it took a
long time to make effective systems to block people from down-
loading software unless they paid for it. Those who are over
thirty will remember the cat-and-mouse game of the internet in
the nineties and noughties, as companies repeatedly tried to
foist adverts and paywalls on people only to be rebuffed by
open-source software that blocked adverts and circumvented
paywalls. These days, platforms are much more strictly controlled, and companies have been successful in getting us to pay
for music, software, videos, storage, podcasts, ebooks – or at
least to sit through plenty of adverts if we don't cough up.
There remains some open-source software that can circumvent

these paywalls if you know where to look, but they are increasingly scarce and are less effective than they once were.*

Dean Baker gives a ballpark estimate that intellectual property rights are costing people in the USA $1 trillion through paying more for software, drugs, fertilisers and pesticides – all of which are covered extensively by laws forbidding others from copying their respective 'recipes'. IP is therefore present in a wide variety of industries, but it has utterly transformed the tech sector. In years past, the hard infrastructure of computers and wires was funded by the government and various enthusiasts tried to provide a service that was free and accessible for as many people as possible. Today, relatively few people and companies extract money from everyone else for using ideas that cost nothing to reproduce – and we are all the poorer for it.[29]

WORKING FOR A BILLIONAIRE

In an awkward video, the late Steve Jobs is sitting on-stage with an Apple computer while attempting to turn a camera on. He seems to be having trouble, until someone from the audience politely suggests he 'slide it and let go'. He replies that he *did* do this, shrugs that it's not turning on, then suddenly throws the camera to (or at) the audience member and says, 'Here … we'll let an expert see if he can turn it on.' Jobs was well known for this level of petulance and rudeness towards people around him, especially his employees. He is visibly annoyed throughout the exchange and while it's fair to be frustrated if your tech doesn't function in a demonstration, taking something like that

* Why are you looking down here? I told you I'm not going to name them.

out on innocent bystanders is recognised by most ordinary people as a terrible personality trait.[30]

The most famous billionaires do not have a reputation for being good with people. Reportedly, Bill Gates was such an insufferable smartass when he was younger that his father once threw a glass of water in his face for being rude to his mother, to which the 12-year-old Gates responded, 'Thanks for the shower.'[31] Decades later in the Microsoft anti-trust deposition, Gates was similarly obstructive and stalled by pretending he didn't know what was meant by everyday terms like 'concern' and 'support'.[32] Steve Ballmer, Gates' replacement as Microsoft CEO and a billionaire in his own right, is famous for allegedly throwing a chair when an employee told him they were leaving.[33] Billionaires largely seek to control the world around them, and that includes those people who refuse to fall in line with their vision: be they parents, opposing lawyers or employees.

Elon Musk has reported that Steve Jobs was once 'incredibly rude' to him at a party, which, while inexcusable, does bring to mind the phrase 'takes one to know one'.[34] Musk is notoriously unfair to his workers, as illustrated even as early as his first company Zip2 – a kind of Yellow Pages for the internet – which expanded quickly with a big investment and started hiring. Reportedly, upon coming face-to-face with the code that made Zip2 tick, newly hired employees complained that Musk had coded in a clumsy manner, making it extremely difficult to fix problems.[35] Even though they had more experience than him on the matter, Musk didn't like the changes they were making and frequently reversed them without informing the coders. They described him as difficult to work with due to his micromanagement and general rudeness, apparently becoming 'really angry' with his employees if they were not working past 9 p.m.[36]

Tesla has numerous documented problems with the way it treats its workers, who are generally expected to work 12-hour days and weekends, with little to no holiday, and are under great pressure to meet the company's exacting targets. The company employs a massive 15,000 workers and contractors in their factory in Fremont, California, which is the largest in the USA. Safety standards are widely known to be lax at Fremont, which has led to a multitude of serious injuries. In one instance, three employees were hospitalised by burns from an aluminium press; in another, an employee lost a fingertip when their glove was caught in a torque gun; in yet another, a worker contracted carpal-tunnel syndrome and after two operations can no longer lift anything heavier than 55 pounds. An investigation by *Forbes* found that Tesla had incurred 54 safety violations between 2014 and 2018, which compared unfavourably to the 18 violations found at every other major automobile factory in the USA *put together*.[37]

Tesla workers clearly have limited control over their own destinies and reports of exploitation are rife at the factories, with many fearful of losing their jobs should they not reach the company's stringent standards. These standards also seem to apply to some more than others: African American workers report having experienced racist abuse at Tesla including slurs, threats and theft.[38] Most galling, though, are the segregated working conditions, with physical labour more likely to be reserved for this group. In one instance African American employees, and only African American employees, were required to scrub the floor of the Tesla factory on their hands and knees. Tesla has faced lawsuits for sexual as well as racial discrimination, with women enduring verbal and physical harassment, unable to report it for fear of endangering their careers.[39] It comes from

the top: Musk allegedly exposed himself to a female flight attendant, who was paid off to the tune of $250,000.[40]

As billionaires and their companies acquire new industries
and new rights like intellectual property, they often become
increasingly able to extract money and ideas from their workforce, who typically have limited outside options. This leads to
further exploitation as the employees are reliant on the companies to get their income and further their careers, even though
they know they should be treated better. Mysterio, the villain
of the film *Spider-Man: Far From Home* is actually a disgrun-
tled faceless scientist from whom Tony Stark (Iron Man) stole
ideas, then claimed credit for them. Similarly, we tend to attri-
bute Apple products to Jobs himself, but as Apple grew, Jobs
comparatively did less and less. As comedian Bill Burr put it, it
was primarily 'faceless scientists' who carried out Jobs' orders,
sending them scrambling with a random idea like, 'I want my
entire music collection in that phone, get on it!'

BILLIONAIRES AND THE MARKET ECONOMY

It is not my intention to paint the plight of exploited workers as
a simple result of a personality defect among those at the top.
These individuals certainly do seem to treat those they come into
contact with poorly, and it is likely that their ruthless approaches
have contributed to their competitive success. You will probably
see more of this type at the top than elsewhere. Nevertheless, billionaires will never meet most of the workers their companies
employ – yet the forces of global market competition will tend to
put pressure on these workers, and that would likely be true even
if billionaires were personally angels. As early as the eighteenth

century, Adam Smith was worrying about the impact that capitalism and the division of labour would have on workers:[41]

> In the progress of the division of labour, the employment of the far greater part of those who live by labour, that is, the great body of the people, comes to be confined to a few very simple operations, frequently to one or two . . . The man whose whole life is spent in performing a few simple operations . . . generally becomes as stupid and ignorant as it is possible for a human creature to become . . . His dexterity at his own particular trade seems . . . to be acquired at the expense of his intellectual, social, and martial virtues. But in every improved and civilised society this is the state into which the labouring poor, that is, the great body of the people, must necessarily fall, unless government takes some pains to prevent it.

It is this back-breaking, mind-numbing, soul-destroying feeling of being a cog in a machine that remains as true today as it was when Smith was writing in 1776. Jeff Bezos is not known for quite the same personality defects as some of the other multi-billionaires, but Amazon sets up its enormous warehouses – ominously named 'fulfilment centres' – at arm's length, mostly in ex-industrial cities where people do not have many other choices. UK journalist James Bloodworth went undercover in an Amazon fulfilment centre in the small town of Rugeley in England. It is clear from seeing how these places work that the mind-bending efficiency of Amazon for customers is built on the backs of its workers.

Bloodworth reported that employees are expected to work 10½-hour shifts with barely enough time to eat. They are heavily monitored using a computer tablet that gives them almost impossible targets and they are admonished when they don't reach them. The turnover of the job is sky-high and most people do not get a permanent contract as they are either canned or leave within one year. Even worse, the promised pay of £7 an hour – already low enough – is riddled with incomprehensible deductions by the agency responsible for the employment, Transline.[42] Bloodworth reported that both his physical and mental health deteriorated while he worked at Amazon, and this is despite the fact that he knew it was only for a few months. Many face this kind of work indefinitely.

Foxconn, the Taiwanese company where Apple products are assembled, famously had nets erected outside their factory to stop their overworked employees from dying after international outcry over 18 attempted suicides in 2010. Although Foxconn made headlines, they are not the only suppliers of these Western tech companies: several other Taiwanese companies provide similar services under similar working conditions. And although Apple was targeted politically for this, Foxconn also supplies Hewlett-Packard, Nokia, Amazon, Intel, Google and Microsoft – among others. At the time of writing, Wikipedia states that the most recent suicide at a Foxconn site was in 2018. Steve Jobs had previously referred to this as 'a pretty nice factory'.[43]

The word 'factories' is actually a misnomer because Chinese and Taiwanese companies build gigantic complexes where workers eat, work and sleep without time for much else. They are generally worked to the point of exhaustion, doing repetitive and monotonous tasks to produce the same part over and over again, while they are reportedly not allowed to speak to one another or even to 'giggle'. Workers stay in the company dormitories together but work different shifts, so they rarely communicate, preferring to use their limited time to sleep – though they still don't get enough. Many of the tasks expose workers to chemicals and other dangers for which they do not get adequate health provisions or even acknowledgement by the company. Workers are expected to assemble 6,400 phone parts per day but their pay is so low that they cannot themselves afford a single iPhone. Many are migrants from the countryside or other countries, which leaves them in highly insecure positions with little to no bargaining power, trapped in the compound indefinitely.[44]

It only gets worse as you travel down the supply chain. The minerals essential to our modern consumer products are extracted under conditions that can only be described as horrifying. Most striking is the mining of cobalt, done mostly in Zambia and the Democratic Republic of Congo (DRC). Cobalt is an essential input for mobile and laptop batteries, in headphones and speakers, as well as to coat computer hard drives. It is all around me as I am writing this sentence. Most of the mining in the DRC today is done at the behest of the Chinese or Taiwanese companies who assemble iPhones and other electronic equipment.

The DRC has been engulfed in conflict for decades, with around six million dying and seven million displaced since 1996. This war actually has its roots in the Rwandan genocide of 1994, which forced the displaced Hutus across the border. Rwanda's Tutsi-led government (the Tutsis being the aggressors during the genocide, while the Hutus were the victims) invaded the area twice: once in 1996 and again in 1998. Since then, the country has been beset by ethnic and political divisions, with warring factions controlling different locations and governments struggling to retain authority over the whole area. After a short period of relative peace, violence erupted once more in 2024 as rebel Tutsi groups took control of several provinces.[45]

In practice, cobalt mines are often run by rebel groups who enslave local populations while forcing women and girls into exploitative sex work. Over one-third of the cobalt miners in the DRC are children – between the ages of 7 and 18 – and they are paid around $2 to $4 per day to work in this potentially deadly occupation. Minerals like cobalt are usually toxic, so as well as being dangerous for these undertrained, under-equipped and overworked miners, they often lead to toxic waste nearby.[46] This kind of thing is not contained to Central Africa, either; the tin mines from Bangka Island in Indonesia saw one miner killed per week in 2011.[47]

Tech companies could be accused of providing a glossy coat over the far darker reality of how their products are produced. Terms like 'the cloud' provoke lofty images of ideas floating around the sky when in fact internet servers are huge blocks of complex circuitry located in warehouses across the world which must be perpetually cooled, an extremely energy-intensive process.[48] Products are assembled by underpaid, overworked labourers in middle-income countries, using minerals mined by people in poor countries whose conditions verge on – and sometimes simply are – slavery. Through low safety standards, lax environmental regulations and above all low pay, Western companies are able to contract out work to poor and middle-income countries while looking the other way.

This brings us back to the issue that puzzled us in the last chapter: are we measuring value created or value extracted? British scholar John Smith has noted that because of their arm's-length relationships with companies like Foxconn, Western companies like Apple can record that they're adding a great deal of value when selling their iPhones. This is despite the fact that they essentially buy the finished product at about half the price that they sell it. Naturally, this benefits well-paid executives and CEOs the most, who pocket about two-thirds of the wage bill in the USA. It also somewhat benefits retail workers at Apple stores who, though not as well-paid as the higher-ups, make a multiple in salary compared to those who assemble the phones themselves. Finally, the entire difference is recorded as GDP for the USA, which gives the country as a whole more economic clout.[49] To be sure, Apple does important things once the phones are in the USA – distribution, sales, logistics – but it is still worth asking whether this warrants profit margins of around 50 per cent *after* buying the fully finished iPhones.

Bernard Arnault's strategy of outsourcing jobs to sell to the global rich had a catastrophic impact on his former workers in Northern France. From an examination of working conditions under these massive companies, we can see an unfortunate bind for these workers. As people are reliant on the market economy to get their income, having no job is even worse than having even a job where you are poorly paid, overworked and generally mistreated. Amazon workers in Rugeley know this, which is why they're happy Amazon set up in the area – after all, some work is better than no work.[50] As the economist Joan Robinson once remarked, 'under capitalism, the only thing worse than being exploited is not being exploited at all'. Far from a defence of said exploitation, this should be interpreted as a call for a sea change in the kinds of choices workers across the world are forced to make.

BILLIONAIRE BENEVOLENCE?

While workers across the world have no choice, the wealthy have so much choice that they're doing whatever takes their fancy. In 2020, the two famous actors Ryan Reynolds and Rob McElhenney bought up the Welsh football team, Wrexham AFC. Wrexham is the oldest football club in Wales and one of the oldest professional football clubs in the world. The team had struggled for a long time, going from competing in European cups to being relegated from the official football league. They were plagued by issues on and off the pitch, including financial problems and mismanagement. At one point, echoing their German brethren, fans sought to depose a chairman who put the club into administration. Moving a club into administration violated football league rules and earned Wrexham a 10-point deduction, which saw them relegated from League One (which is, confusingly, the third-tier league).

Wrexham is a former industrial town which was famous for its mining and its leather industry throughout the Industrial Revolution. The town was hit hard by the gradual decline of British industry in the latter half of the twentieth century and has never really recovered. Wrexham AFC's stadium, the Racecourse, had become dilapidated, a symbol of not only the club's decline but the decline of the town itself. Yet thanks to Reynolds and McElhenney's investment, the Racecourse has been regenerated and there is new life in and around the stadium. At the time of writing, Wrexham AFC have been promoted twice, which comes with it a great deal of funding and esteem. The community are undoubtedly grateful; the chant fans have come up with says it all:

> Less than a mile from the centre of Town,
> A famous old stadium crumbling down,
> No one's invested so much as a penny,
> Bring on the Deadpool and Rob McElhenney

There are two differences between Reynolds and McElhenney and the other characters in this chapter. Firstly, the two are 'merely' multi-millionaires rather than billionaires – with Reynold's fortune hugely outstripping McElhenney's and driving most of the acquisition. Secondly, and more importantly, these two seem to be doing it out of a genuine sense of compassion and curiosity. Admittedly, they did themselves commission the documentary *Welcome to Wrexham*, which follows the takeover, so it's unlikely they'd allow themselves to be portrayed badly. At the same time, there is no doubting that the fans love them, that they've been heavily involved from day one, and that they've achieved results on the football pitch. One fan claims that they've 'transformed' the town as well as the club, which has seen a huge boost in tourism and even had the King of England come to visit.

Welcome to Wrexham illustrates a concerning reality: towns that once had thriving economies are now doomed to decline unless they happen to take the fancy of a handful of rich benefactors. Although it is joyful to see the fans and residents of Wrexham with renewed hope, there are dozens of other such towns that have not received this kind of investment. Wrexham's star striker, Ollie Palmer, was reportedly offered 'irresistible' terms to leave his old club AFC Wimbledon, who have since been relegated from League One themselves. It remains to be seen whether Wrexham AFC, let alone the entire town, will be rejuvenated over the long term by Reynolds and McElhenney's investments. Even if that best-case scenario does happen, this kind of attention should not be reserved for towns that are selected seemingly based on whether they would make a good TV show.[51]

Throughout history and across the globe, people have given to the poor and needy. But these acts of charity are distinct from philanthropy, which is a far more systematic endeavour. Philanthropy means setting up or investing in an organisation with long-term goals and strategies like 'deworming every child in Sub-Saharan Africa' or 'cleaning up the Great Barrier Reef' or even 'rejuvenating Wrexham AFC and getting them a solid footing in the football league'.* Philanthropy is especially popular in North America, but it has had an impact across the globe as the wealth of those at the top has risen.

For example, many of the undoubted health gains enjoyed by poorer countries over the past few decades come partially or wholly from the Gates Foundation, run by both Bill and Melinda Gates – the latter of whom is a billionaire in her own right. The good their investment has done is undoubtable, as they have targeted the eradication of polio, a horrible disease that can cause the limbs to waste away. The legendary British singer Ian Dury was born in 1942 and lived with polio until he died at 58. Even by the time he passed, new cases of polio had become a thing of the past in rich countries. Now the same can be said in poorer countries, too – in part thanks to Dury's own tireless campaigning.

Nevertheless, there is reason to be sceptical of the amount of control this private foundation has over global health. Just because the Gates Foundation have achieved some positive gains, that doesn't mean the money has been put to its best uses. Experts have accused the Gates Foundation of targeting polio at the expense of illnesses like diarrhoea, which countries like India were more interested in solving yet were overruled.

---

*Wrexham AFC is a business that can in principle turn a profit, though it has been a loss-making endeavour up to the time of writing, so it seems to be partially done as an act of philanthropy.

Curing polio makes for better PR because it is comparatively easier to do through vaccination. Curing diarrhoea would require more fundamental changes to public infrastructure in these countries to make the water supply and sewage systems function properly, and these are changes the Gate Foundation is not prepared to make. The fact that such large health efforts are democratically unaccountable to the Indian population may have led to the neglect of important health priorities.[52]

Bill Gates clearly has an eye for public health issues and, for all I know, has good intentions. He actually has a well-circulated TED Talk from 2015 calling for a global vaccine response group, and one can only wish the world had listened. We had no real global coordination when the pandemic hit five years later even though, as Gates stressed, we merely needed a small organisation, which would not have cost too much money. This would have meant teams of researchers collaborating, information being exchanged, lockdown policies being coordinated and crack teams being dispatched to the epicentre of Wuhan, China, as early as possible to understand the virus and contain its spread.[53]

Despite these prescient observations, once the pandemic hit, Gates' decades-old belief in the importance of intellectual property triumphed over spreading the vaccine across the globe. The first Covid vaccine was not actually developed in the private sector but at Oxford University by a team of researchers who did not plan to profit from or patent it. Ironically, Jonas Salk, the American biomedical scientist who created the polio vaccine that the Gates Foundation has relied on so much, also refused to patent or profit from it, insisting that it was for 'the people'. Gates disagreed with this lofty idea. Echoing his practices with software, he insisted that the Oxford vaccine was to be funnelled through pharmaceutical companies rather than freely distributed.[54]

Once more, something that could have cost little to nothing was going to be charged for. This quickly led to what health experts called 'vaccine apartheid', where in 2021 there were 4 doses for every 100 people in poorer countries, compared to 133 doses for every 100 people in wealthy ones. Almost nobody was getting the vaccine in the poor world, while the average person had more than one shot in the rich world.[55] The situation has been gradually improving but it is telling that we frequently speak of the pandemic in the past tense in the West, whereas in poorer countries it remains a pressing concern and large numbers of people are still unvaccinated. In this instance, taking control over ideas led to more than just monopoly power and irritating advert breaks on your YouTube videos.

In response to these charges, Gates has insisted that it was more than just ideas, since poorer countries simply did not have the infrastructure to create vaccines. This claim did not stand up to scrutiny: there were plenty of available facilities from Canada to Bangladesh who were insisting that they could start vaccine production if only they were given a licence to use the patent.[56] The Gates Foundation led the global vaccine response but it was a deeply inequitable failure which led to countless avoidable deaths, largely thanks to Gates' belief that he and others should be able to extract money from the enterprise. He has partially reversed his position on Covid, but the general damage he has done is difficult to overstate.[57]

Another shining example of how apparently generous endeavours often serve the interests of their founders is that many of them seem to be used at least partially to avoid tax. In 2015, Mark Zuckerberg announced that he and his wife Priscilla Chan were putting $45 billion – 99 per cent of their Facebook stock at the time – into an organisation named the Chan Zuckerberg

Initiative. This move received a lot of praise, but oddly, the organisation was not a charity but a limited liability company. Being a company meant few rules or restrictions on what they could do, giving them much more control and influence than a charity might have. It gave them the ability to donate using the Facebook stock held by the initiative, which would reduce the amount of tax Facebook had to pay. Donations in the USA are tax deductible, so Zuckerberg could accrue a lot of credits over time through these stock donations.[58] Needless to say, foundations like the Gates' can serve a similar purpose.[59]

Tax evasion and generally favourable tax regimes are one way that billionaires perpetuate their wealth and power at a time when many governments are feeling cash-strapped. Researchers Emmanuel Saez and Gabriel Zucman estimate that we could get '$1 trillion from 1,000 billionaires' through a one-off tax on their unrealised gains, which are not deemed taxable under the current regime. What this means is that those numbers on the *Forbes* rich list would suddenly be considered real wealth by the tax authorities, and a rate equivalent to the top income tax rate in the USA (40 per cent) would be applied, albeit spread out over a decade. Saez and Zucman argue that billionaires can use their wealth as collateral – as we saw at the start of the chapter, they do this to buy companies – and their substantial shares to fund the tax payments.[60]

BLASTING OFF

It's not just football clubs, philanthropy and tax avoidance: rich individuals have increasingly used their wealth to launch various schemes that are seemingly unrelated to the area through which they became rich. One of the most striking examples in the present day are the billionaires who are trying to launch their own space exploration companies. This industry includes Elon Musk's SpaceX, Jeff Bezos' Blue Origin and Richard Branson's Virgin Galactic – the latter actually being the first private company to make it into space. They all aim to turn space tourism into a profitable industry and eventually to begin mining asteroids and other planets for minerals. Musk in particular stresses that he wants to colonise Mars and possibly even die there, though 'not on impact' he stressed, in a rare example of a good joke from him.

Although Bernard Arnault flies under the radar (literally, in the case of space exploration) and avoids these ostentatious forays, he has been quietly calculated in his acquisition of French media. Arnault applied for Belgian citizenship shortly after then President François Hollande announced a 75 per cent top tax rate in 2012, which naturally led to the popular perception that he was doing so to reduce the taxes he had to pay. This led to the newspaper *Liberation* publishing a picture of Arnault on their front page with the headline '*Casse-toi riche con!*', which loosely translates as 'Fuck off, rich idiot'. Arnault, who doesn't seem to respond that well to criticism, decided to sue the newspaper – though he later dropped the lawsuit.[61]

Arnault may comfort himself with the fact that he has enough influence over the rest of the French media that he can stop other news outlets from saying mean things about him. Arnault once bought up the major newspaper *La Tribune,* but when he was unable to make it turn a profit, he sold it and bought *Les Echos.* Journalists there reported that they were discouraged from criticising LVMH, Arnault, or fellow media billionaire Vincent Bolloré, with whom Arnault has a 'non-aggression pact' not to criticise one another. Workers revolted when

much-loved editor Nicolas Barré departed after a series of art-
icles were published which were not favoured by LVMH
shareholders, including one which delved into the conglomerate's battles with the French tax authorities.[62]

Yet again, Arnault and Musk find themselves at once strange
bedfellows and polar opposites. While Arnault's media acquisi-
tions seem careful and calculated, Musk's purchase of Twitter
was so absurd that it's difficult to know where to begin. Seemingly without thinking, in 2022 Musk tweeted that he was
willing to purchase the company at $54.20 a stock.[63] This price
was a veiled reference to the time of day, 4.20 p.m., which
weed fans have long seen as the appropriate time they can
smoke their first joint. If you are wondering whether anyone
genuinely finds this funny who is (a) over twelve and (b) doesn't
live in the year 2005, I can assure you that the answer is 'no'.
The 54 was, perhaps, a reference to the number of safety violations *Forbes* uncovered at Tesla.

Launching an acquisition based on a meme is generally not a
great business strategy – though it does make a bigger splash
and generate far more attention than otherwise, something
Musk has always excelled at. In any case, he immediately tried
to back out of the deal, making up all kinds of excuses, but a
Delaware court ruled that he had to follow through with the
purchase. Unfortunately, I was a long-term user of Twitter, so I
had to see the consequences of this decision unfold before I
eventually caved in and deleted my account. It is striking how
much Musk has changed the dynamics of Twitter (now X and,
true to its name, increasingly devolving into a porn website),
noticeably altering the kind of information you can find on
it – or not, as the case may be. Like Arnault, Musk is seeking
influence over more than just his home industry.

All of this speaks to an era where we increasingly see billion-aires having control over areas of life that everyone has a stake in. From global health to transportation to both new and old media, the power enormous wealth gives to buy up anything and every-thing should not be underestimated. Many rich people do have a genuine desire to improve the world; moustache-twirling villains who deliberately try to engineer disaster are a thing of fantasy. But intentions are unimportant; a world where billionaires become more and more responsible for our well-being is one where our well-being is subsumed to the interests of those billionaires. Unless such services are delivered by more democratic institutions, these decisions will remain unaccountable to the population.

An especially galling example of what happens when core functions are handed over to the wealthy comes from Starlink, SpaceX's satellite system. This has proven to be a vital system during the Russia–Ukraine War.[64] One especially controversial decision saw Musk deny Ukrainian drones access to Starlink in Crimea, which thwarted an attack on Russian military targets. Musk viewed this as a potential escalation and vetoed the request for access to the satellite system that the Ukrainians have relied upon. Whatever was the right course of action in this specific case, it illustrates the kinds of decisions we have turned over to these private businesses. It seems that as well as business tycoons, media moguls, public service providers and astronauts, billion-aires have also become generals.[65]

BILLIONAIRES AND CLIMATE CHANGE

Musk is uniquely egocentric among billionaires – which is saying a lot, to be sure – because his overarching mission visibly revolves around him as an individual. Jeff Bezos bought the *Washington Post* largely owing to his dislike of fellow billionaire Donald Trump, but he and Arnault still seem largely focused on cornering their own markets. While they are the kings of logistics and fashion respectively, taking over a wide range of related industries, Musk is the king of trying out whatever he thought up at 3 o'clock that morning. As well as being involved with Tesla, SpaceX and Twitter, Musk also created the so-called Boring Company, which drilled tunnels under Las Vegas for his Tesla cars to drive through without using roads. It was originally billed as a futuristic style of transportation that would have us zooming around underground in our low-emission vehicles like something from *I, Robot* or *Futurama*.

If the Boring tunnel sounds familiar, that's because it essentially describes a subway train which, the observant reader will note, already exists. The main difference is that subway trains hold far more people per cubic foot. The Boring Company was pitched as a way to ease congestion in American cities, which are famously car-centric and plagued by crowded freeways. In reality, the Vegas tunnel turned out to be a slow-moving, claustrophobic death trap without viable escape routes.[66] Reports of safety violations have become common, with tunnel workers operating in what has been described as 'skin-burning chemical sludge'.[67] The buzz around the project has disappeared as plans for tunnels in other cities have been slowly but surely abandoned. Even Musk himself appears to have lost interest.[68]

More generally, it is unclear that efforts such as Musk's are the kind of environmental change that is needed to stop feeding either local pollution or climate change. An obvious problem with a company like Tesla is that if most electricity is produced with fossil fuels, then the impact of electric cars is nullified.[69] It's little good swapping your oil-fuelled car for electricity that is produced by oil fuel. Investment in renewable energies is something which is necessary whether or not cars are electric; how green a country's energy grid is will always be the single biggest factor determining its emissions. And public transport almost always results in lower emissions than cars, whether they're petrol or electric.[70]

The uncomfortable truth is that electric cars seem to benefit richer people disproportionately, especially if they are not part of a bigger package of reforms. The cars are not always afford-able: Musk said he'd set the price of the Model S Sedan to $69,420, which, aside from repeating his 'funny number' joke, is pretty damned expensive. One 2018 study showed that the adoption of electric vehicles only reduced air pollution in richer areas – conveniently, those with income at or higher than approximately the price of the Model S Sedan.[71] Richer, often whiter populations could afford Teslas so their neighbourhoods cleaned up – but the electricity was still produced at coal power plants nearby, leading to even more air pollution in the poor neighbourhoods in which these factories were located.

The projects of these billionaires will continue to have nega-tive social and environmental consequences when compared to publicly funded or well-regulated enterprise. SpaceX has a habit of launching rockets which explode, with the footage tending to go viral on social media. Despite the mocking this generates, the explosions are by all accounts a deliberate strat-egy of 'learning from failure' and SpaceX has indeed iteratively improved its rockets so far. They have crossed milestones others have not, such as fully reusable rockets.[72] However, the strategy of exploding until you succeed differs from the much more careful, piecemeal approach of NASA, and SpaceX has attracted attention from the Federal Aviation Administration, with Musk ignoring their warnings to explode yet more rockets.[73] He considers the regulators boring and, having met a few regulators, I can confirm that this is correct. But despite this – or maybe because of it – I am glad they exist.

The sheer volume of fuel used by the rockets leaves a massive CO_2 footprint. The fact that, unlike NASA, SpaceX does not have a clear strategy for reducing 'space debris' is contributing to this growing problem, with used-up rocket parts orbiting the Earth and getting in the way of future attempts at space travel.[74] Musk also chose to locate in Boca Chica in Texas, an area which historically supports an extremely diverse range of endangered wildlife including sea turtles, wild cats and shorebirds. The construction, noise, waste and debris from the rockets have led to local wildlife evacuating the area.[75] Residents have been no less affected, having been subjected to pressure to move out by SpaceX[76], an offer they may find more tempting given that the rocket company's tests might shatter their windows.[77]

BILLIONAIRES AND THE WIDER WORLD

As hard as he may find it to believe, the issue is bigger than Elon Musk. We need to rethink our approach to ownership and control if we are to progress past an economy skewed by billionaires. In fact, the impact that billionaires and their enormous companies have had on the economy is actually less about the individuals than about the broader economic forces that create them and allow them to exert the degree of control they have. They make neat characters, for sure, but the message I want you to take away is – as with the first chapter – about the structure of the economy as a whole. This is the same challenge we encountered in the previous chapter: the billionaire-dominated economy fails to protect and provide for the majority of the population. As a popular modern adage goes, every billionaire is a policy failure.

Ultimately, expecting billionaires and their empires to serve social and environmental interests is like expecting a horse to do a cartwheel. At a basic level, private enterprise has to make a profit, which is not usually the aim of public services. That is precisely why public services are funded by taxes: they are usually loss-making. While companies like Tesla can make a profit on each car sold, public transport is supposed to be accessible to everyone. Reaching a far-out rural route by train is generally going to cost more than it makes in ticket revenue unless the tickets are prohibitively expensive, which would defeat the purpose of a service intended for everyone.

Economists often speak of externalities: effects that extend beyond the parties involved.[78] Negative externalities like pollution or resources depletion are not paid for by private companies. Positive externalities like the broad benefits of transportation are not reaped by private companies. As a result, capitalism gives us too much pollution and not enough transportation. In practice, both positive and negative externalities are so common that it is an ongoing challenge to ensure that everyone is taken care of: neither trampled nor neglected by the market economy. With billionaires and their huge corporations, the problem of external effects is especially prescient. It is no exaggeration to say that these actors have a seismic impact on communities wherever they go.

Expanding transportation through public funding therefore brings broader benefits to the community that are not easily captured by private companies. Germany introduced the 9-Euro-Ticket policy in 2022, which was a monthly pass to literally anywhere in the country for only (you guessed it) 9 Euros. It saw a huge increase in mobility and well-being for the poorest in the country, who felt they had more freedom and autonomy. Many of the beneficiaries used the tickets simply to go shopping or attend medical appointments, fairly basic functions that undoubtedly had benefits beyond themselves through being healthier and happier.[79] In addition, there were clear reductions in pollution which were concentrated in the areas where trains were most used.[80]

It is therefore necessary to reimagine these businesses so that they serve the common good. The original billionaire founder of Twitter, Jack Dorsey, has stated that he doesn't believe social media platforms like Twitter should be privately owned at all. As the common saying goes, 'if it's free, you're the product'. This creates a perverse dynamic where those consuming the service are also the workers, producing the content that others see. Dorsey has argued that prioritising private shareholders has led to an excessive focus on advertising revenue, where getting the most clicks presides over building a holistically better service. While we all fall victim to clickbait, if we were given the time and power to ponder things, we might opt out of having it altogether. Dorsey has previously tweeted that Twitter itself should be a 'public protocol' rather than a company, a kind of open-source software owned by the community.[81]

BILLIONAIRES VERSUS THE BOTTOM

In the last chapter, we investigated who is essential in a modern economy. We looked at how different ways of organising the economy affect the conditions under which things are produced and who gets the spoils of that production. And there is no better example of how our economy has been reconfigured for the worse than the rise of billionaires and their numerous enterprises. Through acquiring industries, expanding those industries aggressively and then venturing into philanthropy or other whimsical investments, billionaires exert a great deal of control over what happens in our economies. This both reflects and reinforces the stark rise in inequality we have seen in so many rich countries, as they lobby for policies that allow them to extract yet more wealth.

Having said all this, the key question on many people's minds is less the impact of billionaires on them, than how they join their ranks. Social mobility – who gets rich, who stays poor, and why – is a burning topic, but our prevailing culture asks all the wrong questions about how to make it big.

CHAPTER 3

WHO CLIMBS THE LADDER?

The Myths of Meritocracy

You don't have to go far to find trite personal advice on how to become rich these days. Podcasts with titles like 'Why you're staying poor and how to change that NOW' are common. A quick Google search reveals a plethora of listicles, documenting behaviours as wide-ranging as: read every day, wake up early, don't watch TV, eat healthily and above all 'change your mindset'. So-called hustle culture asks us to rise and grind, make the most of our time, invest in multiple income streams, and above all to stop complaining about our own shortcomings. If we are not successful, then it is ourselves who are to blame. In the UK, we are less likely to use Americanised terms like 'hustle' or 'grind' and more likely to repeat the sober mantra 'get on with it!'

Even when people push against these ideas, we still seem to have internalised the message that we need to work as much as possible. One trend that has emerged in recent years is the rise of 'quiet quitting', which is defined as simply doing your job and no more. This means not working extra hours, not being on-call 24/7 and not taking on extra responsibilities that aren't considered a core part of your role. While I welcome this trend, it is telling that people doing their job has been called 'quitting'.

Nothing about fulfilling your contractual obligations is synonymous with 'quitting' – clearly, it is the exact opposite, since you are continuing to work in your job. Calling this 'quiet quitting' is like calling walking 'quiet stopping'.

The truth is that while many of us want to move up in the world, most of the advice we see about how to do it ends up missing the point. For instance, one of the many bestselling books that purports to help people get ahead is *The 4-Hour Work Week*, released in 2007 by Tim Ferriss. Ferriss is a successful investor from Silicon Valley who became an author and, inevitably, a podcaster. He is an interesting person who has a wide range of guests on his show and writes lucidly. In the book, he claims that you can escape the drudgery of 9-to-5 working to reach the fabled 4-hour work week, achieving a quality lifestyle and above all, freedom, by following his advice. Making lots of money while working only a handful of hours a week is a pretty wild expectation for most people, so Ferriss must have some world-beating ideas.[1]

The book undoubtedly has a few helpful tips about avoiding the mindset of 'work for the sake of work': not spending too much time on emails or pointless phone calls; thinking for yourself and trying new things; asking yourself whether working 9-to-5 in a terrible job just so you can afford retirement is really worth it. Nevertheless, it is also quite telling about this genre of financial self-help books: most of the big suggestions require some combination of luck, privilege and questionable practices. For example, there is quite a lot written on how you can live like royalty just by moving to a poorer country.[2] Anyone who has been abroad from the West can attest that this is true, but (a) many Western people may not want to do this, and (b) the majority of the rest of the world *cannot*, as they already live in those countries and so cannot benefit from the generous exchange rates.

Unfortunately, this theme continues: large sections of *The 4-Hour Work Week* are about hiring low-paid personal assistants from India to do all of your work for you. These assistants are supposed to send emails, design websites, invent products and even carry out personal tasks like emailing your spouse. In a presumably deliberate twist, sections of the book are actually written by these assistants and other people who aren't Tim Ferriss.[3] Ironically, the book then pivots to selling ideas like self-help books, giving talks and writing on subjects you're barely an expert in. At one point Ferriss directly mocks the idea that an 'expert' needs to have real credentials or smarts.[4] At this stage, it starts to feel like a trick: like the book is mocking *you* for buying it. Needless to say, his advice is not generalisable because if we all followed it, we'd run out of assistants and be overwhelmed by self-help books.

Ferriss' current position results from a number of practices and advantages that just cannot be emulated by everyone. To put it in the parlance of our own book, it seems that a lot of his tips are less about creating wealth and more about extracting it from the rest of us. In fact, his privileged position as somebody who barely works while others do it for him is reminiscent of fourteenth-century feudal lords – or perhaps more accurately, nineteenth-century colonial officials. His naive advice prompts the obvious question: what about the Indian assistants themselves?

Ferriss remains regarded as someone who can give you good career and life advice, having followed up with several other books. And there is a reason that we tend to listen to advice from successful people like this, whether it's proven or not: we strongly believe that our society is one of meritocracy. There is

a widespread perception that, whereas successful people succeed because of their grind and hustle, poor people remain
poor largely because of their negative mentality and self-
defeating habits. In 1757, Adam Smith was already pointing
out the danger of an overly admirative view of the wealthy:[5]

> This disposition to admire, and almost to worship, the
> rich and the powerful, and to despise, or, at least, to neg-
> lect persons of poor and mean condition . . . [is] . . . the
> great and most universal cause of the corruption of our
> moral sentiments.

Instead of focusing on the successful habits of individuals, I
want to show you that a substantial proportion of the lack of
social mobility across the world is created by barriers rather
than different individual efforts and aptitudes. These can take
the form of the challenges of poverty, of inadequate education,
of biases and stereotypes among decision-makers, and of ether-
eal privileges such as connections to the already rich and
powerful. While podcasters may instil us with the entirely reasonable advice to work smart and get on the economic ladder,
it seems that the rungs are a bit more spaced out for some than
for others. Even more so, it is just not possible for everyone to
climb up at the same time.

I WILL SURVIVE

Edgar Cayce's Association for Research and Enlightenment
(ARE) believed that some people had extra-sensory perception
(ESP): an ability to predict the future. To prove this extraordinary

contention, they pointed to experimental subjects who, they claimed, were able to guess randomly selected cards. A group of 35 subjects were asked to predict one of five symbols before the card was revealed. This was repeated for 25 trials and some got it right most of the time. These people were designated to have ESP, whereas those who guessed incorrectly were designated not to.

This sounds impressive, but a moment's inspection reveals this to be a simple matter of chance. With enough subjects, some people are going to guess quite a few of the cards correctly – after all, it's only a one in five chance each time. Only selecting the 'winners' who have guessed correctly and concluding that they have special attributes creates a bias in the conclusion. Including the 'losers' in the analysis would have led ARE to conclude that the results were pure chance and that ESP does not exist.[6]

The name for this phenomenon is survivorship bias and it has implications from economics to statistics to military history.[7] The key point is that we only observe the 'winners' of various historical, economic and social processes and are given to draw sweeping conclusions from their behaviours. We see their success and assume that everything from their morning routine to their opinions on comets is to be emulated, even though these may have played no part in said success. As the below XKCD comic neatly illustrates, being guilty of survivorship bias is like only paying attention to the habits of lottery winners when deciding whether you should buy a ticket, ignoring the countless others whose numbers didn't come in. When we are judging the characteristics of the successful, we have to ask whether we are seeing the full picture.

Survivorship bias applies in spades to the field of economics.

For every adult who claimed, aged four, they were going to grow up to be rich and then actually achieved it, there are a hundred more who promised the same but ended up with an average level of income. For every business that succeeds with some innovative vision, there are plenty, just as bold, that went belly-up. To turn survivorship bias upside down, consider that for every homeless person you see who 'made some bad life choices' and ended up unemployed, suffering from addiction, or hopeless, there are plenty who made similar choices but ended up getting out of it one way or another.

'But surely,' we tend to think, 'those who succeed must just be better at what they do?' The issue is that we have no way of knowing who is 'better' based on some careful consideration of their actual aptitudes, behaviours and ideas. We have simply not evaluated the entire human population on these characteristics and it's unlikely anyone ever will, or even that such a task is possible. All we can see are outcomes like people's income, wealth, stock market values of their companies, and so on. These are precisely the things we are trying to explain: pointing to them as evidence of talent or hard work is like pointing to a puddle as evidence that *those* water molecules were always the best at coming together to form a puddle.

Most people who are successful in one or other dimension can trace it back to some lucky breaks. I myself applied late for a PhD at the University of Manchester owing to my then-awful organisational skills, which are now marginally improved. As not all places were full that particular year, I was allowed in anyway. Had I applied either the year before or the year after, which were both much busier years, I'd not have got in when I wanted. Who knows if I'd be writing this book had I not started my PhD that year? I'll leave it to the reader to decide whether this book is the good or the bad outcome.

Tim Ferriss is clearly a survivor. It's notable that he had already made millions when he wrote *The 4-Hour Work Week*, so he was starting from a wealthy position rather than from scratch. He became rich from an online supplement business, a product called BrainQUICKEN, which has unproven benefits and to which he attached a super-high mark-up.[8] He reports that at one point he went on holiday to London and started limiting his input into the business. Profits jumped 40 per cent.[9] I know some successful entrepreneurs and I can tell you that not one of them has replicated this experience after going on holiday. Profits are much more likely to fall than to rise in their absence.

My point is not that Ferriss or anyone else is uniquely undeserving; it's that individual aptitudes are neither a necessary nor a sufficient condition for success. Rich imbeciles are easy to find (just look at certain members of the British Royal Family) and poor geniuses, while less likely to be on the television, are almost as common – just ask graduate students who attend seminars just to get free food. More importantly, such intelligence is neither a necessary nor a sufficient condition to do something which is good for humanity. If we are asking how to get rich as an individual, my response is that this is the wrong question. We need to look at the whole picture instead of only stories about individuals.

THE LIMITS OF MERITOCRACY

> We all have this idea that we should move up a little bit from our parents' station and each – and each generation should do a little bit better.
> *Eminem, 'Yellow Brick Road'*

The American Dream teaches us that anybody can make it: you can be born in poverty but escape and become rich. Equally, anybody, no matter how much wealth they inherit, can fall from grace and lose their station if they stop working hard and proving their value. When economists investigate whether this dream is a reality, they look at the relationship between parents' and children's income, which is known as intergenerational mobility. This tells us how much people's prospects depend on the birth lottery: if intergenerational mobility were perfect, you'd have the same chance of ending up rich, poor, or somewhere in the middle, no matter your parents' income.

Comprehensive evidence from the USA shows that this is far

from the case. Over 30 in 100 children born poor stay poor, while an even higher proportion of children born rich stay rich. Conversely, fewer than 10 in 100 children born poor end up rich, while just over 10 in 100 of those born rich end up poor.[10] According to my own research, under 10 in 100 of those who are born into the top 20 per cent of income earners in England end up in the bottom 20 per cent, while around 32 in 100 – three times as many of them – stay at the top. Although there is a fair amount of 'churn' in the middle class – meaning you are likely to go from lower-middle to upper-middle, or vice versa – the poorest have a lower chance of ending up out of poverty. Only 14 in 100 of those who are born in the bottom 20 per cent in England end up at the top, while around 29 out of 100 – twice as many of them – stay poor.[11] Mobility is slightly higher across the Atlantic Ocean, which may come as a surprise for narratives about the American Dream.

Although social mobility is limited within richer countries, poor and middle-income countries are typically thought to have it far worse. Data are harder to come by in these countries, but inequality is known to be severe across Latin America, and in Brazil, Peru and Chile, the income of parents is more strongly predictive of their children's eventual income than in any of the richer countries.[12] At the other end of the spectrum, Northern European countries are often celebrated for their high intergenerational mobility. In these countries, your fortunes in life are far less dependent on your parents' income. Norway, Sweden, Finland, Germany and especially Denmark seem to have got close to that ideal of parents' income barely mattering at all for future prospects.[13]

A particularly striking finding came from China. Outright revolution in 1949 had overthrown feudal landlords and redistributed their land to the peasants, in many cases attacking and killing the landlords in the process. The upheavals didn't stop there: the decades-long cultural revolution started 17 years later, dispossessing remaining elites and forcing them out of education. Yet despite these massive changes, the grandchildren of the elites remained richer and more educated than the general population. It seemed that even when completely stripped of their wealth and status, elites had passed down knowledge and retained connections.[14]

All of this presents a puzzle: if individual aptitudes and efforts are the best way to explain the level of mobility, then why do some countries succeed at ensuring mobility while others don't? On the other hand, if mobility can prove so difficult to change even under extreme circumstances, do we really have any hope of doing so? Perhaps mobility in each country is just a long-lasting legacy of stubborn historical forces. To begin to answer these questions, I want to shift focus a little to the barriers faced by individuals. How factors such as poverty, class and discrimination affect our life chances may shed some light on exactly what is driving these distinct levels of mobility.

MARSHMAL-LIES

There is a famous test in psychology known as the marshmallow test, originally designed to understand patience and self-control. In the original experiment, young children were asked to sit in a room with a marshmallow in front of them. The experimenter told them that they could eat the marshmallow now or wait five minutes to get given an extra marshmallow. If the child was able to refrain from devouring the sweet straightaway, they'd soon have twice the amount. The experiment was first devised in the 1960s but has been repeated across the world hundreds of times since then. Unsurprisingly, many children have trouble resisting and just go for the first marshmallow, but a substantial proportion do manage to wait for the extra one.

The reason the experiment became so famous was not for this fairly anodyne finding but because the original experimenter, Walter Mischel, ended up checking in on the children when they were older. What he found was that whether or not they had waited – how patient they had been when they were just children – predicted a wide range of later life outcomes. Children who had exercised self-control in the lab were healthier, earned more and had higher academic achievements than those who hadn't. This wasn't a fluke, either; the finding has been replicated many times. It seemed like the children who were more patient in the lab demonstrated a personality trait which would serve them well later in life.[15]

One of the more uncomfortable findings for the marshmallow test has been that poorer children are much less likely to wait than richer children. This clearly demonstrated that children from poorer backgrounds lacked self-restraint when compared to those from wealthier backgrounds. As children born into poorer families are quite likely to remain poor, while children born into rich families are quite likely to remain rich, this became a popular explanation for why some were poor and others rich. Those who waited for the second marshmallow were able to eat better, study, save more, work harder. The corollary was clear, if not always stated explicitly: being poor was a result of a personality defect.

In recent years, several studies have added some helpful qualifiers to these conclusions, arrived at too hastily by observers keen to blame the poor for their poverty. One experiment re-did the test but additionally monitored the children's vagus nerve. The vagus nerve runs from your brain through your throat all the way down to your digestive system and those who display more activity in the nerve – a higher vagal tone – are usually calmer and more in control, while those who have a lower vagal tone are less in control. The phrase 'gut feeling' is an acknowledgement of the role of things like the vagus nerve in your mood. The new study found that for children from richer backgrounds, a higher vagal tone meant they were more likely to be patient and wait. This would seem like further affirmation that being cool under pressure and making patient, rational, long-term decisions will serve you well later in life.

What destroyed this interpretation was that the result was outright inverted for poorer children. In their case, having a higher vagal tone was associated with *not* waiting for the extra marshmallow. Those children who came from poorer backgrounds and who seemed to keep their cool – as exhibited by their higher vagal tone – were more impatient, not less impatient as their richer counterparts were. This suggests that if you were poor then the rational, calm decision was actually to take the first marshmallow rather than waiting. Conversely, if you were rich, the rational decision was to wait and take the second marshmallow. What was going on?[16]

The original interpretation of the marshmallow experiment seems like a classic case of getting things the wrong way round – or mistaking correlation and causation, if you want to use statistical jargon. It's not that being impatient causes being poor; it's that being poor causes people to be impatient, and for good reason. When you are poor, it is often irrational to wait for things since you cannot rely on them coming. Poor children are constantly told they will get all kinds of things if they just wait: birthday presents, holiday trips, meals. They learn quickly that they cannot rely on people telling them they'll come back with more. In contrast, middle-class or rich children are used to getting the things they are promised, so they're happy to sit and wait for the extra marshmallow.

Another version of the marshmallow test took a different approach, focusing on the children's environment instead of their personality by asking whether children trusted the experimenter to come back. Instead of marshmallows, they first gave the children some old crayons, and the children were told they could colour in using them now or that they would get better art supplies if they waited for the experimenter to go and get them. There were then two possibilities: either the experimenter would return with the new art supplies, or they would come back and say, 'I'm sorry, but I made a mistake. We don't have any other art supplies after all. But why don't you just use these [the old crayons] instead?'

The children were then subjected to the classic marshmallow test, and as you may have expected, the reliability of the experimenter became a crucial factor in whether or not they waited. The children who had been shown the experimenter could not be relied upon were much less likely to wait and would grab the first marshmallow, while those who had been brought better art supplies previously were more likely to wait for the second marshmallow. This experiment was deliberately designed to mimic the unreliable environment that poverty puts children in. It showed how that environment of scarcity and lack of trust can prompt children to take what they can get in the moment.[17]

There is now a wide range of evidence that being poor creates an environment where it is extremely hard to plan forward, not to mention make many other decisions. (Many readers who have experienced poverty will not be surprised by this finding, but sometimes it takes academics a while to catch up.) We have definitive proof that being poor causes people to be more impatient, which is itself an example of how they place their attention on the here and now.[18] Making long-term decisions is not a priority when you need to put food on the table or face eviction if you do not pay rent. This is one reason people in poverty are generally less likely to save and more likely to borrow at high interest rates, since it's no use saving for tomorrow when there may not be a tomorrow.[19] But this is only one way that poverty keeps people poor.

IT'S EXPENSIVE TO BE POOR

In Terry Pratchett's novel *Men at Arms*, the character Sam Vimes comes up with his 'theory of socioeconomic injustice':[20]

> The reason that the rich were so rich, Vimes reasoned, was because they managed to spend less money . . . good boots lasted for years and years. A man who could afford fifty dollars had a pair of boots that'd still be keeping his feet dry in ten years' time, while the poor man who could only afford cheap boots would have spent a hundred dollars on boots in the same time and would still have wet feet.

To take a modern example, many readers will have noticed that buying a mobile phone outright costs less in total than spreading out payments over a 36-month period. For most of us, shelling out £1,000+ upfront is too much to handle, while for richer people it is a feasible option. Poorer people pay £1,500 over 36 months, while richer people pay only £1,000 right away. An outright inability to afford to invest in your future is another good reason to be more concerned with the here and now. The monthly payments become the thing to focus on because paying the overall value is not an option.

It is expensive to be poor – and correspondingly cheap to be rich. At the very top, celebrities and prominent influencers, though typically quite well-off in terms of income, often don't have to pay for things at all. Influencers are regularly gifted by brands in the hope that wearing that make of clothing, using that brand of make-up, or eating at that particular restaurant will count as an endorsement. (This practice may have gone too far – an especially amusing example of this trend was when restaurant owners had to tell influencers to stop 'offering' to eat at their restaurants for free.)[21] And we don't witness this kind of thing only at the extremes; it plays out across the income distribution. The more money you have, the less you need to spend.

Poverty costs people in all sorts of ways because it places constraints and pressures on what they do. One famous study of Indian farmers found that they gained cognitive function after a harvest. Before they reaped and sold their crops, they were poor, but the exact same individual gained around 13 points on an IQ test afterwards. If you're wondering what that means, it is roughly equivalent to the difference between alcoholics and non-alcoholics; or the difference from losing one night's sleep; or the difference from gaining a university degree. The same study showed that experimental participants in the USA performed worse when making a hypothetical decision about their car if there was more money at stake.[22]

We should not confuse this economic disadvantage with irrationality, let alone stupidity. In *Arrested Development,* wealthy magnate Lucille Bluth reveals how out of touch she is when she ponders the price of an everyday fruit to her son. 'It's one banana, Michael. What could it cost, $10?' It turns out that poor people are typically more fastidious with their budgets than rich people, simply by virtue of necessity. In one experiment, people were asked if they'd be willing to travel to save $50 on a $300 tablet, and then asked if they'd be willing to do the same to save $50 on a $1,000 tablet. Most people said they'd do the former but not the latter, but since $50 is $50, this seems to be irrational. The twist is that poorer people were more likely to answer yes to both: since that $50 means a lot more to them, they tend to think about the issue more clearly.[23] Penny pinching is necessary when you have fewer pennies to pinch.

There are well-established ways that poverty makes us all poorer. Those in poverty are more likely to commit crimes; more likely to use healthcare; more likely to claim benefits; more likely to be homeless; more likely to use social services; tend to earn less; and tend to get less education. When you cut spending aimed at reducing poverty, you end up costing not just the affected individuals but everyone else down the line. It's a bit like pushing down a lump under the carpet; it's only going to show up elsewhere. It has been estimated that poverty overall costs the UK £78 billion a year due to an inadequate welfare state and public services, well beyond what it would cost to fund them.[24] Although precise figures like this should always be taken with a pinch of salt, the general idea is not disputed.

Childhood poverty is undoubtedly the most impactful

because it plays out over an entire lifetime.[25] Economist James Heckman has made it one of his life missions to communicate how important childhood nutrition, education and care are for future possibilities. Children who receive programmes which educate them and ensure they have access to resources are more likely to earn more, have better health, and less likely to be involved in crime when they grow up. The 'Heckman equation' emphasises that the earlier, the better: some of the most effective programmes are from birth until pre-school.[26] Many government programmes aimed at young children are so effective that they pay for themselves in the long term through higher tax revenues and lower social costs.[27]

In summary, poor people are constrained in all sorts of ways by the simple fact that they are poor. Poverty disrupts your ability to plan and to invest in yourself and your family, even reducing your cognitive functions. Children born into poverty struggle on a number of fronts because of their lack of access to resources. And to top it all off, as you get poorer it becomes much harder to control your finances – not just because you've got less wiggle room, but because things are objectively more expensive. The main issue with people in poverty is therefore not their lack of hustle, self-control, or their mindset: it's that they just don't have enough money. And this is not just expensive for the poor; it hurts the rest of us, too, through decreased productivity and through public spending to pick up the pieces.

DISCRIMINATION: FACT OR FICTION?

In an infamous 2018 interview, Canadian psychologist Jordan Peterson appeared on Britain's *Channel 4 News*. He was being interviewed by the journalist Cathy Newman about his new status as a famous intellectual, something few academics experience. Peterson's profile had grown massively thanks to YouTube and to some political interventions he made in Canada surrounding free speech. This was a chance to understand the Peterson phenomenon, including his somewhat controversial views on gender. Yet the interview did not go very well, not least because Newman clearly had an axe to grind and repeatedly put words in Peterson's mouth. In contrast, he handled himself well, coming across as knowledgeable and polite despite the hostile interviewer.[28]

In truth, I am less interested in the dynamics of the interview than I am in some of the factual claims Peterson made during it. When Newman argued that women are paid 9 per cent less for the same job than men, Peterson countered that once you break the data down by characteristics like age, occupation and personality type, this so-called gender pay gap 'doesn't exist'. This reflects a pretty widely held perception that lower average pay for women – which is definitively a fact – is just an artefact of the reality that men and women are different. They therefore make different choices about where they work, the hours they work, whether they ask for a promotion, and so on. Given the same job, Peterson charges that men and women will earn roughly the same amount.

As with most complex issues translated into political slogans, there can be some loose talk surrounding the gender pay gap. In the TV show *Rick and Morty*, the character Summer challenges scientist Rick's contention there is no sexism on Earth by saying 'we make 70 per cent of your salary for the same job'. This is, at best, a dated figure which massively overstates the differential pay between men and women in most rich countries. On the other hand, Peterson's contention that the gender pay gap does not exist *at all* within the same job – once you account for all the differences he laid out – is untrue, and evidence from the USA at around the time of the interview suggests that the difference is 9 per cent, precisely as Cathy Newman claimed.[29]

Most important is that accounting for these differences between men and women is not always the right thing to do. As we've seen, poverty inflicts a number of disadvantages on anyone who experiences it, so even if women are employed in different jobs, their lower income could cause issues for themselves and for the broader economy. As it turns out, women working full-time earn 20 per cent less than men on average, partly because the jobs women work pay less. On top of this, women as a whole are less likely to work in paid employment, which means that the average woman in the USA earns about 60 per cent as much as the average man. Women receive substantially less income than men, so regardless of the causes, they have lower access to resources full stop.[30]

One of Peterson's other points is to emphasise that men are more likely to work long hours in high-powered jobs like the legal profession.[31] While this may be true, there is an asymmetry in unpaid work at home: cleaning, cooking and childcare. This work keeps things ticking over – for a functioning economy and society, everyone needs to be fed, places need to be clean and organised, and children need to be raised – but it is not always rewarded by the market economy since it doesn't produce private revenue. Evidence from the USA shows that women do about twice as much of this work as men, which puts the fact that they have only 60 per cent as much income in context. In poorer countries across the world, the total amount of unpaid work is likely to be higher, and the disparity between men and women is likely to be worse. In Mali, Cambodia, Pakistan and India, women take care of more than 90 per cent of the many hours of unpaid work done every day.[32] It's not that they're not working; it's just that they don't get paid!

IS DISCRIMINATION DEAD?

Because people have become dependent on the market economy for income, it is necessary to interrogate who gets preferential access and therefore economic advantages. If discrimination is rife, then those who get fewer opportunities are less likely to be successful through no fault of their own. And most people do not dispute that there has been a long history of sexism, racism, homophobia and other forms of discrimination in most countries. It was only in the latter half of the twentieth century that racial segregation was abolished in the USA, that women entered the workforce, and that being gay became legal. There are people alive today who were born before these changes.

What Jordan Peterson's contentious interview with Cathy Newman highlighted is the modern controversy over whether these issues still exist to any major extent – especially whether they explain contemporary differences in employment, income, access to housing, and so on. Formal barriers to participation have been lifted and, in fact, most previously disadvantaged groups are now protected explicitly from discrimination by legislation. It could even be the case that the pendulum has swung so far the other way that these groups have a relative advantage nowadays, sometimes termed 'positive discrimination'. Investigating this question leads us to, in my opinion, some of the tightest and most illuminating statistical research in social science over the past few decades.

It turns out that because discrimination is usually based on observable characteristics – not just gender but race, immigrant status, disability and even sexuality – it can be quite easily manipulated in studies to see if it is these factors, and these factors alone, that determine people's opportunities. For example, a plethora of famous studies sent out fake CVs to employers which were identical in all but the name. One CV would have a female name displayed in big letters at the top; another would have a male name, but the two CVs would be indistinguishable if the names were hidden. This means that employers will believe that the man and the woman are exactly the same in everything from their education to their employment history to their hobbies. The only reason the employer should make a different choice is because they have a bias one way or the other.

Evidence from these studies shows that employers are indeed less likely to hire women in male-dominated jobs like lawyers, doctors and financiers.[33] One study of scientists found that identical female applicants – which included a full personal statement – were less likely to be successful, were offered less money if accepted, and were rated as less competent than the (seemingly) male applicants.[34] It's not just men driving these decisions, either; everyone is subject to these biases. Evidence suggests female academics tend to discriminate against other women, too.[35]

It goes further than just job applications: an analogous study used an online university course to manipulate whether students thought their teacher was male or female. As the course was purely through written or third-party content online, there were no lectures and so the name alone could determine students' perceptions of the gender of their teacher. Despite the exact same instruction, the 'female' teacher received lower student ratings.[36] The problem even gets meta: when evaluating the very research we are discussing, male academics are more likely to be sceptical of it than female academics![37]

Before we assume that all this gender discrimination only goes one way, we should note an important feature of the findings. Just as women are less likely to be accepted into male-dominated industries, men are less likely to be accepted into female-dominated industries. If you're male, you may have had the frustrating experience of applying to hospitality or secretarial roles as a teenager and being rejected, only to see young women who also have zero experience be accepted. Men are less likely to get callbacks in jobs like hospitality, nursing and administrative or secretarial roles. Some evidence even indicates the level of discrimination here is *worse* than for women applying for male-dominated jobs, possibly due to a lack of social awareness of the issue.[38]

Studies on other disadvantaged groups exhibit the same basic finding that they get lower callbacks, but each iteration seems to have a unique (if depressing) twist. For instance, one of the original CV studies investigated discrimination against African Americans and was aptly titled 'Are Emily and Greg more employable than Lakisha and Jamal?'[39] The CVs were split not only between those who were black and white, but also by quality. Some had more experience, more qualifications, more soft skills like knowing a foreign language, fewer holes in their employment history, and so on. The researchers could therefore investigate four groups: white and qualified, black and qualified, white and unqualified, and black and unqualified.

The study found that Lakisha and Jamal were, in fact, one-third less likely to get the callback than Emily and Greg, even with identical CVs. But the quality element of the study revealed a concerning nuance. While white people with a high-quality CV were more likely to get an offer than white people with a low-quality CV, for black people this factor didn't make a difference at all. African Americans with lots of experience and skills were treated the same as those without. In the words of economist Tim Harford 'it was as though there were three categories: "gifted and white", "ordinary and white", and simply "black"'.[40] The message from this finding is quite clear: why try to escape poverty via education when it won't make a difference?

DAMNED IF YOU DO, DAMNED IF YOU DON'T

This kind of asymmetrical treatment of different groups brings us back to Peterson and Newman. Peterson's academic background lies in personality research and so he is often keen to emphasise these factors in determining different outcomes, whether in employment or elsewhere. As he acknowledges in the interview, differences in personality traits between men and women are not that big, but one that may be a factor is that women are more 'agreeable'. This trait basically means what it says on the tin: whereas women keep their opinions to themselves, men are more likely to voice their opinions and challenge others. Being 'disagreeable' in this way is associated with higher pay as people push for more from their superiors so the natural conclusion is that, since women are more agreeable, they're less likely to ask for a raise.

Once again, though, we see the double bind of being in a group who face discrimination. One study found that women are indeed more agreeable than men, but there are still a fair few who are disagreeable and will ask for that pay rise. However, while being disagreeable was rewarded with higher pay for men, this was not so for women.[41] Being disagreeable may get men somewhere, but it won't work for women. It has also been shown that women are more often expected to take care of menial tasks in the office: taking minutes, making tea, even cleaning the office kitchen.[42] Once more, they are punished should they not display this altruistic kind of behaviour, whereas men are not.[43]

It's clear that individual behaviour and traits do not always produce the same results for different groups of people: studies on both women and African Americans show that they are 'damned if they do, damned if they don't'. For society as a whole, this is an inescapable failure to match would-be productive people to appropriate roles. The individuals who face this discrimination lose out the most, but we all suffer from the wasted talent. The situation is especially insidious because it creates a vicious spiral. Many people are steered away from paths that they would be unlikely to succeed in due to discrimination, which means they don't even bother in the first place.[44]

Although these studies demonstrate discrimination about as clearly as I believe possible, there are some counterpoints worth addressing. For example, in an interview, UK pundit Andrew Doyle highlighted evidence that recruiters are more likely to hire people with the same birthdays as them, arguing that people 'tend to favour candidates who are more similar to themselves'.[45] In other words, the studies detailed above are less evidence of racism and sexism, and more evidence of a general tendency of humans to stick with their in-group, just like football fans or rival departments within a workplace. While this may be true, it amounts not to denying the findings but to explaining them away – not unlike how Jordan Peterson's argument that the gender pay gap is just an outcome of differences in occupation, traits and hours worked. Regardless of the exact causes, the net result is that people who are not in dominant positions – marked by race, class, gender, sexuality, or whatever else – are further excluded.

More fundamental is that this argument completely fails to engage with the question of *why* certain markers are significant. Birthdays are of cultural significance in many Western societies but Quakers and Jehovah's Witnesses abstain; many countries across the world are likewise less likely to celebrate birthdays than we are, including Vietnam, Bhutan, Mozambique and Japan. If you did the CV studies in these populations, you likely wouldn't find employers hiring people with the same birthday because people care less about birthdays in the first place. This raises the question of why exactly race and gender are deemed so important as markers of 'similarity' in our society: is the aim not to make them as insignificant as birthdays are for Bhutanese? As the late economist Bill Spriggs put it, why would anyone:

> . . . assume that an entire set of actors, observing the infinite diversity of human beings, all settle on 'race' as a meaningful marker independent of history, laws, and social norms? And, miraculously . . . only negative attributes highly correlated with 'race'.

Race being a cultural signifier of inferiority is not just a simple in-group bias; it is the essence of racial discrimination.

Underscoring this problem is another counterargument to the studies: that really 'blackness' is just a marker for class, so the issue is class rather than race. But if 'black' names are taken as a marker of being in a lower class, we again have to ask why that is.[46] We have an association between race and class for historical reasons, which leads to the discrimination we observe. All in all, it seems that there is no reason for us to think of race, class or gender as important markers of aptitudes and preferences to do a particular job.

DON'T ASK ME, I'M JUST A GIRL

In *The Simpsons,* Lisa rants to her brother Bart about the new Malibu Stacey doll, whose sayings include 'don't ask me, I'm just a girl' and 'let's buy make-up so the boys will like us'. Attitudes towards gender are quite deep-seated and go back further than the moment an employer looks at your CV. For instance, there is evidence that teachers, parents and peers tend to push boys towards subjects like maths and science relative to girls.[47] A study in the USA looked at how early exposure to these kinds of gender attitudes feeds into occupational choices in adulthood. Girls born into states with more progressive attitudes are more likely to work at all and to work in male-dominated occupations if they do. Boys are more likely to work in female-dominated occupations than their counterparts born into less progressive states.[48]

Such deep-seated biases are undoubtedly difficult to address. Still, there are readily available examples within reach. A perpetual hot button issue in the West is the under-representation of women in the STEM subjects of science, technology, engineering and maths. As of 2023, women in the UK only make up 29 per cent of the STEM workforce;[49] the number is similar in the USA. In contrast, two regions of the world where women have roughly equal representation in science are Arab states and the former Soviet Union. Both have long histories of promoting female entry into the STEM subjects. This can occur through information campaigns: it was not so long ago that adverts for jobs were targeted explicitly at men or at women, depending on the role. Bucking this trend, the USSR regularly displayed posters urging women to become scientists. The USSR also provided childcare, laundries and cafeterias to enable these women to work even through motherhood.[50]

Changing education systems can have long-term effects, too. Instead of allowing children to choose their subjects, Tunisia and Jordan both use test scores and nothing else to allocate children, which organically results in more girls in science.[51] A history of utilising these policies casts a long shadow: to this day, East German women remain more confident in mathematics than their West German counterparts,[52] while in many Arab states women are actually over-represented among science graduates.[53] These countries, of course, still have clear issues with sexism and other biases; it's just that they don't have quite the same associations that we do in the West – which implies those associations can be changed. There is evidence from the USA that simply being exposed to same-sex role models in STEM can make girls more likely to pursue it.[54]

There is a history of female representation in STEM and related industries in the West, too. Anyone who has seen the 2016 film *Hidden Figures* will have learned that African American women played a big role in NASA's space race in the 1960s but were, well, hidden from view. The UK also had a burgeoning technology sector during this period, mostly staffed by women at a time when coding was considered a boring and bureaucratic job where women were paid less for 'girl hours' (no, really). As it became apparent that computers were the wave of the future, women were no longer seen as appropriate for the tech sector and were forced out in favour of men. In fact, the UK Government invested in a labour-saving mainframe so that women would not be needed. As the mainframe was a doomed technology, they ended up destroying the tech sector in the process of evicting women – which is part of the reason we still don't have one today.[55] Once again, it seems that discrimination is bad for everyone.

Today, the most famous technology sector in the world is Silicon Valley in California, which like its UK precursor has become a boys' club. Tech journalist Emily Chang has detailed there is a tradition of lunchtime trips to strip clubs, trips which obviously make many women feel uncomfortable but which they are often compelled to go to. Needless to say, this is less about women's ability to actually do the work and more about the environment they're placed in. Alarmingly, women receive only 2 per cent of venture capital funding in Silicon Valley. As one female tech worker observed, there is a relationship between the lack of funding and the sexism:

> If you do participate in these sex parties, don't ever think about starting a company or having someone invest in you. Those doors get shut. But if you don't participate, you're shut out. You're damned if you do, damned if you don't.[56]

Overall, pervasive discrimination means that groups with a racial or ethnic difference to the majority are less likely to be hired and earn less even when they are hired, restricting their access to resources. In some cases, it is difficult for them to get ahead as investing in education or skills may not be rewarded. In the case of women, they are generally expected to work in 'caring' roles: as a mother and homemaker out of employment, or as a nurse or secretary inside employment. Even when they get access to traditionally male jobs, they may be expected to perform caring duties in the office, making sure the team and workplace as a whole is ticking over rather than pursuing their individual careers. Men are pushed in the opposite direction, and while on average this leads to higher pay and status, it ultimately inhibits their choices and has them doing things that aren't their true calling.

THE PATH TO RICHES

Britain is well known for its 'old boy' network. A famous picture depicts the so-called Bullingdon Club in 1987, an elite all-male club at Oxford University known for smashing up restaurants and paying off the owners, as well as allegedly burning £50 notes in front of homeless people. Among those pictured are future prime ministers Boris Johnson and David Cameron, alongside a wide range of people descended from wealth and who would go on to be barons, bankers and billionaires. In my experience, most people have trouble looking at the picture without a sense of unease. The entitlement spills out from the page, epitomised by the proud stances and matching expensive suits of the all-white, all-male, all-upper-class cast.

Public schools – which are what we call private schools

because our country stopped trying to make sense a long time ago – are one of the key vehicles for getting into the elite in the UK. Most attendees are born rich, which they'd have to be because of the forbidding fees, but the schools still give them a formidable boost. Although their persistence has declined over time, the nine top schools, known as the Clarendon schools, are an alarming 94 times more likely to produce elites than the average British school. It is not mere rhetoric to say that the students at these schools are our future rulers.

It is difficult to overstate the kind of access that the British elite have to resources and education when they are younger. Clearly, they will never want for a meal and would be happy to wait for the second marshmallow – or, more likely, the second packet of marshmallows. They are reportedly told that they are destined to run the country and the fact that two out of three British prime ministers attended Clarendon schools tells you that this is no lie.[57] They have access to an elite network of connections that ensures they will be able to get jobs that offer them money and power. This is why, even if the alumni of Clarendon don't go on to prestigious universities like Oxford or Cambridge, they still have a pretty good chance of reaching the upper echelons of society.

Class is a tricky subject to understand, partially because its definition seems so loose and changeable. According to a classical Marxist definition, anyone who works for a wage is a worker and could therefore be deemed working class. If you don't own land, physical capital, or (these days) digital infrastructure, then you are basically dependent on the 9-to-5 to get by. In many ways, this seems like a reasonable distinction to make: those who work for a living versus those who are in charge of workers because they own things. This Marxist definition of your class position is, incidentally, the same situation Tim Ferriss wanted his readers to escape. Yet as work has changed over the past century or so, some ambiguities have arisen.

Many salaried jobs now have relatively high incomes, meaning that so-called 'workers' may find themselves with as much or more income than some owners. These higher-income jobs – often accessible via higher education – have become less drudgerous and more independent, which has sparked new discussions about what it means to be working class. Is it doing manual or repetitive labour? Is it having a degree? Does it depend on subtle cultural tendencies such as accents? Is it something you can change, or is your own class instead determined by your parents' position in the socioeconomic hierarchy? It may be that contemporary class is a bit like an elephant: hard to define, but you know it when you see it.

Sociologist Mike Savage has created the most comprehensive modern account of class in Britain.[58] Savage argues that class is a combination of economic, social and cultural capital. I would describe these respectively as 'what you have, who you know, and what you know'. Naturally, the Bullingdon elite tend to have all three. They'll have inherited wealth, most likely in keeping with Britain's rich tradition of concentrated land ownership dating back to William the Conqueror. They'll also know plenty of people in positions of power: as one commentator observed when shadowing these people, it is astonishing who they can get on the phone.[59] Finally, their education and upbringing gives them access to quick cultural references that they can drop into conversations: books read, performances attended, historical and geographic knowledge. This last one can sound trivial compared to the other two, but we should not underestimate it in the same way King Henry V was underestimated by the French.

You may have heard of the term 'precariat', which refers to the people at the opposite end of the spectrum to the elites. Around 15 per cent of the UK population have no wealth and low income, generally scraping by day-to-day. Typically, they will flit from short-term contract to short-term contract without really having a career trajectory. They will not go on holidays or dine out and they may not even own things most of us regard as normal, like a home computer. The idea of phoning in a connection to get a job or catch some other break will be alien because their connections are generally to other people who have as little influence as they have. Finally, their cultural activity will largely be informal and local, attending gatherings with neighbours, friends and family rather than paying for something anywhere near as expensive and poncy as an opera ticket.

When the term 'precariat' was coined by British economist Guy Standing in 2011, it became a bit of a cultural phenomenon, with people concerned about whether it was growing in size and whether they were at risk of falling into it. The notion of precarity prompted a whole new wave of research and even some policy initiatives. Yet one of the chilling truths about the precariat is that it has long been a reality for many across the globe. Precarious employment has been the norm for a long time in countries like India, South Africa and Brazil, with a relatively small elite – plus tourists – employing much of the working population in menial services jobs like driving or cleaning. Scholars from these countries have criticised the idea that the precariat is new for this very reason.[60]

CLASS COMPLEXITY

Just as the UK has its class system, India has its caste system. Upper-caste Hindus tend to have the advantage over lower-caste Hindus, while Indian Muslims are increasingly persecuted. As might be expected, this is all reflected in widely disparate economic outcomes, with the lower castes earning less and more likely to be in precarious employment. Although the caste system is palpable and has a long history, it may operate through subtle channels. One CV study in Delhi in 2009 used surnames to signal caste and found that employers did not seem to discriminate much against lower castes. The exception was call-centre jobs, which generally required workers to be able to speak excellent English. It would be absurd to say this means that caste doesn't matter; the takeaway is that these inequalities may not be straightforward enough to uncover just from looking at the moment you apply to a job. Different castes have different chances of being qualified for, or aware of, better-paid jobs in the first place.[61]

Much like the caste system in India, the class system in the UK can be hard to pin down. Most of us in the UK reside between the elite and the precariat, which is where things get more complicated. Many celebrities may be rich, but they have little in the way of social and especially cultural capital – think of footballers or pop stars. Footballer David Beckham is successful and respected, but he may not truly be regarded as part of the 'elite' due to obvious markers like his Essex accent.

Many successful businesspeople who came from working-class backgrounds may find themselves in a similar position, perhaps gaining important contacts but always feeling like outsiders. In contrast, many academics and teachers may have plenty of cultural and social capital, but (as I can personally attest) will lack economic capital.

My own experience in academia has actually illustrated to me how some of these subtle issues can play out. Although I'd never claim to be a working-class hero, we didn't have a great deal of money growing up. And I did not realise quite how 'different' other people's upbringings had been until I started to pursue academia. Many people who I was working with were from families with academic backgrounds and had, effectively, started their training when they were just children. Issues such as levels of background knowledge, familiarity with university spaces and ideas of what was important (much research can seem like an intellectual parlour game when you were raised by a single mum on a salary of £11,000 a year) crystalised as clear markers of who was and wasn't set for a life in academia. To be clear, I didn't feel mistreated exactly; I just found myself in a space that wasn't for me and, ultimately, this contributed to my decision to leave. I watched peers in similar situations gradually drop out. This is the essence of (a lack of) cultural capital.

Economists Anna Stansbury and Robert Schultz have investigated class in the US economics profession. Economics is well known for its under-representation of women and ethnic minorities, and you can add a lack of class representation to the list. Stansbury and Schultz show that parental education is extremely important: a minority of PhD recipients in economics have parents with no bachelor's degree, the worst out of any subject, and this has only got worse over time. Once in, your chances of succeeding are even more dependent on background. Among economics PhDs from top schools – the most likely to go on to become full-blown professors – an eye-watering 79 per cent have parents with a graduate degree themselves. It seems that the economics profession is not so far from the Bullingdon Club: insider knowledge, a privileged upbringing and high expectations all push a certain type of person into the discipline.[62]

Parental background turns out to be a pretty good indicator of class status and its impact goes well beyond academia. It seems that just as there is a gender pay gap, there is a class pay gap. Those whose parents had professional or managerial occupations are more likely to enter those kinds of professions themselves, and these obviously pay substantially more than the average job. What's striking is that the class pay gap is visible even for a given profession. As Mike Savage notes, those from advantaged backgrounds regularly earn 25 per cent more than those from disadvantaged backgrounds. In 2011, a UK lawyer whose parents worked in senior management could expect to earn £86,363; one whose parents worked in a manual occupation could expect to earn £65,583. Add to this how much less likely the latter is to be a lawyer in the first place and you have a hefty penalty for being born into the wrong class.[63]

The CV studies we discussed earlier have not investigated class as much as race and gender, precisely because it is so difficult to measure. It is not usual to put your parental background on a job application, so some researchers have experimented with other ideas. One study in the USA sent applications to law firms and used indicators for class such as surnames, whether an applicant had received financial aid at university and hobbies (sailing versus football). Sure enough, upper-class

CVs received more callbacks and were perceived by lawyers as better fitted to the elite culture of their firms. As always, there was a twist: upper-class women did not get higher callbacks than lower-class women, perhaps because employers perceived them as less committed to their careers.[64] In this instance, higher social and cultural capital only seemed to provide a boost for men.

INSURING SUCCESS

Think back to what Tim Ferriss was trying to achieve for individuals in *The 4-Hour Work Week*: income, stability and insurance. It turns out that the modern case for the welfare state is just this: an all-encompassing insurance against the shifts and shocks of income that have always characterised market economies.[65] Whether through recessions, the rise and fall of different industries, ageing, discrimination, class, sickness, bad luck, or even undoubted personal failings, the aim is to create a kind of 'corridor': your income won't get so low that you experience poverty at any point, even though this means higher taxes reducing the highs at other points in your life.

It may be that focusing on social mobility is not enough as long as the inequalities detailed in this chapter persist. Yet some economists use the fact that people move up and down in the income distribution to play down concerns about inequality. For instance, the economist Thomas Sowell has argued that it is often a mistake to talk about 'the rich' and 'the poor', since people move in and out of the different categories: of those Americans in the bottom fifth of the income distribution in 1975, 19 out of 20 were out of that bracket by

1991; similarly, those initially at the top of the income distribution saw their income fall.[66]

While a world of some income mobility is surely preferred to
a world where people are stuck at the station they are born in
for life – as was the case under chattel slavery or feudalism – it
may only be of passing relevance to discussions of inequality.
Whether a perfectly mobile but perfectly unequal society is
desirable is actually the premise of a Spanish film called *The
Platform*, where people are randomly assigned to different
levels of a prison. For one month at a time, your assigned level
determines your access to food and those at the top feast while
those at the bottom starve and tear each other to pieces. The
following month, the positions might be reversed – but this
barely matters to those at the bottom, many of them consigned
to death. It is clear that we may not want some types of
inequality, even if people can easily move around to become
richer or poorer.

The social insurance corridor is illustrated in a less extreme
fashion by age, which is one of Thomas Sowell's other reasons
that concerns about income inequality are overblown.[67] It is
fair to say that most people see their income rise as they grow
older. Comparing a teenager who works in a fast-food restaurant to a senior executive at a bank is questionable because the
latter has much more experience and is invaluable to the organisation. According to Sowell, those who are poor when young
but who have high-income career trajectories are not truly the
dispossessed, even though treating their income as a snapshot
without considering their age and future prospects may leave
that impression. It is for this reason that many economists consider income over the so-called 'life cycle' equally important as
income in a given year.

The argument can be exaggerated. In the UK, young lawyers earn plenty of money while older teachers barely get a premium.[68] Regardless of how important age is for income, once more I fear the focus on mobility misses the point. One of the contemporary justifications for the welfare state is precisely to redistribute income not only from rich to poor people, but between the same person across their life cycle. Just as we redistribute from the rich to the poor in the current moment, we redistribute from someone when they are a senior banker to that same person when they have their first job at McDonald's. In practice, this means that at any moment, older workers will be paying taxes to support younger workers, but each will have the assurance that the system supports them throughout their lives. To this end, the banker will be protected after retirement, at which point the former teenager will effectively be paying taxes to fund their pension.

Having a guarantee that you will not fall below a certain level of income in any given year is known as *social* insurance. The difference is that Ferriss' advice to contract out your work to the low-paid is not generalisable, whereas social insurance – almost by definition – assists *everyone*. The word 'insurance' provokes images of private companies (likely unfavourable ones), but this kind of insurance is much more general than that for your home or car. In fact, private companies have historically failed at providing social insurance for predictable reasons.

Firstly, reducing your own 'inequality' across your life typically requires borrowing huge amounts when you are younger, and many people – especially the poorest – just do not have access to that kind of credit, let alone the appetite to take on such a big burden. Secondly, there are well-observed human tendencies to save too little for the future, sometimes known as 'present-bias'.[69] Even the children who wait for the marshmallow are unlikely to manage to fund their whole retirement on their own, which is why forced savings via government compulsion are the only reliable way to fully fund pensions.[70]

Thirdly, buying outright insurance against the possibility of unemployment or ill-health can be difficult because private companies do not want to insure everyone.[71] This is especially true of those who need it most because those people are likely to be the costliest. For this reason, private insurance against unemployment is a pretty small market – many of you may be surprised to find out it exists at all, after a quick google. The company will reason that if you have to ask for it, chances are that you're hiding something important about your situation. The process of the riskiest individuals selecting private insurance only to be rebuffed or charged exorbitant amounts is called 'adverse selection', and it is one reason that private health insurance, too, can fall apart without public funding and regulation.[72]

Finally, there are simple economies of scale to having the insurance pool as large as possible. Insurance converts an unpredictable event – am I going to lose my job? – into a predictable payment schedule for the individual. It is a well-known feature of these risks that a larger population means that the annual payments are going to be more predictable, which is the same reason denizens in blocks of flats pool their money against emergencies. You turn what might have been a massive out-of-pocket payment for one person into a steady stream of small payments for everyone. While it may turn out you personally do not face too serious an expense, you cannot know that beforehand and you have peace of mind for a relatively small, continuous fee. This is the overarching logic of having a fully funded and functional welfare state.

Social insurance is perhaps most important for those who are out of work on a longer-term basis. In fact, around half of the US population just do not work and this group is primarily made up of children, homemakers and the elderly.[73] Most countries provide payments to these groups in one way or another, but there is not enough appreciation of the role this plays. It ensures that the unevenly distributed income of the market economy goes to those who are not working in the market. In addition, a well-functioning welfare state provides money for the invisible work done cooking, cleaning and raising children in the home, which benefits not just the recipients but everyone who lives in a better-functioning economy as a result. Currently, we are failing to invest properly in the population and are causing untold human harm while doing so.[74]

'ESCAPING' POVERTY?

In the last chapter, we discussed the rise of billionaires and how they dominate the economy. Many have a tendency to idolise the individuals who get rich and aspire to join them one day. This is completely understandable, but if we do it too much we risk becoming 'temporarily embarrassed millionaires', living in denial of not just our situation but that of countless others. Innumerable barriers are faced by individuals in poverty and by certain demographic groups, which means that getting to the top is much more difficult, even impossible, for some than for others. Even more than this, it may be the case that pursuing mobility is not going to solve all of these problems; social insurance is necessary even under conditions of perfect meritocracy.

Most people who believe in meritocracy probably do not

realise that the idea was first coined as satire by the sociologist and activist Michael Young in 1958. Young foresaw the splintering of classes into those who excelled in formal education and those who did not. The former would end up in well-paid jobs with authority and power, whereas the latter would be in more menial and lower-status occupations. In essence, Young was wondering if a separation into ruled and rulers would be justified if based on academic ability – and he thought not. He successfully campaigned for universal compulsory education in Britain, in opposition to the preferential system of grammar schools at the time, which had pupils take the notorious 11-plus tests. The previous school system separated out and elevated those who scored well over those who scored badly. In doing so, it explicitly laid out the future paths of both groups at the mere age of eleven based on merit.[75]

We have been focused in this chapter on what individuals earn and how mobile they are in the income distribution. But it is worth pausing to reflect on the challenge raised by Young: are some kinds of inequality harmful, no matter their justification? Despite some progress, global inequality remains high and so does inequality within countries. We may strive for equality of opportunity, but do we want to condemn anyone to a life of poverty and drudgery? The simple fact is that most of the world lives in poverty by any reasonable definition. Investigating poverty and inequality in themselves, along with their consequences, leads us to a distinct set of questions to the ones raised about mobility.

CHAPTER 4

IS POVERTY GETTING BETTER?

How Poverty Manifests Across the World

There has been a rising tide of so-called 'New Optimist' books over the past few years, which emphasise how well our world has been doing despite widespread pessimism. One of the top sellers is Hans Rosling's *Factfulness*, which details through count-less graphs how things have been getting better on numerous fronts: health, poverty, literacy, the environment, airline safety, scientific research, and so on.[1] Rosling enjoyed testing his audi-ence and finding that they almost always got it wrong. People think that global poverty and other ills have worsened, when in fact they have improved. Steven Pinker's *Enlightenment Now* is an attempt at a more scholarly exposition of these facts.[2]

Many of these trends are indeed worth celebrating. For much of humanity's history, most children did not survive into adulthood; now even people in poorer countries can assume their children will live past the age of five. Many curable dis-eases have been vaccinated against and issues of basic health, nutrition and education do genuinely seem to be getting better. There are several success stories in the global economy: coun-tries such as China, South Korea and Japan have catapulted up the economic ladder since World War II. Other countries such as Bangladesh, Mongolia, Ghana and Rwanda seem to hold some promise of repeating this feat. These are just a few of the changes that have happened over my lifetime that I can look at with genuine joy.

On the other hand, we should always be wary of TED Talkers bearing impressive-looking graphs because they often hide biases. The truth is that the global economy is far too complex to be reduced to one graph, or even to several graphs. When we look beneath the surface, there are myriad issues with where the data come from, which measures are chosen and what alternative indicators tell us. To take a simple example, consider probably the most famous graph of all, beloved by people like Rosling: the one that depicts the decline in the number of people living below $2.15 (USD) per day. At $2.15 a day – which is how the World Bank and others define extreme poverty – the proportion of the global population in poverty has declined by almost 30 per cent since 1990 and is now below 10 per cent overall.[3]

Share of population living in extreme poverty, 1990–2022

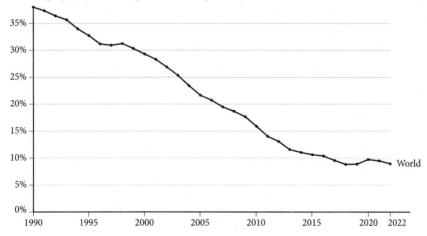

This graph is undoubtedly eye-catching and should not be dismissed outright. Anyone who tells you statistics like this are simply meaningless is not inhabiting reality: the numbers are painstakingly gathered from real people. At the same time, any outright triumphalism about this finding is misplaced. For a start, if you express this poverty line as an annual income it comes to only $784.75 a year, which is an unimaginably small sum for most people reading this. Earning $2.15 a day, this book would have cost you a week's income, almost 2 per cent of your annual salary. For the average Westerner, spending that proportion of your income would enable you to buy over 500 books, typically considered enough to start a small library.

Any poverty line worth its salt should be based on a sober assessment of whether humans have access to our basic needs – food, water, shelter – but the $2.15 a day line simply is not. It was cobbled together from various national poverty lines in six poor countries simply because those were the ones with acceptable data. Taking poverty lines from poorer countries tends to low-ball the real threshold for poverty in richer countries, even with the various adjustments made by statisticians.[4] More concerning is that this specific value seems to have been chosen not because it is genuinely representative of poverty around the globe, but because it makes organisations like the World Bank and United Nations, who are nominally responsible for ending global poverty, look good.

Scholars who live in or have visited countries around the globe have commented that the World Bank's numbers do not pass the laugh test. Egypt is down as having 1 per cent poverty, yet its own government – having observed the large number of people who scrape by in slums in precarious employment – put the figure at one-third of the population; something similar applies in Turkey.[5] The 1.4 billion people in India are done a massive disservice by these statistics since they seriously understate poverty in the world's largest country. In one case, the stats indicated that almost everyone in rural Indian villages had personal toilets.[6] Anyone who has seen hit films such as *Lion, White Tiger,* or especially *Slum Dog Millionaire* will recognise that this is a rose-tinted view of the toilet situation in rural India.*

When we are trying to understand inequality across the entire globe, we need to abandon simplistic narratives about poverty reduction. The spread of material progress over the past century is real, but it is marked by several important historical complexities. We need to understand more about where poverty comes from, how we measure it and how it might be alleviated. This leads us to a more critical perspective on the recent history of global economic development.

WHAT ARE WE MEASURING?

> ... it measures everything in short, except that which makes life worthwhile.
>
> Bobby Kennedy on GDP

We all know that Gross Domestic Product (GDP), which is usually what people usually mean when they say 'the economy', is not the be-all and end-all of life. One of the main issues with GDP, which Bobby Kennedy was well aware of, is that it is

---

* In *Slum Dog Millionaire*, a child is locked in the communal toilets – which are simply poised above trenches full of faeces – and to get out, he jumps through the toilets straight into the trenches, an image which still haunts me to this day.

basically neutral on whether the economic output it measures is good or bad. Felling a forest to sell wood may increase GDP, but there can be a devastating effect on local ecosystems. Most people would consider a divorce to be a difficult and regrettable process, but since it generally costs money in the form of legal fees, it counts towards GDP. If you break your leg then paying for the scan, operation, cast and continued care will count in GDP. On the other hand, things we widely regard as good – art, good personal relationships, intelligence, fresh air, a sense of purpose in life – do not contribute directly to economic growth numbers.

GDP measures the market value of the final goods and services produced in a given country. In other words, it is first and foremost a measure of activity within the market economy. If it increases over time (after adjusting for inflation), then the idea is that there is more market activity, so there are more goods and services. The idea of calling these 'final' goods and services may seem odd to anyone unfamiliar with the definition, but it is important as it stops double counting. If a lumberjack chops down a tree, then sells it to a carpenter, who goes on to sell the chair made from the wood, counting both sales in GDP would mean the tree went in twice: once as lumber, then again as a chair. In practice, the cost of the lumber is deducted from the cost of the chair so GDP only measures the 'value added' by creating the chair.

When we're looking at historical development and how countries escape poverty, we often try to estimate GDP over long stretches of time and for a wide range of countries. You may, for instance, have seen the 'hockey stick' graph of world GDP, which shows it flatlining for almost all of human history before exploding exponentially at the advent of capitalism. The message is simple: humanity lived in the muck for a long time,

Global GDP over the long run (US$)

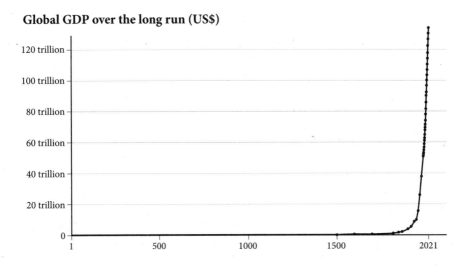

with the resources available to most people at paltry levels compared to today. In fact, the argument goes, many kings in the olden days were materially worse off than the average person in a rich country now. While the latter point is hard to verify, the increase in living standards is real and should not be underestimated or glossed over.[7]

My favourite comparison point is that of bathing and cleanliness. Roman baths were famously collective venues, where people would wash in the same large body of water. Although this was a valued social ritual accessible to all, by modern standards the water was not particularly clean, with the sick and healthy bathing together and the tepid standing water a breeding ground for bacteria.[8] In Shakespearean times, long after the Roman Empire collapsed, people were still using the same collective baths, prioritised by class in typical English fashion. Kings, lords and barons would go first, then the middle-class, and by the time the poorest were allowed in it was questionable whether the bath would make you cleaner or dirtier.[9]

It wasn't until the Victorian era that we started to see running water, which meant separate cubicles in town baths that people would visit regularly, and which were once again more accessible to the wealthy. These weren't used daily like the Roman baths, but the fresh, hot water at least guaranteed you would be clean – helped along by the advent of soap.[10] A famous episode of the sitcom *Steptoe and Son* from this period

sees the elderly father bathing in a tiny bath in the living room, prompting his son to reflect on how 'degrading' the situation is.

It's easy to forget just how modern, modern cleaning habits and facilities are. The British classic *Quadrophenia*, set in the 1960s, shows the main character still using a stall in a town bath like those built in Victorian times, and most British homes, as demonstrated in the image above, did not have a separate bathroom around this time.[11] These days even the very poorest in rich countries would expect to have their own porcelain bathroom in their house, accessible whenever they need it. Running water is available to everybody and a hot shower is both a way to keep us all clean, as well as a source of therapy. Roman emperors or King Lear would not have been able to imagine the convenience, cleanliness and efficiency of a modern bath. The same goes for things like washing machines, dishwashers and toilets.

Material progress is real. Nevertheless, there is a degree of false certainty which pervades these historical estimates of poverty and living standards. Anthropologist Jason Hickel, who is known as a staunch critic of the narrative on global poverty, has noted that GDP data just isn't available for most times and places. Western countries have been gathering reliable data on GDP since World War II, but elsewhere or before that the data just doesn't exist. Hickel highlights that there is no African data whatsoever before 1900, and only for three African countries before 1950. The enormous continent of Asia, which contains most of the world's people, only has data for three of its countries before 1950, and the same goes for Latin America.[12]

As countries were brought into global capitalism, which was often a violent and tumultuous process, measured GDP could increase because more 'final goods' were being produced and sold in the market economy. For instance, as Britain colonised India in the nineteenth century, much of its agricultural sector was repurposed to mass produce and export grain. Previously, the land was owned in either small or collective plots, produced for local consumption. Transforming these situations, where few market transactions took place, into modern industrial agriculture was undoubtedly registered as an economic boom. Yet from 1870 to 1920, it is widely recognised that tens of millions of Indians died of famine and average life expectancy in the country declined.[13] Though an extreme example, this makes it clear that measured GDP does not always mean higher living standards.

Gathering granular data on poverty this far back is an extremely difficult task. In fact, when you hear a narrative of declining poverty, you should know that most of the data before 1981 – which is when the World Bank started measuring poverty itself – is based on GDP. Economic historian Robert Allen engaged in some painstaking work when he instead tried to look at how much food households actually consumed in England and India before each transformed into market economies. He found that poverty was indeed common: by his calculations, fourteenth-century England and nineteenth-century India both had around 25 per cent of their populations in extreme poverty. But this is still less than the World Bank estimates, which would put almost everyone in these eras below the poverty line.[14]

Allen's story shows that, rather than GDP growth gradually taking off as the hockey stick depicts, there was progress in reducing poverty beforehand, with periods of flatlining poverty in some times and places and rising poverty in others. By the seventeenth century, just before the Industrial Revolution, England had only 5 to 10 per cent of its population in poverty, and the average Indian was also living on a par with much of Western Europe. Indian poverty doubled during British colonialism, while England saw neither progress nor regress during the early days of the Industrial Revolution. This complex picture is just not visible from looking at long-term graphs of GDP rising relentlessly, nor more recent ones of poverty declining precipitously.

Arguing that colonialism was a terrible crime may not be especially controversial and it does not necessarily mean that modern capitalism is equivalent. What I want you to take away

is a degree of scepticism of simple narratives about how countries got rich that are sold by people like Rosling, Pinker and
Bill Gates – the latter having roundly endorsed New Optimism.
And the issues with the numbers go beyond the historical
record: while the World Bank's poverty data after 1981 are
leaps and bounds above the sparse historical data we've discussed, they still have unacceptable gaps. Poverty researcher
Morten Jerven summarised the problem as:

> 'when it comes to studying economic development, our
> knowledge based on numbers is doubly biased: we know
> little about poor countries and even less about the poor
> people who live in these countries'.[15]

Almost half the countries in the World Bank's database either
have no data on poverty or have it for only one year. It's difficult to speak about a reduction in poverty when you don't have
a comparison point from the past, and even more difficult when
you don't have any data at all. Only a minority of countries can
be said to credibly track poverty over time. This is true not just
of poverty indicators but of ones measuring progress in health
and education, too.[16] We need to take care with how we use
these statistics and make sure we are seeing the broader historical picture.

At the same time, we do not want to endorse an equally simplistic narrative that things are actually getting worse. Allen's
own meticulous estimates, though they put the amount of
remaining poverty in the world higher than the World Bank,
still show a clear decline in recent decades, as do different methods by other researchers trying to verify the numbers.[17] In fact,
the overall decline in poverty since 1981 seems to be a fairly

stable finding: whether you use different ways of estimating poverty, or increase the poverty line (e.g. $5.50 a day instead of $2.15 a day), or even look at other correlated measures like nutrition and undernourishment,[18] hardship has really been reduced for the average global citizen. Despite this, there are plenty of people across the rich and poor worlds who have struggled over the past few decades, and it is worth looking at them in more detail to better understand these trends.

REALISM OVER OPTIMISM

In the twenty-first century, China has emerged as an economic superpower, achieving growth rates of 5 to 10 per cent for decades and a huge growth of its middle class. While China is not the world's only economic success story, most of the growth from poor countries since World War II has come from nearby. Smaller East Asian countries, starting with Japan, have seen even more economic success for the average person, reaching levels of income that were previously reserved for Western countries. This success was emulated to varying degrees by Taiwan, South Korea, Malaysia, Hong Kong and Singapore.[19] All of these countries have built impressive economies such that we now recognise many of their products as household names: Hyundai, Nintendo, TikTok, Samsung. This has lifted their populations out of absolute poverty almost entirely, with the proportion of East Asians living below $2.15 a day going from around 80 per cent of the population to virtually zero per cent since 1980.

Nevertheless, billing the trajectory of these nations as a success story for *global* poverty implies that their success is emulated around the world, which is not reflected in the data.

If you take China out of the equation and use a higher poverty line, the level of poverty rises hugely and the decline all but disappears. At $5.50 per day – still only an annual income of $2007.50 – poverty around the world has not declined outside of China, and the poverty rate today is still almost half of the globe.[20] Some recommend using an even higher line – for example, development expert Lant Pritchett thinks it should be $15 a day.[21] Using this line, you only see a decline from 80 per cent to 70 per cent of the globe in the past few decades, and that's including East Asia.[22]

When we think of global poverty, many people's minds will instinctively go to poor countries in Africa, but many of the world's poorest are in middle-income but highly unequal countries such as those in Latin America. Brazil is a good example of how easily we can be misled by graphs of average poverty decline. Having experienced solid growth, Brazil is a middle-income country with a GDP per person of $15,000, about one-fifth as much as the USA and just under one-third as much as the EU. It joined the so-called BRICS (Brazil, Russia, India, China, South Africa) as an example of 'up and coming' countries in the global economy. Yet Brazil's income growth hides a number of concerning shifts that have beset the country, particularly the decline of the manufacturing sector and the rise of inequality.

As development experts David Oks and Henry Williams have reminded us, almost no countries – absent a few oil-rich nations – have managed to get rich successfully without solid manufacturing bases.[23] Making stuff you can 'drop on your foot', while seen as a dated view, is still by far the most common path to sustained development. Rapid growth in manufacturing provides undoubtedly tough but well-paid and reliable employment for much of the population. It increases productivity as skills and technology advance, driving down prices while driving up the quality of the manufactured goods. A set of ideas in economics known as Kaldor's Growth Laws state that higher growth in manufacturing kick-starts the virtuous cycle of industrialisation, leading to further growth not only in manufacturing but in the rest of the economy, too.[24]

While we should never romanticise these jobs, the central historical role of manufacturing remains a fact to be reckoned with and it has serious consequences for poverty. Brazil hugely expanded its manufacturing sector from 1960 to 1980, over which time GDP per person increased by 140 per cent. Had this continued until 2000, it would be richer than most European nations today; in reality, in the twenty years after this, Brazilian GDP had increased by only 20 per cent as the country's industry flatlined. Brazil was a leader in both vehicles and electronics and although these industries remain, they are nowhere near the powerhouses they once promised to be. Brazilian analyst Alex Hochuli actually coined the term 'Brazilianization' to mean 'modern but not modern enough', facing relative stagnation in an economy which is nowhere near on track to joining the ranks of the industrialised rich countries.[25]

Brazil is just one example of how the rise of East Asia has been accompanied by a decline in manufacturing elsewhere in the world. The country has instead relied on booms in raw commodities such as iron, meat, soy and oil – some of which directly fuelled industrialisation in East Asia. Relying on raw commodities leaves a country exposed to the vagaries of international markets, with massive fluctuations causing sudden plunges in income. While manufacturing booms deliver broad-based growth for the population, booms in commodity prices tend to enrich a small segment of the population, with the rest hoping to get scraps from the table in terms of menial service jobs serving the upper or middle classes. Hochuli notes that Brazil's entrenched elite, living in luxurious fortresses with advanced private security, actually benefit from the lack of industrialisation because it means they get to keep their housemaids.

India de-industrialised much earlier than Brazil, during the era of British colonialism. Ever since independence, India's economy has been billed as a rising star; an unusual example of skipping the manufacturing stage and going straight into advanced services. India has indeed grown in recent years and boasts some impressive universities and technological achievements, including their satellite mission to Mars. But the reality is that the tired stereotype of the Indian computer scientist or call centre worker only ever applied to a small part of the population. As we discussed in the last chapter, precarity is the norm in India, which has long struggled to draw its people into reliable formal employment in markets: 9 out of 10 jobs created since 1991 have been in informal, unreliable work, like the unlicensed taxi drivers that transport tourists around for minimal pay. Dutch sociologist Jan Breman once called these workers 'wage hunters and gatherers', which reflects the mobile, transitory and poverty-stricken nature of their existence.[26]

Indian economists Snehashish Bhattacharya and Surbhi Kesar have noted that most of the businesses in the Indian economy are pretty different to ones in the West. Remember Marx's M-C-M', as businesses pay their workers, make out with a profit, then use the remaining money to expand? It doesn't apply everywhere. The Indian economy is an illustrative example: many of these enterprises are scraping by and just don't have the money to reinvest. Since they are generally family businesses, they use the little money they make to take care of everyone while holding onto any extras for insurance in case something should go wrong in the future. The boundary between household, business and community is far more blurred than in a business in the West. As Bhattacharya and Kesar are keen to emphasise, it's not that these 'non-capitalist' enterprises are somehow yet to develop into fully capitalist ones; it's that the changes since 1991 have actually created them *alongside* the capitalist parts of the economy.[27] What we often call 'economic development' can be pretty uneven.

Economic growth need not be a zero-sum game and the global economy has seen huge increases in wealth, both over the long arc of history and in recent decades. But it is undeniable that recent positive trends in the global economy have driven the relative (and in some cases, absolute) decline of manufacturing which used to form not only the basis of strong economic growth but strong communities in countries like Brazil. For countries like India, these sectors never really took off in the first place. The effects are visible in the countless underemployed young men on the streets of Delhi or Sao Paulo, scraping a living by washing cars, cleaning shoes, or stealing. In fact, it turns out that the situation of the poor in these countries has more in common with 'precariat' in richer countries than you might expect.

THE ILLS OF INEQUALITY

The seaside town of Blackpool in England has long been a tourist destination. Starting in the nineteenth century, workers from cotton mills across the country would travel there during their summer breaks. As tourism pushed Blackpool to grow, its famous piers were opened, where visitors could dance and watch plays. Blackpool was one of the first towns to embrace full-scale electrification and the annual Blackpool Illuminations Festival – akin to Christmas lights, though held in September – remains famous to this day. Blackpool Tower, then the tallest building in Britain, was built in 1894, and from the top you can sometimes see the Isle of Man, almost a hundred miles away. The theme park Pleasure Beach, opened two years after Blackpool Tower, still boasts the tallest rollercoaster in Britain.

Despite its picturesque location, plentiful attractions and long history as a vibrant city, Blackpool has fallen into decline in recent years. Today, the level of deprivation is clear from a journey through the city centre. There are boarded-up shops, buildings and roads are in disrepair and many people are struggling with serious mental and physical health issues. As of 2017, Blackpool had one of the UK's highest prescription rates for anti-depressants and among the highest rates of alcoholism, obesity and smoking. Blackpool contains the single largest proportion of people on disability benefits in the UK. It has become a sort of migration destination for those struggling: people on benefits often arrive from elsewhere in the country, while those who have employment opportunities leave for greener pastures.

The doctors in Blackpool have taken to calling the affliction that ails many of their patients 'shit life syndrome'.[28] This may sound a little mean, but that is not the intention. The reason GPs came up with this name is because they typically have a mere 10 to 15 minutes with their patients, so they are unable to solve problems with the patients' broader economic and social environment. Dr Arif Rajpura, the director of public health, argues that '80 per cent of health is determined outside the health service; it's things like whether you've got a job, whether you've got a decent home, whether you've got social connections and friends'. There is some pretty solid evidence behind what Dr Rajpura is saying.

Earlier in the book, we saw Karl Polanyi's description of the 'great transformation' of many countries into market economies. What this transformation meant was that people came to rely on formal employment, working 9-to-5 (or more likely 7-to-7 during the nineteenth century) for a wage. Before the Industrial Revolution, people may have done at least some farming themselves, survived based on informal odd jobs, or used things collectively produced by their village. Many individuals and communities had ways of growing food, making clothes and building or repairing houses that often did not involve the exchange of money. Social gatherings were more regular and basically costless, as was a direct connection with nature. The point is not to romanticise these eras; it's just that much of life did not depend on the exchange of money.

As the market economy spread, people came to depend on income from what we now consider a typical job and used this money to buy their essentials in the form of commodities. On top of being the main way to ensure you don't starve, having money has increasingly become the way to participate in social life. Whether you are going for a pint at the pub, visiting the cinema to see a film, or travelling to the countryside, engaging in social activities typically entails spending. As the market economy became more widespread and people congregated in cities, many aspects of life that previously did not have a price tag came to have one. In big cities like London, where I live, it can feel like even leaving the house incurs a charge.

All of this is to say that there is a clear explanation for shit life syndrome. In a city that previously thrived from industrial capitalism, many of the informal economic and social bonds that people had in the past have been shattered to make way for market relationships. People were dependent on the economic success of their town to get gainful employment, to survive, and to participate in social life. As Blackpool has seen a relative decline in these opportunities, people have found it difficult to make ends meet. Without traditional ties and safety nets to fall back on, this leaves them not only in economically precarious situations but often socially isolated, with little self-worth or recognition from the rest of society.

The residents of Blackpool seem to understand the problem. Gavin Phillips, who was suicidal for months, has benefited from joining the community groups that have tried to fill the gaps left by the failed market economy in recent years. He says that at one point he was having a 'really bad struggle', so he met up with a friend for a cup of tea and a chat. 'And I was fine and done!' His friend Chris Hopkins, who moved to Blackpool because it had the lowest rent he could find in the country, agrees. 'We need some kind of community, some sense of camaraderie . . . you must have your colleagues, whether you get along with them or not. But with isolation, you fall into that deep despair pit.' When social ties break down, it may lead to serious problems for the individuals who are no longer connected to the world around them. At the regimented Foxconn factories in Taiwan, some workers cited not just the demanding work, but the lack of community as a potential reason for the suicides.[29]

IT'S ALL RELATIVE

In his book *Enlightenment Now,* Steven Pinker makes the claim that unlike health or wealth, 'inequality is not a component of human well-being'.[30] Everyone agrees that if you ask people how happy they are with their lives overall, then first and foremost it matters how well they're doing in an absolute sense. If people don't have enough money to eat, to afford rent and to pay the bills, this has a huge detrimental effect on their well-being. Yet a wide range of evidence shows that it also matters how much they have compared to others in their country, workplace, or local area. Along with health, people's self-reported happiness depends on where they stand relative to those around them.[31] When our low income shuts us out from the rest of society, we suffer. Pinker's claim is therefore straightforwardly wrong.

It has long been recognised in public health that inequality can 'get under the skin' and create a special kind of anxiety known as status anxiety. Status anxiety is a reflection of your position in society and may go back to our natural instincts as primates organised into hierarchies. 'Where do I sit in the pecking order?' we wonder, and nowadays our income is the most readily available measuring stick.[32] As you might expect, within a given country, those who earn a lot have less status anxiety than those at the bottom. Earning £50,000 in the UK will mean you are much less likely to suffer from status anxiety than someone earning £20,000. But it's not just 'the rich' versus 'the poor': earning £60,000 will make you less anxious than someone earning £50,000, while earning £10,000 will make you more anxious than someone earning £20,000.

Each country shows a clear pattern across the whole distribution: more income means less status anxiety. The most striking finding, though, comes from comparing different countries. Although the poor suffer within every country, *everybody* feels the burden of higher inequality. In countries with higher inequality, someone who is at the top of the income distribution experiences more status anxiety than someone at the same point in the income distribution, but in a more equal country. It is therefore the case that the rich in Germany have less status anxiety than the rich in the USA, simply because the former is more equal overall. So, too, do the poor in Germany have less status anxiety than the poor in the USA. Inequality gets under everyone's skin.[33]

The result of all this is that many social problems are much more pronounced under conditions of high inequality. When people are shut out, this tends to show up in numerous ways which are detrimental for them and for the rest of society – not to mention the economy. People who are lower in the economic pecking order are more likely to suffer from a variety of health problems: in some cases, you lose ten years of life expectancy going from the richest to the poorest. As with status anxiety, at every step you will lose some life expectancy – even when going from £100,000 a year to £90,000 a year, your life expectancy drops. Suffering is not confined to the very poor; everyone's position in society affects their health.

It turns out that relative comparisons are deeply ingrained in how humans understand the world. For example, it is quite difficult for someone to judge the temperature of a bowl of water by placing their hand in it unless they can place their hand in another bowl of water, which is at a different temperature, to make a comparison. Similarly, we cannot judge how bright a light is in an absolute sense – guessing its brightness in 'lumens' – but we are extremely good at judging its brightness relative to another light. Comparisons are simply how we make sense of the world and if you reflect on this, you may realise how difficult it is to judge many things at all without making a comparison.[34]

KNOW YOUR PLACE

In modern society, this facet of human nature has taken new forms. The boomer expression 'keeping up with the Joneses' refers to the endless modern drive to make sure that we are doing as well as those around us. We may jealously eye up a friend's car or new pair of shoes; we might feel hard done by if a co-worker gets a raise and we don't; and the American Dream makes us all believe that we should do a bit better than our parents. All of these comparisons affect us deeply and they are one reason that inequalities of various kinds can have pernicious effects. When we feel we are not keeping up with the Joneses, we feel that we have failed ourselves and those around us. Adam Smith recognised this back in the eighteenth century:[35]

> A linen shirt, for example, is, strictly speaking, not a necessity of life. The Greeks and Romans lived, I suppose, very comfortably though they had no linen. But in the present times, through the greater part of Europe, a creditable day-labourer would be ashamed to appear in public without a linen shirt, the want of which would be supposed to denote that disgraceful degree of poverty which, it is presumed, nobody can well fall into without extreme bad conduct. Custom, in the same manner, has rendered leather shoes a necessary of life in England. The poorest creditable person of either sex would be ashamed to appear in public without them.

Our ability to live without things deemed normal by our society is limited and these needs change over time and place. Almost one hundred years after Smith, Friedrich Engels was observing – not without some prejudice, it must be said – that Irish workers could get by happily on much less than English workers.[36] Over the course of my lifetime alone, the internet has gone from a curiosity for nerds to a vital requirement for basic functions like working, banking, socialising, navigating and paying for things. Streaming services like Netflix were considered essential during the pandemic despite humanity surviving for hundreds of thousands of years without them. Humans need entertainment, and streaming is the modern way to provide this – even more so during lockdown.

The saying that the poor 'must know their place', while arguably implicit in countries like the UK and USA, is frequently said out loud in Brazil, which is an extremely unequal society, with the top percentage of earners likely getting more as a proportion of total income than any other country in the world.[37] This is reflected in explicit elitism: items like branded clothing are markers of status and poorer children speak hopefully about owning them one day. However, elitism is so ingrained that merely owning them is not enough. Poor or non-white Brazilians who manage to afford the clothing usually reserved for the middle classes will be sneered at, denied access to places, or accused of stealing. In fact, buying and proudly wearing a pair of sneakers is practically an act of resistance for those in poverty.[38]

The economist Robert Frank has shown that people often mimic those better off than them to gain social status and avoid shame. What Frank and his co-authors call 'expenditure cascades' show how inequality can affect everyone's behaviour. Evidence from the USA shows that the rich first expand their spending, which then causes those below them to follow suit, and so on, as the effect 'cascades' down to the poorest. Startlingly, a rise in inequality in a local area can cause a spade of bankruptcies among poorer families, a raft of divorces and even a spike in commuting times as people work more to keep up.[39] As in Brazil, the shame felt by the poor for not being able to keep up with the rest of society can be palpable.

Some may dismiss concerns about inequality as the 'politics of envy', wanting what we can't have and don't deserve. But the issue is deeper than this: our ability to live our social lives depends on our economic surroundings. For example, I have a number of friends who earn substantially more than me. It is not that I am nakedly envious of them (they work longer hours than me, so it's swings and roundabouts) but that they participate in a number of activities which are pretty expensive by my standards. Whether these are holidays, fancy restaurants, or expectations about clothing, it is difficult to avoid these entirely if I want to spend time with my friends. Simply turning my nose up at all of this would be a signal that I didn't want to be friends with them, which is not a signal it's reasonable to expect any human being to send.

Higher taxes are usually billed as a way to address inequality through redistribution. Progressive taxation would straightforwardly take money from the rich and give it to the poor, whether directly or through programmes that help poorer communities. This would boost the income of the poor so that they would be better able to keep up with the level of spending necessary for them to be lifted out of poverty and to participate in society. Whether in decaying towns like Blackpool or the slums of Brazil, it could serve the basis of community restorations which expand economic opportunities and social cohesion.

Frank has drawn attention to one less obvious – but no less significant – benefit of higher taxes: reducing the income of the rich would mean that those who earn less would have less to 'keep up with' in the first place. If people have a lower level of disposable income, their social habits will adjust accordingly. This is to say that although richer people will be less able to spend money on super nice things – with apologies to my friends – there will be less of a drive to do so just to take part in the expectations that surround them. If everyone is less able to afford that fancy restaurant, then a group of friends can have just as much fun at a normal one – which are often just as good if you ask me, though maybe I just lack cultural capital.

Inequality in Brazil is special in another way: through its tax system. A series of unique exemptions and privileges mean the rich are taxed less than the middle class. The Brazilian tax system does not tax profits or gains from selling financial assets as highly as it taxes the incomes earned by most people in their day jobs. The result is that, instead of spreading the wealth and enabling a broad swathe of society to enjoy those sneakers as equals, the Brazilian government takes the time to make the burden on the middle class higher relative to their wealthy peers. The very poorest are (rightly) taxed at a low rate, but the Brazilian tax system still stands out for how ineffectively it manages to achieve any real level of redistribution, scholars agree is the number one barrier to addressing inequality in the country.[40]

In summary, poverty in Brazil and in the UK illustrate why we should see global inequality and local inequality as part of the same problem, with similar solutions. Several programmes in Brazil that have expanded healthcare, education and employment to the population have seen noticeable successes in bringing poverty down. Using these programmes, the state Santa Catarina reduced the number of individuals living in poverty by 46 per cent in just one decade.[41] The effort to improve bathing facilities in Victorian England was also largely public; these things don't happen organically as a consequence of economic growth.[42] This is why any hope of alleviating poverty means thinking seriously about aggressive redistributive measures within both rich and poor countries. [43] As with the poor in rich countries, redistribution and good public policy hold a lot of promise for the global poor.[44]

MS HELEN AND MS LEAH

In 2023, I am in my home office on a patchy Zoom call connected to some Rwandan villages. The charity GiveDirectly, who do exactly what their name says, transferring large sums of money to the poorest people in the world with no strings attached, have helpfully arranged the call. They take us through conversations with some of the villagers, each of whom the charity is giving around $800 – well above their annual income. We visit three villages: one where the villagers have just been informed they will get the money; one where they are close to receiving it; and another where they have already received it and put it to use. Through a translator, me and other participants are able to ask the villagers questions about what the money means to them.

Rwanda is a country that has seen a lot of successes, as mentioned in the introduction. Their GDP growth has averaged around 5 per cent a year while health and education have improved massively. As of 2023, Rwanda stood out as having one of the highest levels of gender equality in Africa and actually ranked twelfth in the world, above many richer countries.[45] Over half its parliament was female, while 80 per cent of women were either working or looking for jobs. Given its extremely violent history, which is still in living memory for much of the population, Rwanda has progressed a lot in the past thirty years.

Despite this good news, strong growth from a very poor starting point may not translate into much of a recognisable gain to
an onlooker, especially when that growth is concentrated in urban
areas. Half the population of Rwanda, most of them in rural
areas, still live in extreme poverty. Since this is defined as less
than $2.15 a day, most citizens have started from so little income
that 5 per cent growth for twenty years has probably netted them
less than one dollar more per day than they previously had. Give-
Directly inform me that Nyanza, the district we are calling into,
is the fifth most malnourished district in the country, with an
astonishing 50 per cent prevalence of stunting in children under
five years old. Rwanda is at once a success story for the global
economy and a sign of how we need to do much, much better.

One of the women we speak to, Ms Leah, grows bananas on a
subsistence farm. She is getting older and hopes that the money
will help her to support her children and give them chances she
never had. She says that they currently have trouble sleeping
when it is raining as the water seeps through: as she points out
to us, the roof has been seriously damaged by the wind. To my
eye, it seems like her and her son's house is not only damaged
but on the verge of collapsing; the hole in the roof is gaping.
Currently, they borrow their neighbour's cow, a common practice in Rwanda, but once they get the money they will be able to
buy their own. They may also join a savings group in their village, which often emerge following these programmes.

Ms Helen owns a farm and was similarly poor, though she has
now received the transfer. Whereas she had no cows or goats
beforehand, she now has two of each, which means she has
plenty of milk and can also breed more. She says that the money,
which is roughly my monthly rent, has changed her life. When I
ask her about her plans for the future, she becomes more

animated and says that, like Ms Leah, she wants to renovate her house. She hopes to have an outdoor kitchen so that she can cook for her family out in the open. These goals are evidently quite modest, but the shift between Ms Leah and Ms Helen from having so little to having, well, something, is staggering.

JUST GIVE PEOPLE MONEY!

The idea of a Universal Basic Income (UBI) has grown in popularity in recent years. This would be a simple cash payment to everyone in a country, irrespective of how much they earned, every month, for as long as they lived. Traditional welfare is means-tested: 'Do you have children?' 'Are you unemployed?' 'Do you have a disability?' and so on. UBI would do away with all of that administration – which is costly in itself and also a huge burden for those needy individuals having to navigate a labyrinth of conditions – and with one simple policy, alleviate the worst of poverty for the citizens of a country.

Naturally, people are often concerned about free money. Among the concerns are: how will we pay for it? Won't people just laze around all day? Will it not just lead to inflation, making the payments worthless? Won't they just spend it all on chips and cigarettes?* For instance, when the Scottish Government proposed an annual UBI of £25,000, it was met with outrage and incredulity. This incredulity was misguided. At this stage, extensive trials have been conducted in both rich and poor

---

* This not to say that recipients of redistribution should not be allowed to indulge. In the words of Australian comedian Steve Hughes, 'What do you think I was going to spend it on?'

countries and one thing is clear: UBI works wonders, effecting virtually none of the laziness or slobbery people worry about.[46]

In Kenya, just a short distance from Rwanda, cash transfers of around $1,000 to 10,000 poor households – which totalled a boost in income of a massive 15 per cent for the average participating village – created largely positive effects. Naturally, the money helped to reduce poverty and the spending had positive knock-on effects on the local community. As with Ms Helen and Ms Leah, people invested in things they needed, like livestock and housing but, according to the study, didn't buy cigarettes or alcohol – despite them being readily available. Inflation didn't really budge, implying that these economies have plenty of room to expand as people increase their material standard of living. Following GiveDirectly's policy, these transfers were only one-offs rather than a true income, but they give us an idea of what people actually do with free money.[47]

In Canada, the province of Ontario experimented with a proper UBI for two years, which was around C$1,000 per person. Those who took part in the experiment reported improved physical and mental health – one participant noted that beforehand, their mental health issues 'would really cause me to stay in bed or drain me of any will to do anything. When I got basic income, the stress was gone, and it was just easier.' A 57-year-old man reported that he used the financial resources to enrol in an adult education course, which he successfully completed, while another participant even attributed finding a partner to the scheme, stating that their poverty beforehand had made them too miserable to be with. Direct cash transfers are simply the best way of stopping people falling into poverty, whether in rich countries or poor countries.[48]

Absolute poverty of the type you see in Rwandan villages or

Brazilian slums is not the same as the kind of poverty that might be experienced in Blackpool or Ontario. In richer countries, people typically do not starve to death when they lack resources, since social safety nets already prevent them from falling below a floor that would put them under even the highest absolute poverty lines produced by the World Bank. But this is precisely the point: UBI, enacted globally, would make sure this applied to everyone. The reason poor people are poor is because they don't have enough money – no matter where they are. And when previously deprived people have access to resources, it makes all of us richer.

THE MAGIC OF REDISTRIBUTION

Has there been a fall in global inequality over the past few decades? Many would answer yes. The famous 'elephant curve'

Growth incidence curve, 1988–2008

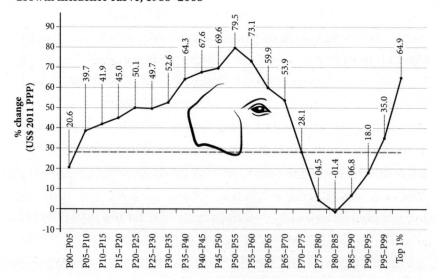

created by poverty researchers Christoph Lakner and Branko Milanovic in 2013 shows the income gains across the world. At the bottom, corresponding to countries like Rwanda, there have been small but real gains in income of 20 per cent: the tail of the elephant. In the middle, corresponding largely to China, there have been much bigger gains of 50 to 80 per cent: the head of the elephant. Towards the top, corresponding to those in poor regions of rich countries like Detroit and Blackpool, people have gained little or even slightly lost out: the bottom of the elephant's trunk. Finally, the very richest in the rich countries have gained substantially: the top of the trunk.[49]

The elephant paints a picture of globalisation as a largely positive, albeit flawed process, compressing the global income distribution by creating a much larger global middle class while neglecting the middle classes of the rich world, who have seen high and possibly rising income inequality within their own borders. But the graph hides an assumption which is pervasive in these debates: these are relative changes, expressed in percentages.

Economic growth means a certain percentage expansion in GDP every year. If I earn $2 a day and you earn $20, then even a doubling of my income – a 100 per cent increase – will not match a 20 per cent increase in yours. Doubling my income will mean I gain $2 a day, while increasing yours by 20 per cent will mean you gain $4 per day. This is exactly what has happened globally over the latter half of the twentieth century. In fact, due to the different starting points of the richest, growth is extremely ineffective at reducing inequality when you look at the actual dollar amounts instead of percentages. Jason Hickel has calculated that it would take over two hundred years for growth to end global poverty entirely.[50]

Absolute global income growth, 1988–2008

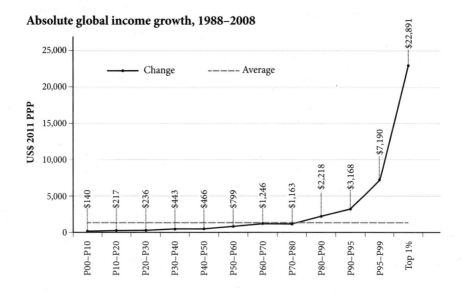

As shown in Lakner and Milanovic's original paper (albeit not circulated as widely), graphing the raw changes in income show the changes are largely flattened at the bottom of the distribution and the income gains take a familiar 'hockey stick' shape, albeit with a slight bump in the middle due to the impressive growth of China and other Southeast Asian countries. From this vantage point the gains in poorer countries look much less impressive and you can understand why the progress in global poverty feels so distant when you speak to the residents of Nyanza in Rwanda.

The great fortune of living in a world which is already wealthy is that alleviating the remaining poverty is well within our grasp. We don't have to wait to get rid of poverty: the massive growth in aggregate income is the basis for redistributing it to the poor. Philosopher Peter Singer famously argued that if you would save a drowning child – even at the cost of missing a meeting and getting your expensive clothes muddy – you should be giving generously to solve global poverty.[51] While I'm not here to admonish any one individual for not doing this, there are clear ways of achieving it at a systemic level.

GLOBAL RESPONSIBILITY

Redistribution through charities like GiveDirectly has achieved notable poverty reduction where it's been done, but more than this it has demonstrated unequivocally that such a policy is a good idea. It is rare to say this in economics, but it is very difficult to find an example of such a trial failing to achieve its aims or backfiring somehow.* Redistribution by governments within highly unequal countries like Rwanda or Brazil can help to achieve some of this poverty reduction, but sustained global efforts will be needed. The idea of global redistribution may seem like a lofty goal, but the truth is that the global economy is extremely integrated and already has global institutions responsible for governing it, so it is natural to wonder why it isn't governed according to similar principles as nation states. Outright taxes from rich countries and transfers to poor countries are something to aspire to, but there are more subtle ways to achieve the same aim.

For example, those governing international institutions are universally skewed towards the interests of richer countries. At the World Bank (WB), which is ostensibly responsible for

---

* As this book goes to print, a study of UBI in the USA backed by OpenAI has been released and it seemed less successful than previous attempts. However, as it was conducted from the period 2020–2023, it is difficult to infer much due to the pandemic, lockdown, and massive additional transfers made by governments during this period.

global development, votes are proportional to GDP so that poorer countries, who by far make up the majority, have under half the total votes. The USA has effective veto power at the International Monetary Fund (IMF), which is responsible for lending to poor countries and often imposes conditions on the types of policies they can enact. The World Trade Organization (WTO) determines the terms and conditions of trade between countries. Even though the WTO is more nominally democratic than the IMF or WB, many poor countries simply lack the resources to engage meaningfully in trade negotiations.[52]

Democratising these institutions so that they operate less on a 'one dollar, one vote' and more on a 'one country, one vote' basis is a first step to giving poorer countries a seat at the table. This could simply mean changing their constitutions, but it will likely necessitate providing every country with an equal footing in terms of expertise and access, too. Although it is not a direct way of achieving redistribution, there is absolutely no doubt that poorer countries would benefit. The most simple example are trade deals which could see them reimbursed more for their products, as currently richer countries have the edge in these negotiations, to say the least.

It goes further than just fetching a higher price for your wares. Dean Baker has noted that although trade deals might seem like a simple case of 'you give me semiconductors, I give you cars' in reality they are anything but. They are complex webs of legal agreements which often tend to favour corporations, including use of our old friend intellectual property rights.[53] The infamous investor-state dispute system lets corporations sue countries who create policies that impact their profits negatively. If the agreements were instead rejigged to favour workers – for example, with minimum wage laws – it would see a massive shift in distribution from the top to the bottom.

The final and probably most effective way to equip global governments with the means to end poverty is by addressing tax evasion. As the global economy is generally dominated by companies from richer countries, failing to collect taxes from them represents a de facto transfer from the poorer countries to the richer ones. Journalist Nicholas Shaxson has estimated that low-income economies lose about $200 billion a year in corporate tax revenue due to tax havens, which is more than they receive in aid.[54] And that's before you factor in other tax evasion schemes pursued by wealthy individuals, which are of similar magnitudes. Taxing properly is a case of enforcing policies that already exist on the books.

In practice, achieving this may require big changes in how we tax corporations. One popular proposal is the idea of unitary taxation. This is a commonsense proposal that many might mistakenly think is already in place. Unitary taxation asks: instead of taxing companies based on legal fictions, why not tax them based on their economic activity? Currently, companies are taxed based on their legal form: where they are registered as a company, which may just happen to be a tax haven. Unitary taxation treats each massive corporation as a single entity instead of a collection of separate entities operating in different countries. For example, as Apple hires Foxconn to build their iPhones, the revenues, workers employed and profits that they make in China and Taiwan would be counted as taxable under those jurisdictions. Similarly, the disproportionate mark-up they apply when the iPhones reach the West would result in taxation in those countries.

Currently, these companies are taking advantage of the fact

that the legal maze of ownership allows them to extract wealth by evading taxation. Remember Katharina Pistor's example of a freelancer getting tax advantages from becoming a corporation? This is that, on steroids. It favours only the largest companies who can afford an army of accountants and lawyers to take advantage of a complex and outmoded tax system. This system was developed in the twentieth century before companies became quite as legally fluid as they are today. Even when it was developed, its limitations were recognised and with them the need for a more coherent, centralised tax system.[55] By tying the taxation of companies to the places where they produce and sell their products, we stop them from reaping all the benefits of operating in stable, civilised societies without incurring any of the costs.

In the first section of this book, we have mapped out our uneven economy: from the underappreciated role of essential workers in the economy, to modern dominance by billionaires and their enormous corporations, to the barriers faced by so many individuals on their hoped-for way to the top, to the fact that despite real progress, entire areas of the globe seem to be stubbornly stuck in poverty. We have centred the failure to take care of everyone who is neglected by the market economy and powerful actors within it.

In the second half of the book, I want to turn to more specific issues in economics, all of which are intimately linked to what we have already discussed. To develop a full understanding of how the modern economy works, including where it seems to go wrong, we need to look at more than just the big picture. We need to see how dysfunctional so many of our markets really are.

PART II

THE DYSFUNCTIONAL ECONOMY

CHAPTER 5

WHAT ON EARTH HAS HAPPENED TO HOUSING?

A sector with many problems, but even more solutions

The start-up Established Titles offers people the chance to send their loved ones a remarkable gift: the status of Lord or Lady, titles generally confined to a select few with unique heritage. The company owns around two hundred acres of land in Scotland and they'll happily sell you a small plot, varying from just one square foot to twenty. It was originally claimed that the plot of land would confer an official peerage as part of a 'historic Scottish land ownership custom, where landowners have been long referred to as "Lairds" ', which is the Scottish equivalent of Lord or Lady.[1] From 2022 to 2023, Established Titles were advertising their business all over the web and especially on YouTube, with various large channels partnering with them for sponsorships. They reportedly made millions of dollars of profit from selling these titles – until several prominent people called them out as being a scam.

As detailed by American lawyer Devin Stone, there were several reasons to believe that Established Titles was a scam.[2] For a start, Scottish courts had already specified way back in 2012 that buying Scottish land does not officially confer upon you the title of Laird, so the central selling point of the business was false. It gets worse, though; the company wasn't even selling you the land. You can't sell land in one-foot-squared parcels in Scotland because that's just too small for the legal system to bother with. Instead of an actual deed, Established Titles were selling you a 'contractual dedication' to the land, whatever that means. You did not own the land in any meaningful sense and would not be able to use it or sell it on.

The US-based company insisted that the product had never been anything but a wacky gift which shouldn't be taken too seriously. The CEO Kat Yip argued that you are free to give yourself the title of Lord or Lady if you want, as long as you don't use it to try to get a loan or some other kind of economic gain. Of course, this is true of someone who doesn't own a small plot of Scottish land, too. I'm free to call myself Lord Moran in everyday conversation, although it would probably isolate me socially. Yip acknowledged that Established Title's advertisements may have been misleading and that they should update their marketing. Their website now makes the fact that the whole thing is a joke clearer and that nobody with one of their titles has the 'right to rule', has a peerage in the UK, or is in any way linked to the Royal Family.*

The point is not to target Established Titles themselves, not least because they are only one of several companies to do this; it is what the company reveals about how we see land. That

---

* It still leads with 'become a lord today' but now adds 'most hilarious gift of the year': 'Purchase a personal Lordship or Ladyship Title Pack with dedicated land in Scotland.*' but the asterisked comment reads 'This is a purchase for a personal dedication for a souvenir plot of land. You may choose to title yourself with the title of Lord, Laird or Lady.' https://establishedtitles.com/

they were able to advertise a tiny plot of Scottish land as conferring on the buyer special privileges illustrates two truths. Firstly, North Americans still seem to view all of Europe as a kind of magical land full of kings, wizards and elves, where it is possible just buying land will turn you into a character from *Game of Thrones*. Secondly and more importantly, there is something unique about land. Almost everyone recognises that owning a plot of land is far more significant than owning, say, a set of high-quality speakers, even if the two were to cost the same.

While the idea of 'land' is something we don't talk about much anymore – it conjures up images of feudal lords, images Established Titles took advantage of all too well – we do still talk about location. The phrase 'location, location, location' has long been a hallmark of estate agents and is even the name of a popular reality show in the UK which follows people trying to find a house somewhere in the country. Much of a house's value is derived from its location and we need to understand why this is if we want to understand the housing market. The construction of the house itself can easily rise into the tens of thousands and possibly hundreds of thousands of pounds/dollars/euros. But this pales in comparison to the value derived from the land.

Whether we call it housing, land or location, we might rightly wonder how we've managed to get it all so wrong. Concerns about housing rank highest on most people's list of economic worries. If you name a country, I'll name a country that is regularly talking about its housing crisis: one report found that 94/94 housing markets across the rich world were some variety of 'unaffordable'.[3] From the extortionate rents in London and Manhattan to the shanty towns of South Africa to the 'favelas' of Brazil, housing seems to be a source of disquiet everywhere. Even European countries like Germany and Austria that people hold up as shining examples have serious problems with their housing. Most people feel somehow insecure in their dwellings, many feel ripped off by their rent and large numbers of young people are unable to purchase a home. Those at the sharp end of all this are either rough sleeping or living in completely unacceptable conditions. Something has to give.

THE MYTH OF THE FAVELA

Brazilian favelas are one of the enduring images of the country. The sprawling slums sit just outside major cities like Sao Paulo and Rio de Janeiro, stretching up and over steep hills. They are populated by box-like homes of varying sizes and degrees of quality. The blockbuster film *City of God* stamped an image of the favelas on people's minds across the world: a symbol of Brazil's poverty and inequality. The seeming physical ugliness of the favelas, especially when contrasted with the comparative glitz of the cities, contributes to this image – they were once described as 'syphilitic sores on the beautiful body of the city'.[4]

Beyond this superficial narrative lies a complex truth: life in favelas is just as varied as life in the rest of the cities. There is no doubt that living in the favelas is hard for many, but they are not unique in being poverty stricken; in 2001, the World Bank acknowledged that 'residence in a favela is not significantly related to poverty'.[5] The people who live in the outer parts of Brazilian cities are just as poor as those in the favelas. Perhaps more surprisingly, there are relatively well-off people in the favelas, too. In terms of residential amenities, access to electricity, sewage, water and waste collection, it is surprisingly similar in favelas and in non-favela areas. While the very richest do inhabit the city centres, living in a favela is not such a clear disadvantage for the majority of the urban population.[6]

The true difference between favelas and non-favelas is their location. Favelas tend to cluster near the city centres on land that was originally unclaimed by official landlords. That the favelas are relatively contained isolates them from richer areas and provides a clear target for aggressive policing. Favela residents are uniquely discriminated against, being denied jobs or even deliveries to their homes due to their place of residence.[7] At the same time, their location provides fairly good access to the cities, with all of the benefits that entails: jobs, shops and festivals. In comparison to the far-out poverty-stricken regions of Brazilian cities, the favelas are quite close to urban life.

The favelas emerged as a result of mass migration from the countryside to the cities, starting in the 1950s and '60s. The rural population of Brazil had been exposed, mostly via radio, to the possibility of a world beyond their highly restricted local boundaries. Instead of a lifetime of back-breaking farming in the area they grew up in, surrounded by a small community of people they had always known, with little to no modern technology, they could now travel to the cities with the promise of variety and opportunity. Such mass migration from the countryside to the city was a pretty common event at this time across poorer countries and had already happened a century ago in richer ones.[8]

Sadly, city life did not always deliver on its promises. It often meant squatting on plots of land that were not legally sanctioned by the government. This meant relying on more 'informal' ways of getting access to housing, with the areas usually governed by organised crime. The bosses would aid with massive, often illegal housing projects, which nevertheless made up a massive half of all housing built in Brazil at the time. These informal and illegal settlements cannot be thought of as some kind of unnatural blight on the landscape of the cities; they are long-term residences with their own, sometimes thriving communities and economies.[9]

Early on, one of the things which surprised outside observers of Brazilian favelas was how effectively they came together to manage their collectively owned spaces:[10]

> Favela residents were socially well organized and cohesive and made wide use of the urban milieu and its institutions . . . and they built their own houses and the physical infrastructure for their communities. Politically, they were aware of and keenly involved in those aspects of politics that affect their lives, both within and outside the favela.

Since then, there has been a marked decline in these kinds of communal activities and management. This is partially owing to broader economic issues discussed in the last chapter, with Brazil's faltering manufacturing sector leading to less reliable employment for the poorest. It is partially due to the misconceptions surrounding the favelas and the resultant discrimination faced by residents. It is also partially due to the drug trade and the criminals who thrive off it. Whatever the reasons, many residents are no longer active participants in their communities.

Although the term 'favela' remains unique to Brazil, these dynamics are similar across many poor and middle-income countries. Anyone who has seen the TV series *Narcos* will recognise that the drug lord Pablo Escobar played a big role in expanding housing (as well as other aid for the poor) in his hometown of Medellin, funding favela-esque neighbourhoods that still sit on the beautiful hillsides of Colombia. In South Africa, so-called shanty towns are typically much flatter and there is an especially pronounced racial dimension to housing, with the slums on the outskirts of major cities being home for much of the black population. Those who have visited Thailand will not have failed to notice the extensive shanty towns lining the motorway on the way from the airport into the centre of Bangkok, skipped over by tourists coming to visit.

What favelas, shanty towns and slums teach us is that location is absolutely fundamental to people across the world. A mass of historical, economic, political and geographic forces plays a role in deciding where we are located, which in turn dictates huge parts of our lives. Not only the simple quality of our residence but our access to related needs such as water, electricity and waste disposal are determined by our location. Our neighbourhood dictates the extent to which we are exposed to crime, as well as the behaviour of police who are (hopefully) trying to address that crime. Job opportunities and social circles are largely dependent on location, especially for the poorest, who may not be able to afford transportation. There are few areas of life that are not touched by where we live.

THE TRAGEDY OF THE COMMONS?

One of the central challenges of governing land is how directly one person's rights and behaviours can conflict with another's. At a basic level, if I am living on a plot of land then you are unable to live there, too. But even if I am living on the plot of land next to you, what I do with my land can easily affect you – whether through the noise I make, how my home obscures your view, my truck hogging the adjacent road, my cat disrupting local wildlife, my use of water reducing the power of your shower, and so on. Local woodlands and reservoirs must be maintained so that everyone can use their fair share without them being depleted. Every single community throughout human history has had to come up with ways to manage the competing needs that arise from using the location they're in.

One text that has left a big imprint on how economists think about managing collectively owned land is Garrett Hardin's *Tragedy of the Commons*. Hardin imagined a field that a community of farmers needed for grazing their cattle – the field being the so-called 'commons'. As the field was not owned by any one individual, each farmer had to make their own, individual decision about whether to bring more cows onto the field. Having a cow graze on the field would benefit the farmer directly through more milk, meat and therefore money; but it would degrade the field slightly. As the large benefit to each individual farmer outweighed the small cost to the field as a whole, each farmer would gradually add more and more cattle until the field was overcrowded, depleted and unusable. This was the 'tragedy' of the commons.[11]

According to Hardin, private ownership would better align benefits and costs: a farmer who had to worry about the entire field would think more holistically, populating it with cattle only until the point it could be sustained indefinitely into the future. Since they were the only one who would benefit, having legally excluded other farmers, they were prepared to account for the potential long-term costs of overgrazing. This was generally considered a good reason that private ownership trumped collective ownership when it came to economics. When farmers were incentivised by the profits they could make from having ownership over the whole field, it would not only benefit them; it would be better for the environment, too.

Unfortunately, Hardin's thought experiment was just that; it had no basis in reality. He relied on armchair reasoning instead of visiting actual sites where land was collectively owned to see how farmers might manage it. His reasoning was also illogical: somehow, the farmers would continue to add cows to the field without noticing that something was going wrong and taking individual and collective measures to prevent it. They would fail to communicate and abide by even basic rules like 'no more cows this year' to guarantee sustainability. The economist Amartya Sen once called the individuals in this type of thought experiment 'rational fools', because although they abide strictly by a rational economic logic of pursuing large benefits (one more cow) over small costs (grass depletion), they somehow cannot manage to take a perspective which is more rational over the long term.[12]

Hardin's approach followed a long tradition we have in Western philosophy of thinking about our approach to land as the correct one, even using it to justify outright conquest. Philosopher John Locke famously argued that, because Native Americans had not managed to increase the productivity of their land for mass production, they did not own it and Europeans could rightfully take it from them. This had its origins in the logic of the market economy, along with the idea of productivity and profit, that had emerged in the English countryside around the sixteenth century. That the European approach was superior was basically assumed by Locke, rather than proven, which may have been related to the fact that he oversaw and personally benefited from the process.[13]

In stark contrast to Hardin and Locke, the social scientist Elinor Ostrom spent her life detailing how communities across the world have come together to manage land and the resources that so often come attached to it. She found that the tragedy of the commons was almost never observed. From the water industry in modern California to farming in Nepal to forests in Colombia, people came up with patterns of rules that allowed them to take advantage of what they had without endangering the environment or other members of the community. There were certainly challenging tendencies that had to be quashed: individuals who exploited the shared resources, difficulties in coordinating the movements of different members, and how to keep track of exactly what was going on. But these were all more surmountable than Hardin's essay let on.[14]

The work of Ostrom and, to a lesser extent, Hardin, raises the crucial question of how we manage our land, housing and cities. Although it was not Ostrom's central focus, several scholars have extended her work to urban spaces and found that it was readily applicable. These are, after all, collectively owned spaces where taking up residence has an impact on everyone else: as one person put it, 'the city analog to placing an additional cow on the commons is the decision to locate one's firm or household, along with the privately-owned structure that contains it, in a particular position within an urban area'.[15] When we decide where we live, we are immediately concerned with questions about what is going on in that area: transport links, local parks, access to utilities, neighbours, schools, hospitals, jobs, shops. All of these are in our collective interest to maintain.

It is natural that humans have come up with a wide range of

different approaches to managing land. Groups like the Aboriginal Peoples of Australia may roam across vast territories that they claim as their own, though no patch of land was owned by any one individual.[16] In modern capitalist societies, we prioritise private ownership, where an individual, business or family will have exclusive rights to their land. Even in these cases, though, the necessity of communal management makes itself heard: whether through rules and regulations like zoning, the construction of adjacent public spaces, community initiatives, or market prices themselves, we have to come up with some way of deciding how the land is used. Perhaps paradoxically, understanding land as a collectively managed commons helps us to make more sense of our prevailing approach of private land ownership.

LAND: THE ULTIMATE MONOPOLY

Buy land AJ, 'cause God ain't makin' any more of it.

Tony Soprano

In my economics degree, one of our lecturers taught us about the concept of 'local monopoly'. While international monopolies such as Amazon, Microsoft and Louis Vuitton are impossible to miss, local monopolies are just as pervasive and can easily abuse their market power. The example my lecturer gave – which has always stayed with me – was that of a kebab shop at 3 a.m. Sure, there were about a thousand kebab shops in Manchester, but were you really going to go to another one at that time, when you were drunk and ravenous, or were you going to put up with the inevitable slow service, low-quality meat and high prices – not to mention the other equally irritating drunk teenagers – that your local kebab shop had to offer? Billionaire Peter Thiel defined monopoly in exactly this way:[17]

> By 'monopoly', I mean the kind of company that is so good at what it does that no other firm can offer a close substitute.

Private ownership of land fits neatly into the local monopoly category. Each location is unique in terms of its access to schools, work, friends, parks and other amenities. Even two houses that are side by side can be quite different inside due to an accumulated list of renovations and decorations. Moving location is a significant event in a person's life and entails substantial financial, social and psychological considerations. The fact that most buyers are attached to their location and face substantial costs of moving means that whoever owns the land has the advantage of reduced competition. Just like the customers of the kebab shop, residents of a house cannot reasonably threaten to go elsewhere. There is no substitute for a unique location.

Another feature of land which makes it different is that the total amount is fixed: as Tony Soprano remarked, we don't make it anymore. There are some isolated efforts to create land, including the expansion of already tiny Hong Kong and Singapore, as well as the slightly offensive efforts in Dubai; Elon Musk's colonisation of Mars may yet expand our square acreage, if he gets there; and longshore drift gradually both builds and destroys land (shout out to my secondary school geography teacher, Mr Howlett, for that insight). But for the most part, we accept that the total amount of land available to humans cannot change. When a lot of people want to buy apples, farmers can respond by planting more apple trees, hiring more apple pickers and using more productive farming methods. When a lot of people want to buy the land in a specific location, it is difficult to expand the amount available and please everyone. In a market economy, the result is that the price goes up.

Land is probably the most fundamental human need. We simply have to reside somewhere – to exist in physical space – so it follows that whoever has the rights to that particular location will have some degree of power over us. They could extract money from us; they could order us around; or they could get favourable treatment from the community. For this reason, those who own land, especially a lot of land, will usually have a substantial advantage when compared to those who own little to none. The fact that land is both necessary and that it naturally belongs to no-one makes it the ultimate monopoly.

Simultaneously the worst- and best-kept secret of housing is that it is less about the house itself than about the land it is built on. To see this, imagine buying two houses that are of similar size and quality for your needs: each has two bedrooms, two bathrooms, a garden, a nice kitchen, is near a good school, has minimal crime in the area, has neighbours who don't play music as loudly as mine are while I'm writing this, and so on. The only difference is that one of them is in the centre of a major city while the other is in a rural area. Now ask yourself the question: which one has the higher price? The answer should be obvious: it's the house in the city. Despite the fact that the two buildings are virtually identical and that the two neighbourhoods are of similar quality, you could see yourself spending a multiple of the value of the rural house if you moved to the city instead.

There is an idea in economics known as 'rent', which is related to but distinct from the rent you pay for your house. The idea behind rent is that it is an excessive charge; over and above what can feasibly be justified from the efforts and skills of whoever produced a given product. Anyone who overcharges for something, such as a monopoly exploiting its customers, is potentially extracting rent. As economist Cecilia Rikap has emphasised, many examples of intellectual property, profiting from ideas that are not inherently scarce, are rents.[18] It is often difficult to discern where the line is between a fair price and a 'rent', but the clearest-cut case is land ownership. It is no coincidence that the term is the same as the everyday one we use to pay for housing.

High rents for land are difficult to justify, either from a moral perspective or from one of cold, calculated efficiency. While we may speak of the value of land, much of this value is not attributable to the owner but to the community. When a carpenter builds a beautiful table, they can be certain that the price it will fetch is largely a reflection of their own efforts and how desirable the table is when compared to other tables. In contrast, when the price of land goes up, it's usually because the local area has become more desirable in some way rather than because the landlord has done anything. Maybe there was a big regeneration project; maybe a big new employer opened up; maybe that area is just 'up and coming', to use the watered-down term for gentrification. You may recall Adam Smith's charge that 'landlords . . . love to reap what they never sowed'.[19]

LAND GAMES

The board game Monopoly was originally created to illustrate the extraction of rent – in both senses of the term – by inactive landlords from the rest of the economy. As those who have spent tedious hours playing this game will know, it generally ends up with one person owning all of the property on the board, which was supposed to reflect the reality of untethered capitalism. These monopolistic dynamics of land ownership were seen as a justification for taxing land, so that the value the community generated would return to that community. The original name of Monopoly was The Landlord's Game and there was an option to play with a tax which redistributed rents to all the players, to teach people about the benefits of land taxation. While mentioning land taxes may not make you the life and soul of the party – even if it is the type of party where people actually want to play Monopoly – it remains one of the most important solutions to our housing woes.

Land taxes come in a few different forms, with the traditional idea being to have the landlord pay some percentage of the value of the land every year. To make sense of what exactly a land tax means, we need to distinguish between the owners of the land and the modern term 'landlord', who usually owns a specific residence. This type of landlord may actually carry out some duties such as construction and maintenance of the property. They certainly come in good and bad forms (more often, it seems, bad forms) and I've had my share of serious issues with my own landlords. But the historical usage of the term landlord really refers to the land itself rather than the dwelling constructed upon it, and that's what would be targeted by such a tax.

It is rarely argued that taxes increase efficiency: any business owner who has had to pay the numerous, opaque, confusing taxes levied on companies will attest to the potential inefficiency of taxation. As we've seen, despite their purported inefficiency, taxes still have various justifications in terms of redistributing from rich to poor. The moral case for a land tax is clear because landowners are generally richer than everyone else and because their income is not justified by their efforts or ideas. Yet the land tax is unique in that it is argued not only to redistribute wealth and to reflect just desserts, but to increase efficiency, too. This applies to any tax on 'economic rent', but the land tax is the sharpest tool for taxing rent alone.

The difference between a land tax and most other taxes is that because the amount of land is fixed, taxing it doesn't affect how much there is. If you tax investment, then you tend to get less of it. If you tax work, then people tend to work less. The logic is that the capitalist or the worker are getting less bang for their buck as the tax is imposed and will take lengths to avoid it, including both accounting gimmicks and genuine reductions in their economic activity. With land, taxing it will not discourage the creation of new land because such a thing is impossible. The landowner has the legal right to the land but they did not create it and they must pay the tax no matter what they do. The rent extracted by landowners is absorbed into the tax and can be used for various public spending projects or for reductions in other taxes (like the much-hated council tax in my own country).

It goes further than this: land taxes may actually *encourage* economic activity. That's because having to pay a levy will light a fire under the feet of any landlord who is not doing much with their land. If they want the privilege of land ownership but are not engaging in productive activity to help them pay for the revenue, they will make a loss. The result is that they will either do something worthwhile with the land or sell it to someone who has better plans for it. One natural corollary of this is that a land tax will tend to reduce speculation, because holding onto land and waiting for the price to rise is much less profitable when you're getting charged every year you hold it. The practice of hoarding land without using it, known as land banking, would be discouraged by this. Hoarding land has long been a problem in countries all over the world, with Jamaica and Colombia among the countries who have historically tried to tax land to reduce widespread speculation.[20]

While they are effective in theory, land taxes are politically difficult to implement. This is simply because landowners have quite a lot of political power, partially owing to their economic clout but also because land ownership often comes with a great deal of historical privilege. In the UK, the landed gentry can trace their heritage back for generations and generations, the most obvious example being the Royal Family tracing their heritage back to William the Conqueror. It was Winston Churchill who first called land the 'mother of all monopolies' and claimed:[21]

Roads are made, streets are made, services are improved, electric light turns night into day, water is brought from reservoirs a hundred miles off in the mountains – and all the while the landlord sits still. Every one of those improvements is effected by the labour and cost of other people and the taxpayers. To not one of those improvements does the land monopolist, as a land monopolist, contribute, and yet by every one of them the value of his land is enhanced. He renders no service to the community, he contributes nothing to the general welfare, he contributes nothing to the process from which his own enrichment is derived.

Churchill was instrumental in attempting to enact a land tax in the UK in 1909. Unfortunately, the UK tax was unsuccessful due to various legal and logistical challenges, buoyed by staunch opposition from the landed gentry. Fortunately, other parts of the world with less powerful vested interests have successfully put these taxes in place and evidence seems to show that they encourage rather than discourage economic activity.

You may know that the singer Joni Mitchell famously sang 'they paved paradise and put up a parking lot', but you probably haven't understood the song's relation to land value taxes. The lyrics were actually inspired by Hawaii's experience after they introduced such a tax in 1963. It resulted in so much development that Hawaii's income went from 20 per cent below the US average in 1959 to 25 per cent above the average in 1970.[22] The tax was largely abandoned in 1977, primarily because officials perceived it as having resulted in *too much* growth, with its critics citing environmental concerns about high density. I'm not saying that Mitchell was wrong to be against overdevelopment in Hawaii, but it is a testament to the power of land taxes if we were to use them in the right places.

In the USA, the city of Pittsburgh in the state of Pennsylvania near-quadrupled its land tax relative to other cities nearby in 1980. According to one study it was 'the only city to have experienced a large and significant increase in levels of building activity during the 1980s', despite being on a downward trajectory before the tax.[23] This seems to have been because the land tax had no negative effects on investment, but allowed the city to reduce the taxes that did. In the state of Victoria, in Australia, switching over to land taxes resulted directly in a huge increase in building on underutilised land as developers scrambled to make money from their land to pay it.[24] All in all, land taxes are one of the most elegant and effective policies out there and are advocated by a wide range of experts and people from different political traditions. There is no good reason not to have them in place.

EXTREME MAKEOVER, UK EDITION

We are all aware that estate agents are not to be trusted. In *The Simpsons*, Marge temporarily has a job as an estate agent. She is initially introduced to the job with smiles and high hopes, told to match the right home to the right buyer. As she suffers for her honesty, unable to make a sale, her boss Lionel Hutz tells her 'the truth': the right house is the one that's for sale, and the right buyer is the one who's looking. A small house is 'cosy'; a dilapidated house is 'a handyman's dream'; a house on fire has a 'motivated seller'. Marge is informed that she needs to sell a house soon – any house, to anyone – or she's out. All that matters is the money, rather than getting people into good homes.

There are quite a few reasons why the housing market seems to be so problematic, but one is that there are few avenues through which consumers can express discontent: there is poor feedback from buyers to sellers. Most people can probably count the number of times they've moved house on one hand. Conversely, can you even count the number of times you've bought something like a tea mug, a pencil, or an apple? When things are bought and sold regularly, people get an idea of what they like and they can 'vote with their feet', taking their business elsewhere if a particular brand or shop is no good. When things are bought and sold rarely, people do not have that option readily available. You're unlikely to return your house or buy a new one next week from a different estate agent.

With a purchase as rare and complex as housing, people are also much less certain about what they should expect and which common traps to avoid, which leads to what we could call 'poor market feedback mechanisms'. We all understand what rotten fruit is, and if you're as British as I am, you have a pretty good idea of what makes a good tea mug. But what makes a 'good' house? There are so many characteristics to worry about: the location, the quality of the bathroom and kitchen, the number of bedrooms, the presence of weird smells, and so on. It's difficult to find one house that is truly the best when compared to all the others, and there will always be things you didn't notice. Estate agents therefore have a tendency to draw your attention to the positives while failing to mention the negatives. That's not really possible with groceries (though I guess you can turn apples over to their 'good' side in the display case).

It's not just poor market feedback mechanisms; owning a house comes with a wide variety of legal and logistical challenges. Whether you buy or rent a house, you need people to navigate you through the process of signing contracts that dictate your various rights and responsibilities. Owning a pencil is straightforward: it's your pencil and nobody else can use or take it. Owning a house is a bit more complex. You are free to snap your pencil – as many an edgy 12-year-old schoolboy discovers – but you are not free to demolish your house. You can give your pencil to someone else, and while you can allow others into your home, even to live, legally transferring ownership is complicated. All these complications are multiplied when getting a mortgage, and few people can navigate all of this without legal assistance.

Renting leads to another whole set of complications from both the tenant's and the landlord's perspective. In these cases, legal ownership becomes fuzzier and both parties have to understand what exactly it entails. For example, in the UK landlords technically own the house, but while it's being rented they can't do what they want with the space. Tenants have a right to 'quiet enjoyment', which means not being disrupted endlessly by unexpected visits from the landlord. Landlords do have a right to continued payments from the tenant, and they are entitled to check up on the house every so often, but there are limits. Who can truly say that they know the numerous rights and obligations of tenants versus landlords in their own country?

For all of these reasons and more, moving house has been deemed as one of the most stressful things a person can do.[25] The headache of negotiating buying or renting houses is just one example of how convoluted our approach to this fundamental need has become. While having our housing dominated by private ownership and markets seems natural to us, it has actually become incredibly burdensome for both individuals and for society. In the UK, people have been struggling on numerous fronts for well over a decade and one of the key drivers of these difficulties is the housing market. House prices have risen relentlessly since the 1990s and, despite temporary blips, seem to be continuing their upward march. It's not that rising house prices are the result of a generally thriving economy; many people are struggling to make rental payments. The amount most people spend on housing has risen as a percentage of their income, making it more of a burden over time for families.[26]

SAFE AS HOUSES?

One of the choices we've made in the UK, alongside other English-speaking countries like the USA and Australia, is to make housing not just a place to live but a financial investment. When people buy a house, they expect it to appreciate in value. They are willing to borrow precisely because of this reality: paying interest on your mortgage can only really be justified if your house's price is increasing steadily. It is a major fear of homeowners to go into what's called 'negative equity' and have the value of your house drop below the value of your mortgage. Conversely, if everything goes according to plan then a home can serve as a kind of quasi-pension, with essentially zero housing costs in old age, plus something to pass on to your children.

In the 1980s, Margaret Thatcher famously sold off social housing owned by the state to individual families at a heavy discount to create a 'property-owning democracy'.[27] Social housing had expanded massively following World War II, but Thatcher's premiership saw its expansion grind to a halt as private home ownership rose. Social housing is by far the cheapest option for most people and its decline has played a big part in increasing housing costs for everyone. In 1979, even one in five rich people lived in social housing, but these days that number is essentially zero. The UK Government still supports people who can't afford housing, but these days it is more likely to be about subsidising their ability to pay rent or a deposit than supplying the houses themselves.[28]

Privately owned housing has never been evenly distributed: those who have managerial or professional jobs, are white, and/ or are native Brits have long been more likely to own their homes.[29] Housing costs are higher for those who are renting privately, who are disproportionately the poorer classes in urban areas.[30] The historical force of accumulated wealth, which falls along predictable social demographic lines, is a big factor in whether somebody can afford a deposit or will even be given a house outright. Among those who have mortgages, those with the largest debts (relative to income) are usually the poorest. The 'property-owning democracy' was never truly one.

There is also an emerging generational divide, with owning a house a distant dream for many people in my generation. One study in Australia found that households earning average levels of income in 1985 would have been able to afford a deposit after two years, but by 2023 it would have taken five and a half years.[31] Such an 'average' household would only have access to just over one out of every ten homes, compared to triple that in the past. In the UK, getting older is no longer a clear pathway to gaining a home. As millennials grow up and have children, they fail to become homeowners: almost one million more households with children live in rented accommodation than in the past.[32] Many younger readers will be familiar with the reality that without assistance from the older generation, a deposit is basically out of reach. In this respect, it seems that my generation is poorer than that of my parents or grandparents.

FINANCIALISATION AND HOUSING

We have also seen the financial sector get more and more into property, with the result being serious instability. It was not until the late twentieth-century wave of financial deregulation – which, contrary to popular belief, came in the early 1970s, before Thatcher – that 'regular' banks could now get into the mortgage business more freely.[33] Land's status as desirable for banks actually goes back to its key characteristics: since it is essentially permanent and immobile, it makes good collateral for banks. People cannot hide land or their ownership of it as easily as they can hide other assets, so the bank can take it off you relatively easily if you fail to keep up your payments. This is why a 'secured' loan is precisely one that is collateralised with property and therefore land. For the same reasons land is a desirable thing to tax, it is a desirable thing to lend against.

These days, banks do the majority of their lending for commercial real estate. After the first wave of deregulation in 1970, houses experienced a short and sharp boom-bust cycle, with a big drop in price after 1973. This led to restrictions on lending, but Thatcher removed these in 1979 and this led to another boom-bust cycle, with the bust in 1982. There was yet another crash in 1990, which brought down the housing market. Despite these issues, when New Labour were elected seven years later, they continued to treat housing in a similar manner. Gordon Brown's famous refrain 'no return to boom and bust' was ceremoniously belied as housing became the epicentre of the 2007–9 financial crisis, which at the time was the biggest crash for almost a century.[34]

In the past, most lending for home ownership was done by community-owned building societies which had been around since the eighteenth century. These saw citizens in a local area pool their savings to help other members of the building society finance construction of their homes – if you've got a good memory, you might recall these as a variant of the credit cooperatives so common in Germany. In many cases, they were temporary and once every member had a home, they would dissolve. Building societies had rarely experienced bank runs in the past. In an illustrative shift, the UK bank Northern Rock arose from a series of mergers of building societies and by the new millennium it famously sold mortgages at 125 per cent of the market value of a house. Northern Rock was the first to go in the 2007 crash.

The economist Josh Ryan-Collins has argued that our approach to the housing market creates a vicious cycle: banks lend money to buy homes, which bids up the price of land since it is largely fixed in quantity, especially in desirable areas. As house prices rise, people have to borrow more to buy a home. High house prices are also good for banks' balance sheets, so they end up lending even more, bidding prices up further. Far from funding the building of new homes, most of this credit seems to go towards pumping up the price of existing properties. To further perpetuate this cycle, people have increasingly used remortgaging as a way to buy big consumer goods like cars, so mortgage lending ends up driving other spending in the economy, too.[35]

Many people blame the rich for our housing woes and they're not entirely wrong. People will generally reach a point of satiation with most goods – you're not buying twice as many bananas if your income doubles. But with space, people always want more. Evidence suggests that an increase in income will lead you to spend disproportionately more on square footage. For instance, a 1998 UK study found that a 10 per cent increase in income led to people spending over 15 per cent more on square footage.[36] It is therefore no surprise that richer individuals have sought more of the limited space, especially in cities: in Manhattan the average price per square foot increased from $324 to $767 between 1995 and 2004.[37] As in the UK, foreign investment into the housing market has grown and these investors are generally among the global elite.

The more uncomfortable truth is that it's not just the rich; the entire population is invested in the idea of housing as an investment. In the UK, the average person has become much more likely to become a landlord, with buy-to-let (BTL) properties growing in popularity since their introduction in 1996. Many of these landlords are indeed quite wealthy, or are corporate landlords, but many of them have fairly similar levels of income to their tenants and are essentially using their properties to make a living. Private landlords own one in five homes in Britain and the rise of BTL has been associated with an increase in house prices.[38] Letting is a sensible decision for many individuals, especially as they approach old age, but it may worsen the housing crisis overall.

TO CONTROL OR NOT TO CONTROL?

In many cases rent control appears to be the most efficient technique presently known to destroy a city – except for bombing.

Assar Lindbeck, Professor of Economics,
Stockholm University

Navigating smarmy estate agents, negligent landlords and rip-off mortgages are all parts of the type of housing market we have chosen to create in the Anglo-American world. Elsewhere, things are somewhat better thanks to a few smart policy choices. Countries like Germany and the Netherlands, for instance, see most of their population renting from private landlords. Looking at Anglo markets, you might expect this to be associated with more expensive housing, but the opposite is true. These countries may have problems, but many residents seem to enjoy stable access to housing despite less political focus on home ownership.

The truth is that access to housing does not depend on having ownership of it, and these countries take that reality seriously. Germany has the lowest home ownership proportion in the OECD (a group of rich countries) at around 50 per cent and in Berlin it is a mere 15 per cent. This compares to about two-thirds in the USA, UK and France. While private renting is more common in Germany, even among richer individuals, renters enjoy a wide range of guarantees including controls on rent and security from eviction. In Berlin, landlords can rarely increase rents above the level paid by the previous tenant. Canada, Spain, the Netherlands and several US states have followed similar policies.[39] Although rent control is a controversial policy among economists, it is interesting how it challenges our perceptions of ownership.

Fetishising home ownership in and of itself can end up mistaking financial wealth – the value of the home – for actual access to housing. Economist Josh Mason notes that because Anglo-American populations have much of their wealth tied up in housing, the statistics could lead one to conclude that the people of Germany or the Netherlands are less wealthy than those in the UK and the USA just because their homes are worth less in financial terms. But this would be a case of just looking at the balance sheet and ignoring the concrete reality of access to housing (pun intended). Germans who rent are about as secure in their dwellings as the average UK homeowner and many have no intention of buying for this reason.[40]

These countries would seem to prove that a well-regulated rental market is one workable way to approach the housing problem. But one of the issues many economists have with these strict protections is that they can put landlords in a straitjacket. The more difficult and expensive you make renting out a home, the argument goes, the less likely landlords are to invest in homes or even bother renting them out in the first place. Owing to ballooning rents, Berlin itself introduced quite a strict rent-control policy in 2020 – so strict, in fact, that it was ruled unconstitutional around a year later. While active, the policy reduced rents in the affected homes – 83 per cent of households rent in the city – but it also resulted in a dramatic reduction in vacancies as landlords withdrew.[41]

Most rent-control policies across the world are looser than Berlin's, for example by allowing landlords to raise rents if they engage in serious renovations. This is a sensible modification to the policy which ensures that rent increases are matched by increases in the quality of homes. So-called second generation rent control also excludes newly built houses and the evidence is clear that this more flexible form of rent control does not reduce new construction.[42] It is better thought of as 'rent stabilisation' because it protects existing tenants from sudden increases in their rents that are unjustified by investment from the landlord.

Given that this variety of rent control doesn't reduce the total amount of housing, it is worth bearing in mind that the homes are still used, either by tenants in rent-controlled apartments or by new homeowners to whom the landlords sell. As housing economist Cameron Murray has emphasised, getting landlords to sell up to first-time buyers might be considered a desirable consequence of rent control, while them selling to other landlords is a moot point. It's just a change in ownership; it's not like the home suddenly becomes unavailable.[43]

One study showed that when rent control was abolished in Cambridge, Massachusetts in 1995, it had little effect on the total volume of housing built.[44] There was no construction boom as landlords took advantage of fewer restrictions on what they could do. Meanwhile, the prices and rents of the previously controlled houses rose substantially, pricing many people out who had previously enjoyed controlled rents. However, landlords *did* rent more homes out (as opposed to selling them or sitting on them) and they also invested slightly more in the maintenance of their existing properties, providing a boost to the market. It's fair to say that the consequences of these policies are so complex that they are not easy to judge at first glance: even the rise in house prices can be perceived as good or bad, depending on whether you own a home or not.

The major worry with this more flexible form of rent control is that it creates a two-track housing market: some enjoy the protections, while others are displaced due to the higher rents in the unprotected market. In San Francisco, rent control resulted in 15 per cent fewer rent-controlled flats, with landlords either selling homes or investing enough that they were allowed to rent their flats at a higher rate. One famous study found that the benefits to residents who enjoyed rent control were equal to the costs to those excluded from rent control, who faced higher rents.[45] In other words, the winners and losers of this modern form of rent control roughly offset each other, so the policy is basically a judgement call. It depends on whether you want to protect existing residents with rent control or to entice new residents with lower rents for other, usually newer properties.

We also need to delve into the landlord-tenant relationship, instead of treating the behaviour of landlords as a law of nature. After all, if landlords are in the business of extracting unfair rents, then we may want to regulate them more, not less. In Berlin, it seemed that many landlords were sitting on empty dwellings while waiting to see if rent control would be abolished, something which would be less likely if a land tax were there to light a fire under their feet.[46] In San Francisco, the Ellis Act allows landlords to suddenly remove all their units from the market and evict tenants. This is exploited by landlords to escape rent control – but is this the fault of rent control, or the Ellis Act?[47] Were tenants as well-protected as in Germany or the Netherlands, evictions would surely be lower. Massachusetts also boasted greater protection from evictions in its laws.[48]

Any poorly designed or overly restrictive policy can have unintended consequences, and rent protections are no exception. However, there is plenty of scope for making rental a less costly and more reliable option with rent stabilisation, plus rights to prevent landlords from evading regulations and evicting tenants. You can grant flexibility to landlords where it's warranted and take it away where it's not. The track towards well-protected tenancies as an alternative path to private home ownership can work, although secure tenancy regulations can only ever be a part of the picture. The fact remains that rent control and strong tenants' rights have at best a neutral effect on the total amount of housing available, so they are not going to solve the housing crisis alone.

BUILD MORE HOUSES!

Since the year 2000, France has enacted *Loi Solidarité et Renouvellement Urbain*, which translates as the Solidarity and Urban Renewal Law (SRU). Unlike the USA and UK, widespread home ownership in France is substantially driven by social housing. The so-called SRU law required most cities to make sure at least 20 per cent of housing is low cost and this was upped to 25 per cent in 2013, with an accompanying increase in fines for non-compliers.[49] This is one of the most aggressive pro-housing laws in the world and it seems to have worked. The social housing share has more than quintupled in the wealthiest French cities: Paris, once famous for its social segregation, now boasts widespread affordable housing in desirable neighbourhoods.[50] Across France, neighbourhoods have become less segregated by class and ethnicity as social housing is no longer confined to poorer communities.

The most direct way to expand the amount of low-cost housing is for the government to build it directly and provide it affordably for anyone who needs it. Another set of countries who have maintained a deeper commitment to social housing are the Nordics. Sweden has 1 million units of social housing in a country with only 8 million people.[51] In Finland, they've taken an even more direct approach: just give everyone a home who needs one. Housing giveaways to the unhoused have been a hugely successful policy in Finland, working to house four out of five individuals over the long term. Just as having money makes people not poor, it seems that having a house makes people not homeless.[52] Far from being an expensive giveaway, the policy probably saves money as having a stable home helps people get back on their feet and into work instead of falling into rough sleeping, crime and addiction.[53] It seems like an easy win for everyone.

Vienna, the capital of Austria, is famous for its approach to social housing. In 1928, the average household paid 5 per cent of its income on rent, and no that's not a typo. Housing in the country was rationed by the government depending on need, and rents were not allowed to change for decades. Today, private rentals are permitted, but half of Vienna's inhabitants live in cheap public housing as the government continues to take responsibility for construction. Nearby, Poland also has a history of widespread public housing, owing to its communist legacy. More than 70 per cent of households own their home outright, with no mortgage.[54]

Some East Asian countries take another approach: the state continually intervenes in land, housing and credit markets. Since World War 2, Japan's Government Housing Loan Corporation has supported people with low-interest rate mortgages should they need them. Local governments started to take responsibility for land and public housing around the same time, which has improved the options for their citizens. In South Korea, the Korean Land Corporation (KLC) carries out about half of all residential development, making sure that idle land is used to build housing. The KLC buys up vacant or idle land and either develops it or sells it to someone who will. The cost of housing in Korea has declined substantially thanks to the KLC.[55]

In Singapore, a country whose housing situation is better than most, the government owns almost all the land and the private sector leases it from them. This successfully provides the population with housing and yields revenue for the government. Singapore is the king of the 'public option', with the Housing and Development Board providing a cheap home to any adult couple who applies. It is similar in spirit to the way public health systems like the NHS operate: it's there if you need it. Successful housing policy is one reason Singapore has transformed from majority slum conditions to a wonderful place to live that boasts a 90 per cent home ownership rate.[56]

Secure access to housing, then, does not depend on owning it privately, the growth of which is a recent phenomenon which is especially pronounced in Anglo-American countries. In fact, although owning housing privately may give the illusion of security for some, it has resulted in worse outcomes for those countries that have pursued it. Many people find themselves with large mortgages which they struggle to pay in the hope that they will own the house far into the future. People depend on home ownership not only for their access to shelter but for their access to other consumer goods, and people increasingly even use it as a pension. Private home ownership is a major driver of differences in living standards and, to top things off, has been at the epicentre of catastrophic economic crashes.

Those countries that have better housing markets have taken land ownership seriously, as something that incurs obligations to the community, whether through rules and regulations or through payments that return that value to everyone else. In many cases, the state steps in to provide housing or at least the land necessary for its construction. The utter failure of Anglo-American countries to fulfil housing needs is a choice that stems from the emphasis on private ownership, supported by numerous policies in both the public and private sector. These issues have come to a head in recent years, and many people are actively debating solutions.

THE BATTLE OF THE XIMBYS

A few years ago, residents of my street complained in the WhatsApp group that a house on the corner was being converted to flats. According to one resident, it was a shame that their family couldn't stretch to the £1.4-million house solely as a residence for their nanna, who currently lived with them. With no disrespect meant to her personally, I'd argue that housing several people in London, a city with a serious housing crisis, should take priority over one woman who clearly already had a residence.

In this instance, I felt like I held the moral high ground: I was in favour of the type of housing that would take care of as many people as was feasible. Yet at my current residence, I have repeatedly cursed a nearby construction site – ostensibly building a similar block of flats to the one coveted by the nan – as the noise interrupts my work. When housing construction affects me personally, it seems that my moral high ground rapidly disappears.

My internal struggle reflects an interesting debate which has emerged in recent years: the NIMBY versus the YIMBY. The former stands for 'Not In My Back Yard' and it emerged as a pejorative term for people who would not let any housing or infrastructure be built too close to them because it would be noisy, disrupt their view, cause pollution, cause overcrowding, put pressure on local infrastructure, and so on. The ire directed at NIMBYs stems from the shortages of housing and good infrastructure faced in many places, particularly cities, and the idea that their petulant protestations are the main obstacles to improvement. As you may have guessed, YIMBY simply stands for 'Yes In My Back Yard' and welcomes higher-density housing and any legal reforms which make building it easier.

The NIMBY/YIMBY debate is a cute way of framing disputes over zoning regulations which, even ten years ago, would have seemed like one of the dullest topics around for most people. Seemingly because of the pandemic and lockdowns, people rediscovered how important their residence and the space around it was. The truth is that there are few things more important than the idea of living in a great house in a great area, and this is a life goal for many of us. As activity in city centres disappeared during lockdown, everyone was struck by the peacefulness, the lack of pollution, and even the return of wildlife to urban environments. The intensity of this debate may also have had something to do with the fact that people also spent a lot more time online during Covid, where, having nothing better to do, they could separate into warring online factions like NIMBYs and YIMBYs.[57]

The call for more construction and shifts in zoning regulations certainly has reasonable foundations. Cities in the USA and Australia are notorious for their urban sprawl, with suburban areas featuring grids of houses that look exactly the same, stretching as far as the eye can see. Blocks of flats which would house more people, especially those who are younger and renting, are typically disfavoured over the traditional suburban house you might have seen in *Malcolm in the Middle* or *Modern Family*. Zoning laws do not permit shops near the houses, with the result that people have to drive to nearby mall complexes to get even basic goods and services. A lengthy car journey to a shopping complex may be necessary just to get some milk, a situation that most Europeans would look upon with raised eyebrows.

In the USA especially, there is a long racist history behind the suburbs, which are dominated by the white population. 'Redlining' during the 1930s referred to the practice of designated zones where no African Americans were allowed to live, and if you look at maps of major US cities today, you'll see that the pattern of races persists. Despite the issues noted above, the white suburbs are relatively wealthy, spacious and low on crime, while the inner-city areas suffer from a variety of social and economic disadvantages. The term 'white flight' refers to white residents exiting the city centres out of an explicit desire not to live among the black population.[58] White flight actually gave rise to the 1950s stereotype of the traditional American suburb, mocked in the show *It's Always Sunny in Philadelphia*. Friends Dennis and Mac move to the Philadelphian suburbs, only to gradually lose their minds at the sterile and lifeless area, the infuriating commute into work and the rift that opens up between the stay-at-home partner (Mac) and the working partner (Dennis).

YIMBYs often contrast the segregation and rigidity of these suburbs with the vibrance of many continental European city centres. From Berlin to Bordeaux to Barcelona, flats stand side by side with shops, restaurants and other commerce. Many areas are pedestrianised or at least have few cars when compared to American cities. These cities are often better looking aesthetically, more socially and economically vibrant, and crucially house more people per square mile than NIMBY-ridden American suburbs. A rich history certainly doesn't hurt here: taking a photo in almost any habitation in Italy will net you a good postcard because of the sheer beauty of the structures prevalent across the country. YIMBYs reasonably claim that at least some of this magic could be emulated elsewhere with a few smart changes to zoning.

To this end, there are places in the USA which have experimented with reforms with some success. The city of Minneapolis is the pioneer in this regard, since in 2018 it enacted an aggressive series of reforms which aimed to supplant the traditional single-family home of the suburbs with apartment blocks and other multi-family housing.[59] The consensus is that these reforms have been successful: since then, the city has approved 9,000 new housing units and rents have barely grown at all, which contrasts with the rapid pace at which they've grown across the rest of the country. Echoing Hawaii's experience with the land tax, the reforms were actually struck down at the behest of environmental groups because they were seen to have resulted in *too much* building.[60] Creating more housing, using zoning laws that are not arbitrarily limited to one kind of building, is a sensible and proven policy.

MAKING HOUSING COMMUNAL AGAIN

In the words of Australian economist Matt Cowgill, this debate raises the question: 'What do you buy when you buy a house?'[61] Do you buy the local neighbourhood, including the exact shape, colour and height of the nearby houses? Do you buy the transport links you rely on to get to work? Do you buy the proximity and type of shops or other local facilities? Even when we pursue private ownership of homes as aggressively as we have done, the communal nature of land and location come back to bite us. The cry of the NIMBYs cannot be altogether dismissed.

NIMBYs may point out that YIMBYs can be hypocrites: despite their progressive bent, they do tend to be professional, white, middle-class city-slickers who focus mostly on the type of development that might benefit them.[62] This means prioritising an expansion of private housing, which tends to be more expensive, over social housing, which could benefit poorer families. Minneapolis may be the big contemporary success story but the city remains one of the worst places in the country for racial inequality.[63] In addition, NIMBYs frequently argue that YIMBYs are really YIYBYs: as in 'Yes In *Your* Back Yard'. They are not necessarily talking about aggressively building near where they live and may even revert to becoming NIMBYs themselves should such a possibility arise.[64] As UK journalist Tom Utley once put it: 'I hate NIMBYs . . . but I hate the new lean-to on my neighbour's patio even more!'[65]

Hypocrisy aside, NIMBYism versus YIMBYism is a debate where I can see both sides. Zoning laws in many English-speaking countries seem to disfavour the housing that is so desperately needed. On the other hand, residents of an area have the right to participate in the decision-making processes that govern their local commons. Before the Kowloon Walled

City in Hong Kong was demolished in 1993, the area had no planning regulations (except for a height limit of 14 stories to accommodate planes landing in the nearby Kai Tak Airport), so the residents favoured high-density housing. Density at its most populated point was 1.9 million people per square kilometre.[66] Even from a simple look at the so-called 'walled city' above, you can see that it must have been an extremely difficult place to live. Although new housing does effectively increase supply, it transforms the location – in this case, largely for the worse.

One of the quirks of YIMBYism and NIMBYism is that they both fall victim to the same obsession with private ownership of land. The reason people rightly complain about NIMBYism is because property owning, middle-class families in the suburbs use their status to block out construction which will bring in housing that will benefit poorer people, who have less economic and political clout. At the same time, the YIMBY focus on marking out zoning for private developers can help to fuel processes like gentrification, sometimes even outright displacing of poorer residents, as happened with a set of YIMBY reforms in San Francisco.[67] Better modes of organisation which would allow broader swathes of society to manage their land and housing would help to solve this problem.

As an example of what not to do, the UK has an utterly bizarre approach to planning that seems to combine the worst of both worlds, having been dubbed 'Socialist Thatcherism'.[68] Because of the 1947 Town and Country Planning Act, growth is deliberately curtailed by the government, with new developments having to go through several opaque planning procedures.[69] This allows NIMBYs to stick their oar in at every stage, which is just one reason why the current High Speed 2 rail project was roughly halved in size after coming in massively over cost.[70] Green belts which strangle the growth of cities have few of their purported environmental benefits while reducing housing construction and increasing prices. Even though private construction is made exceedingly difficult, the government refuses to fill the gap itself.[71]

Elsewhere, in real countries, there are a growing number of organisations which directly tackle the challenge of building housing that works for entire communities. Community Land Trusts (CLTs), for example, take land into collective ownership and are democratically governed by their members. These include the residents who build housing or businesses on the land; the nearby community; and other interests such as charities, public officials and businesspeople. CLTs often endeavour to ensure there is low-cost housing for the poorest in the community and prevent house prices from spiralling out of control. But evidence across a wide range of cases shows they are also prepared to mix their goals with commercial uses, public spaces and environmental purposes. They are especially popular in North America, with many US cities using them to take control of their land.

In other cases, it is the housing itself which is taken into collective ownership through 'housing cooperatives'. In these organisations, every member who buys in has the right to one home, and each member gets one vote on the collective management of the homes. There has been a boom in housing coops in Switzerland over the past few years, which is probably related to the fact that the capital, Geneva, is one of the most expensive cities on the planet. Housing cooperatives are not typically allowed to make a profit and rates are simply set at the cost of building and maintaining the homes, with many Swiss cities having more than one in ten houses in coops. Residents favour them because they offer an alternative to high private house prices while allowing for more direct democratic input than public housing built by the government.[72]

In practice, these efforts tend to come together. Porto Alegre, the capital of the Brazilian state of Rio Grande do Sul, has historically seen sustained efforts to build these kinds of alternatives in poor communities to provide low-cost housing and amenities to the favelas there. This has involved cooperation between community groups, labour unions and the government. The housing cooperatives in Porto Alegre have bought up the plentiful unused land in the area and have used financing from their members, the unions and sometimes the government to build collectively owned housing and infrastructure. While this is far from a silver bullet, it has helped many communities avoid the kind of decline seen in favelas elsewhere in the country.[73]

More generally, organisations like MTST and MST (which

roughly translate to 'the homeless workers movement' and 'the landless workers movement', respectively) are trying to change things across Brazil by building housing communities. The former mostly operate in urban areas, the latter in rural areas, but both have the same basic mission and strategy, which is to provide housing for those who are struggling by utilising unoccupied land. MTST and MST will simply occupy the unused land and build homes and communities on it, citing the Brazilian constitution as support, which explicitly states that land must have a social function and purpose. Although it may not be law elsewhere, this is an important principle to bear in mind when thinking about the housing debate. These community-led efforts address the problem of private land monopolies head-on.

HOUSING: SPOILED FOR SOLUTIONS?

In the first part of the book, we looked at the difficulty of being in poverty and the drivers of inequality and poverty across the planet. Housing and, more broadly, location, is a key driver of inequality across the world. From poor Brazilians who face the displacement and discrimination of the favelas to elites buying an apartment in Manhattan big enough to house a swimming pool, our accommodation and location make up key parts of our lives. Location should be thought of as a shared commons and in many cases, an excessive focus on private ownership simply warps and distorts our housing rather than magicking its collective reality away.

You may have noticed that I have offered a large number of solutions to the issue of housing, more policy solutions than at any other point in this book. I appreciate the policies may have been difficult to keep track of, and in some cases, they are con-tradictory: you can't have both government and community groups owning land, for example. In others, they are comple-mentary: legislation to protect renters may work best paired with government expansion of housing supply. The reason for offering such a wide range of solutions is that each country has a unique history with land – indeed, each country *is* a unique land – so it is not always possible to enact certain policies in certain places. There is no one-size-fits-all solution to arguably the defining economic issue of our age.

Nevertheless, each and every country could better house its residents and reduce the outsized cost of housing for them with these policies, making housing a significant example where most of us are much worse off than we should be. In Brazil, community groups like MST and MTST seem to be growing once more, as does social housing under the presidency of Lula. Many other Latin American countries have seen a growth of these kinds of organisations, including Colombia and Vene-zuela. European countries like Germany and the Netherlands may continue down the legislative route, enacting carefully designed rent controls and protections, while housing coopera-tives remain popular in Switzerland and Denmark.

It seems like the USA's hopes for solving its housing crisis lie in YIMBYism, supplemented by community organisations, an altogether localised approach which fits well within a federal system. In the UK, vested interests prevent a serious land tax (or anything that threatens homeowners) from being enacted, so the options have to be pro-building. As with the USA, planning laws have to be changed drastically, albeit in slightly different ways – multi-use zoning for the USA; an easier set of procedures for the UK. Given my country's lack of investment gumption, a UK

Infrastructure Bank was launched in 2021 by the Tories[74], while a national wealth fund was launched by the incoming Labour Government in 2024.[75] A national land bank, in the vein of Korea's KLC, could get things moving in housing, too.

Lack of housing and rising housing costs is one of the most important economic problems facing people across the world, but it is far from the only one. Land is just one of Polanyi's 'fictitious commodities' that marked the advent of the market economy in the English countryside. Another is money: nowadays, money increasingly dominates our lives and we need to understand it to understand how the contemporary economy is failing us. How money is created, who it goes to, and how we manage it, are all crucial questions which are too often misunderstood by laymen and experts alike.

CHAPTER 6

WHERE DOES MONEY COME FROM?

The ins and outs of the lifeblood of the market economy

When I asked my mum at age twelve where money came from, she told me the following story. People have always had different occupations and so they had to trade, initially bartering one thing directly for another. I might be a chicken farmer while you crafted chairs, so we exchanged a few of my chickens for a couple of your chairs and were both better off. But this proved to be too complicated – how can you guarantee the person who has what you want, wants what you have? Maybe I have chickens and want chairs, but you actually want a hammer, and the person who makes hammers wants a blanket, and so on.

Direct barter requires a so-called 'double coincidence of wants': a match-up between what you want and what I have, and what I want and what you have (you may have to read that last bit twice). Money can solve the double coincidence of wants, since everyone agrees to accept money for everything. I pay you for a chair, you pay me for a chicken, then you go and buy a hammer while I go and buy some candles. People invented money precisely because bartering is so inconvenient, my mum insisted. Twelve-year-old me was presumably happy with this answer and moved on to incessant questioning about another topic.

People used to barter, then invented money, then much later on came debt and modern financial systems, or so the story goes. But in his book *Debt: The First 5,000 Years*, the anthropologist David Graeber showed that the historical record indicates the exact opposite. Debts to one another are something deeply ingrained into human societies of all kinds: 'you owe me one' is a phrase most people will recognise. What exactly 'one' meant was usually vague and enforced by social norms. Henry might owe Joshua one for gifting him a pair of shoes and would be mocked if he paid him back a mere loaf of bread.[1] In lieu of wages, industrial workers used to run up a tab at a bar until they eventually settled it when they got paid in bags of nails.[2] The things exchanged were intertwined with traditions and they were rarely precisely equivalent in the sense exchanges must be today. These exchanges were also separated by often lengthy periods of time.

Settling more precise debts of specific amounts of money came to require a common monetary standard, which was typically enforced by states and bureaucracy. These institutions could keep count of precisely what people owed each other so that they had to pay back precisely that amount of money. This was exactly the role of the accountants and scribes that emerged in civilisations like Ancient Sumer, keeping track of owed amounts of grain and volumes of precious metals. From this came modern 'spot exchange' where people simply bought things in one-off transactions which were settled straightaway, such as buying tools from your local blacksmith. Graeber calls the story my mum told me the 'myth of barter' and shows that it has been decisively refuted by evidence across a wide range of times and places. He states that, throughout history, no-one has ever been able to find evidence of a transaction like, 'I'll give you twenty chickens for that cow.'[3] Take that, Mum.

It's fair for a social worker to get the story of how money came about wrong, presumably just as I'd get the strategy for helping a disadvantaged client who suffers from a heroin addiction wrong. What is less understandable is professional economists also getting the origin of money so wrong for so long. Economists have relied on explanations similar to my mum's since the days of Adam Smith – often considered the father of modern economics – despite the fact that it is largely speculation. The myth of barter basically takes our existing economic system and transports it back in time, then takes money out of the equation but assumes everything functions the same, albeit slower. As Graeber puts it in his critique of economics textbooks:[4]

> Historically, they note, we know there was a time when there was no money. What must it have been like? Well, let us imagine an economy something like today's, except with no money. That would have been decidedly inconvenient! Surely, people must have invented money for the sake of efficiency.

When you start to think about the myth of barter even a little bit, it breaks down. To be a chicken farmer I'd need feed, land, chicken coops and so on. How would I get these without having any chickens to trade in the first place? Specialisation of the type assumed by the myth of barter requires a functioning economic system with money and, crucially, debt – so that people can get the materials for production before they have anything to sell.

This kind of thinking has long been absent from explanations that preach the myth of barter, often content to indulge in thought experiments over actual historical evidence. A historical account of money helps to avoid these kinds of errors, not least because they have led to catastrophes from economic depression to hyperinflation to chronic underperformance. It goes beyond just the myth of barter: misunderstandings of money have made us all poorer.

What Good is Money?

Homer: Aw, twenty dollars. I wanted a peanut.
Homer's brain: Twenty dollars can buy many peanuts.
Homer: Explain how.
Homer's brain: Money can be exchanged for goods
    and services.

Money is, in essence, a useful fiction. Paper notes and coins by themselves are largely worthless and only have value because we know they will be accepted by others, whether chicken farmers or not chicken farmers (the two types of profession). Money has worth because we all buy into the idea that it has worth. Two of the most important roles of money, which are typically underpinned by law, are that it is accepted by banks to pay our debts and by governments to pay our taxes. Yet even the supposedly hard truth of the law has to be commonly accepted for it to work. If banks or governments are not trusted, the whole system can break down – as we'll see.

Many people believe money is still backed by gold or other precious metals. My agent admitted as much when she first read this, and polling shows that she is joined by at least 30 per cent of people in the USA.[5] In fact, modern money is simply created via the printing press – or, more accurately these days, by entering numbers into a computer screen. If you take a close look at any note, for example the British £20 note below, it will typically have scribbled on it a promise from the country's central bank to pay you . . . the exact amount of money on the note. If you head into your country's central bank with a note worth 100 of the currency in your country, they'll happily exchange it for a similar note of 100, or two notes of 50, or 100 coins of 1, and so on. The whole system is essentially built on the promise: I owe you one.

Noting that something is a fiction does not imply that it is completely arbitrary. Rules in sport are historically changeable – in the UK, rugby is separated into the two games of Rugby League and Rugby Union, which differ on a number of dimensions. At the risk of infuriating my American and Australian readers, by my reckoning both games of rugby bear more than

a passing similarity to American Football and to Aussie Rules Football. Rules can differ while the spirit of a game remains the same. Having said that, we can all appreciate that there are some rules which would make no sense at all, such as if teams started the game on the same side they were supposed to score – every kick-off would just result in a try, touchdown, or goal. Having absolutely no rules would be equally unworkable as the game would have no meaning and may well descend into chaos. We have designed Rugby, American Football and Aussie Rules Football in slightly different and sometimes arbitrary ways, but that doesn't mean anything goes (though Aussie Rules isn't far off, if you ask me).

Rules surrounding money and the financial system can be thought of in a similar way. There are rules which govern how much money is in the system, how this money can be used, who gets access to it, and when. These rules differ between countries: the UK, USA and Australia have different currencies as well as different approaches to their respective currencies. Countries outside the rich world face major additional constraints, as we will see. Central banks are fundamental to the modern money system and are one of the main characters of this chapter, but they did not always exist. We have to continually update and refine the rules to make sure that the financial system is functioning effectively.

You may reasonably ask (with more than a hint of sarcasm): 'When you say the financial system functions effectively, what do you mean exactly?' The financial system has crashed several times in my lifetime alone and has been bailed out to the tune of trillions of (pick your currency) each time. As we've seen, despite these clear failings many in the financial sector are paid much more than the average person and this disparity seems to be growing. Lending for productive investment, especially to small businesses, has lagged behind lending for credit cards and mortgages,[6] and consumer debt levels have risen to unmanageable levels for many families.[7] As we saw in the last chapter, this has also fuelled house price increases.[8] To top it all off we have experienced bouts of high inflation recently, eroding the incomes of people who were already struggling. Is this a functioning financial system? The answer is, of course, 'no' by any reasonable standard, but understanding how it works and the thinking behind its rules is the first step towards fixing it.

In my opinion, anyone who tells you they *fully* understand the financial system is usually either mistaken or trying to sell you something. Finance is extremely complicated, at once global but with important differences between countries. There are multiple financial institutions – retail banks, individual investors, hedge funds, governments – who interact continually. There are a plethora of different types of money or other financial assets, from simple notes and coins to bank deposits to more exotic instruments like Credit Default Obligations and Credit Default Swaps. By the time we've written down something about the financial system, it has probably changed. This is all accompanied by a thick layer of jargon: equity, reserve ratios, tranching, diversification. It's enough to put people off, and it's not unreasonable to suggest some in finance may benefit from such a low level of public scrutiny. Needless to say, we are not going to get to all of these details in a single book chapter.

Money has always been used by humans in one form or another, but it has become ever-more essential to us following the expansion of the market economy depicted by Karl Polanyi. Instead of just 'owing each other one' we now get paid in precise amounts, are taxed automatically based on our pay, have bills and rent come out of our accounts almost as automatically as taxes, and have a precise amount of money left to spend freely on what we like – our disposable income. The hope is that the various rules around how money works allow the amount of money in the economy to grow and shrink in line with what is needed for businesses and families, going where it is needed and disappearing from where it isn't needed.

A key principle we need to know to understand how the financial system works is 'double-entry bookkeeping', where everyone's books have to balance. This doesn't sound like the sexiest of ideas but if we can get our heads around it, many seemingly complicated aspects of the financial system will fall into place. Depending on your point of view, double-entry book-keeping can seem fishy, or it can seem like magic. To keep it simple to start with, imagine your own balance sheet as an individual. Assets are things that you own, while liabilities are things that you owe to others. Say you had £1,000 worth of gold – an asset – but also owed your friend Tracey £1,000. Then your balance sheet would look like this:

Your Balance Sheet #1

Assets	Liabilities
£1,000 gold	£1,000 loan from Tracey

Because the two amounts are equal, your books balance.

You may point out that your average bank or individual does not owe exactly as much as they own, and you'd be right. The above scenario is a rare one of perfect harmony between assets and liabilities. But how does the balance sheet look without this harmony? Imagine you still own £1,000 in gold but instead owe £500 to Tracey, so that you have a net positive position. Your balance sheet now looks like this:

Your Balance Sheet #2

Assets	Liabilities + equity
£1,000 gold	£500 loan from Tracey £500 equity

We take the difference between what you own and what you owe and, if it is positive, then you have your equity of £500 – which you can think of as your financial cushion or net worth. Equity may look evil because it is in the liabilities column, but actually it's a good thing (remember how I said the rules are kind of arbitrary?). As per the last chapter, you may be familiar with equity in the context of home ownership – is my house worth more than my mortgage? – but it is a far more general principle. It is literally *always* the case that 'assets = liabilities + equity'. As long as this equity is positive, you have what is shockingly called 'positive equity' and you're doing just fine. On the other hand, if equity is negative – say, you owe Tracey £5,000 – then you have 'negative equity' and you are possibly facing insolvency. Equity ensures the books always balance and is a core tenet of our financial system.

Double-entry bookkeeping seems like a simple idea, but it wasn't invented until thirteenth-century Italy, or quite possibly in Arabic states before that.[9] The Church had originally banned the charging of interest on loans, but double-entry bookkeeping facilitated modern credit systems which got around this and possibly even facilitated the growth of capitalism itself. Commercial enterprises grew beyond the scope of an individual to understand them informally, as in David Graeber's historical examples of local communities owing each other chickens and tools. Double-entry bookkeeping was an innovative way for merchants to keep track of how much they had, how much they'd sold, and crucially the profit they'd made. Suddenly, huge financial flows could be recorded, and debts could easily be created or cancelled in a consistent manner.

MONEY FROM NOTHING?

Where the magic comes in is that double-entry bookkeeping, as well as other elements of our financial system that we will soon learn about, allows banks to create money 'out of nothing' when they make a loan. Let's imagine you ask a bank, call it Bank Aussie Rules, for a £100 loan to buy a loaf of bread – which, following the cost of living crisis, is not looking too far off. If the bank agrees to the loan, it will deposit the money in your account. The result is the bank has an asset of £100 for the loan that you need to repay them, but it also has a liability of £100 for the deposit. Since there is £100 on each side of the balance sheet, they cancel each other out and the loan has not affected the bank's financial position. Equity is zero once more because assets and liabilities are equal.

Bank Aussie Rule's Balance Sheet

Assets	Liabilities + equity
£100 loan to you	£100 deposit from you

The idea that a deposit is a loan from you to your bank might seem strange at first because we think of deposits as our own

money. In fact, you have given money to the bank on the promise of getting it back some day: a loan. It is certainly a different
kind of loan to the one the bank has made you, since you can get
a deposit back whenever you want, rather than having it paid
back to you over a specific period of time. It is also guaranteed
by the government through deposit insurance. Nevertheless, it *is*
a loan, and like most loans it does typically carry interest with it.
You are being paid to lend the bank money!

You may wonder if there are any limits to how much money
banks can create. The first thing to be aware of is that just
because banks create money, it doesn't mean they can simply
create as much money as they want and give it to themselves –
even if it might seem that way sometimes. One of the key factors
here is that there needs to be a willing borrower: the bank can't
create money without people who want loans. Equally, the bank
won't create money if it suspects you won't pay your loan back –
that would make the 'assets' part of the above balance sheet a
little shaky, raising questions about the bank's solvency. Money is
created as credit to potential borrowers, but the number of cred-
ible and willing borrowers is limited. Furthermore, creating
credit this way doesn't automatically translate into higher profits
for the bank if the loans they make are rubbish ones to people
who won't pay them back.

So how do banks make money? Their business model is
essentially to create money for borrowers, in return for which
the borrowers have debts in the form of credit cards, business
loans and mortgages, etc., on which the borrowers pay interest. Banks typically charge more interest on these loans than
they pay to depositors and the difference makes them money.
It seems like a simple money-making machine, but the difficulty lies in (a) making sure the loans are actually going to be

paid back, and (b) making sure the bank has enough cash so that they don't face a bank run. These two things are linked: if customers and investors suspect that a bank has made a lot of dodgy loans, they will all try to withdraw at once and cause a bank run. This is precisely what happened with the queues outside Northern Rock in 2007, as well as the 1930s Great Depression before it.[10]

It is natural to be slightly puzzled by the money system. The economist John Kenneth Galbraith once remarked that 'the process by which money is created is so simple that the mind is repelled'.[11] Money is culturally regarded as the ultimate hard truth: it doesn't grow on trees, or so the saying goes. This is completely understandable, since a single parent feeding three children cannot magic up money out of nowhere in the same way private banks can. In truth, the amount of money created in the economy depends not just on the activities of private banks, but of central banks, governments, businesses, plus the single parent themselves. These different actors do not behave independently of each other but interact in interesting and sometimes unpredictable ways. We need to understand every piece of the monetary mosaic before we can put them all together.

THE MONETARY MOSAIC

Everyone can create money; the problem is to get it accepted.
Hyman Minsky[12]

Look back at your balance sheets from before. What is the difference between you and a bank? In principle, there is nothing stopping you announcing that you will take in 'deposits' from people like Tracey, which they can get back from you any time they like, and also announcing that you will grant loans to them if you deem them likely to pay them back. It's easy – just enter it all into a balance sheet as above, call yourself 'Bank Rugby' and you're away. But there is obviously something wrong with what I'm saying: neither you nor your customers will be confident that you can fulfil these obligations. You would need a lot of money to get started, and even if you did manage to get started there's a good chance you would encounter issues if you lost confidence and there was a bank run, with Tracey and your other customer knocking aggressively at your door hoping to withdraw money you just don't have.

Enter central banks. The best way to think about central banks is as the 'bank of banks'. Just as you have an account with your bank, banks themselves have accounts with the central bank, where they hold special money called 'reserves'. Reserves are an asset for the bank, just as your deposits are an asset for you. Arguably the defining feature of a modern private bank is that it is allowed to hold an account with reserves at the central bank of its country. What is important about reserves is that banks are allowed to swap them for hard cash at any time. If Bank Rugby asks for £1 million of its reserves to be converted to currency, the Bank of England will send a truck full of money to them to fulfil this request.

There are rules surrounding how many reserves banks must have, which are related to how much lending and borrowing the bank has been doing. This is with the aim of ensuring the whole system functions smoothly so that the bank can carry out its business of borrowing and lending to the rest of the economy. Let's understand this with some more balance sheets – I sensed you were missing them – by imagining that you are paying a building contractor £10,000 for a housing extension. When you pay the contractor, you transfer deposits from your bank account into theirs. But behind the scenes, your bank will be making sure to pay the contractor's bank in reserves.

Your Bank's Balance Sheet

Assets	Liabilities + equity
- £10,000 reserves	- £10,000 your deposit

Your Contractor's Bank's Balance Sheet

Assets	Liabilities + equity
+ £10,000 reserves	+ £10,000 contractor's deposit

Looking at the balance sheets above, you can see that £10,000 is subtracted from your bank account – which, remember, is a liability for your bank because they owe it to you – while £10,000 is added to the contractor's bank account, which is similarly a liability for their bank. At the same time, your bank will shift £10,000 of reserves from themselves to the builder's bank to match the change in assets to the change in liabilities. Your bank previously had £10,000 in reserves to match your deposit; now your contractor's bank has the same in reserves to match your contractor's deposit. The books therefore balance, and the contractor's bank can be sure they have the reserves to back up the new money if it is withdrawn.[13]

The difference between your account with your bank, versus your bank's account with your central bank, is that banks effectively have a licence to create money. They may not always have reserves to hand, just as you may not always have enough money deposited at your bank to pay your bills. However, private banks know they will be backed up by the central bank, which routinely creates and destroys money in the form of reserves to make sure that private banks can settle transactions like the one above. Banks can also lend and borrow reserves from each other so that they have enough at the end of the day.

When people first hear this, they're understandably outraged. 'When banks don't have enough money, the central bank just . . . creates it for them?' This is where things really start to sound fishy: why can't the central bank just create money for you and me when we fall short on this month's bills? In principle, central banks can create money for any purpose, including paying off your bills. The economist Nathan Tankus noted that when he attended a central bank conference, they created the money to reimburse his travel expenses.[14] Yet this is a drop in the ocean in terms of the entire economy. When we are talking about systematic creation of large amounts of money, we need to have clear rules otherwise the value of the money will become uncertain or worthless. We need to think carefully about the central bank's more impactful interventions surrounding money creation, which are known as *monetary policy*.

WHERE GOVERNMENTS FIT IN

Another crucial piece of the monetary mosaic are governments, which raises the thorny political issue of government debt. Government bonds are the primary way governments go into debt because they are how people and organisations loan those governments money. You yourself may well own some of these bonds because they are considered a safe investment. Over the bond's lifetime, which is usually between 1 and 20 years, a government agrees to pay you back with some interest. The interest payments are stretched over the bond's lifetime and when the bond reaches the end, the government gives you back the amount you originally paid. When you see headlines about government debt, know that it is primarily in the form of these bonds.

Traditionally, the central bank's primary tool to control the amount of lending done by banks is to engage in what are called 'open market operations' (OMOs) where it creates reserves with which to buy bonds sold by the government. The fact that the central bank uses the reserves it creates to buy these bonds, instead of directly giving the money away to private banks, makes the whole process seem slightly less outrageous. Let's look at how this works using balance sheets again. Imagine the central bank creates £1,000 in reserves and wants to buy £1,000 worth of government bonds from 'Bank American Football'. In this case, the balance sheets of the central bank and Bank American Football look like this:

Central Bank's Balance Sheet

Assets	Liabilities + equity
+ £1,000 Government Bonds	+ £1,000 Reserves

Bank American Football's Balance Sheet

Assets	Liabilities + equity
- £1,000 Government Bonds + £1,000 Reserves	

Again, we see the suspicious magic of double-entry bookkeeping. The central bank has a licence to create money in the form of reserves, while Bank American Football has a licence to hold reserves, and the whole system has agreed to follow the principles of these accounting balance sheets. From here, the central bank can 'magically' create money and the private bank can 'magically' have more reserves, making it less vulnerable to a bank run. Hopefully, this filters down to everyone else through more bank lending and indirect effects which shore up the balance sheets of companies and households.

Government debt is a thorny political issue, with politicians across the world regularly promising to keep the debt down. But this is much more complex than these politicians let on; many do not understand the basics at all. An additional benefit of the dynamics we just outlined – and I stress that what I am saying is truer for richer countries with well-established currencies, an issue we will interrogate shortly – is that central banks can directly finance government borrowing on a large scale. I will spare you a further, larger set of balance sheets but imagine what it would look like if we included the government above and they were creating new government bonds. They could issue the bonds, selling them directly to the central bank in exchange for reserves – the government is allowed to hold an account with the central bank, too – and use this money to fund government spending. There are intricate legal nuances concerning how exactly the government can do this, but in practice something close to this is happening across the world.[15]

Unfortunately, many discussions of government debt are hysterical and do not properly grasp how crucial it is for modern economies to function. Government debt is not owed to a single angry loan shark knocking on the government's door; it is a set of slow-moving payments owed to numerous households and businesses and is an integral part of the financial system.

Government bonds are the primary way for central banks to engage in monetary policy to facilitate banks' lending. They underpin the financial system by acting as a safe asset for investors, helping them to benchmark against other, riskier investments like stocks. Economist Stephanie Kelton has said that when she asks US politicians if they want to eliminate their government's debt, a majority of them agree. When she asks the same politicians if they want to eliminate government bonds it elicits puzzlement, even though bonds and debt *are exactly the same thing*.[16] This doesn't mean we can't ask challenging questions about government debt, but, as with the rest of the monetary system, we need to understand how it works before we do so.

With the plumbing of the money system outlined, we can return to the question of why central banks don't just give people money directly. Could we all have accounts with central banks, the way private banks do now? Let's start by taking things to an extreme and imagine that every time anyone needed money, the central bank simply credited their bank account. This would seem fantastic at first, but it is easy to see that the long-term effects would be disastrous. You could buy what you liked and pay whatever was asked, but so could everyone else – which would likely lead to shortages as everyone flooded to buy anything that took their fancy. Prices would increase because of the extra demand, then people would credit more money into their bank accounts, leading to an inflationary spiral which ultimately would render money and prices completely meaningless. This process is known as hyperinflation and it is so catastrophic that its presence in Weimar Germany in the 1920s is often associated with the subsequent rise of the Nazis.[17]

In short, central banks cannot create as much 'real' wealth and 'real' income as they want simply by increasing the numbers on a spreadsheet, or by printing notes and minting coins. Such an act is equivalent to changing the measuring stick to make yourself taller. Nevertheless, we shouldn't take this point too far and conclude that creating money cannot aid the economy at all. Too *little* money in the economy is associated with falling prices, wages and growth, something known as deflation. This can be just as painful as hyperinflation, and during the 1930s in the USA deflation was a big feature of the so-called Great Depression, which saw years and years of economic turmoil until the US Government and central bank started to get more money flowing through the economy through various means.[18] Managing monetary policy so that we have neither excessive inflation nor deflation has been a key challenge throughout central bank history.

A BRIEF HISTORY OF CENTRAL BANKING

David Graeber's myth of barter taught us that it is important not to depend on fables when trying to understand the global monetary system. A firm grasp of the history of money shows us that things have not always been the way they are now. This naturally leads one to scrutinise historical changes in monetary arrangements and to ask how they could be different in the future. Nuances in the monetary system can have subtle yet important effects and we need to update our understanding continually. Indeed, one of the frustrating yet fascinating things about the monetary system is how often it seems to change, with us as economists scrambling to keep up.

A simple fact which gives us a bit of perspective on central banks is to know that they haven't always existed. Many countries operated without central banks for a long time, and naturally their monetary systems looked quite different to ours. No central banks didn't mean no backups should the financial system teeter, though; there were various private mechanisms in place to shore things up. Still, private banking systems were more likely to allow banks to fail, which meant that some customers lost their money when their bank went belly-up. This proved to be too much for many countries to stomach politically, which led to the creation of central banks to guarantee deposits and generally back up the financial system. Advocates of abolishing central banking argue that this has damaged a key feedback mechanism of capitalism – bankruptcy – contributing to the 'too big to fail' situation we have in banking today.[19]

Each country's central bank was established at a different time and for different reasons. The first-ever central bank was the Swedish Riksbank, established in 1668 to assist governments and commercial banks. Not too much later, in 1694, the Bank of England was established primarily to fund government debt, though it was privately owned until it was nationalised in 1946. The French central bank was established by Napoleon in 1800 after hyperinflation following the French Revolution and civil wars. The Federal Reserve in the USA (the Fed) was not established until 1913. The private Bank of England had previously been the template, but the Fed created a new template with a much more active role in managing the economy. To this day, it and central banks across the world set a common currency for the entire country and use it to manage employment and prices.[20]

During this era, central banks still used gold or other metallic standards. This tied their hands by fixing the amount of money they could issue to the limited amount of gold they owned. The logic was reasonable: governments might abuse the power to print money from nothing. Yet as the economy and the population of a country grew, it required more money to circulate to keep up, but the fixed amount of gold prevented expansion. For this reason, the famous economist John Maynard Keynes openly called the gold standard 'evil' in the only surviving video of him.[21] He correctly believed that escaping it was the only way to end the deflation of the Great Depression, and the UK recovered much more quickly than the USA having followed his advice.[22]

Because of how much the gold standard restricted economies, it slowly died over the course of the twentieth century. But the desire to restrain central banks' money-printing abilities survived. The 1970s/80s doctrine of monetarism attempted to target the total amount of money in the economy. The idea was this: if the economy was growing at 3 per cent, why couldn't the volume of money just grow at a similar rate? This might retain the discipline of the gold standard without becoming a straitjacket. Central banks were licensed to print more money, but only up to a point: they'd have to stay in line with a rule that it grew a set amount, year on year.

Monetarism was adopted as a policy by the USA, UK and Chile and, though intuitive, it quite clearly failed. In the face of the high inflation of 1979, the Bank of England set itself a target of a 7 to 11 per cent increase in the money supply, but it actually increased by 22 per cent.[23] Essentially, they discovered that the amount of money in the economy cannot be controlled absolutely by central banks – in fact, less than 11 per cent of money was created by the Bank of England in 1979. Today that number is closer to 3 per cent, which means that 97 per cent of money creation in modern economies is done by private banks in the way we saw earlier: by creating it 'out of nothing' when they make loans.[24]

Most modern central banks sprung up over the twentieth century and by the end of this century many settled on inflation-targeting as a policy which constrains money creation without throttling the economy. Currently, most central banks target 2 per cent inflation by managing interest rates, which trickles through the financial system in ways we've seen. When inflation looks to be getting too high, the central bank cuts back on its open market operations (selling instead of buying government bonds) and this makes reserves scarcer and more expensive for banks, resulting in less lending down the road. If inflation is too low and/or the economy is sluggish, the central bank expands its OMOs, which hopefully facilitates more lending and boosts the economy.

Inflation targeting has generally coincided with central banks becoming independent of governments. New Zealand pioneered the policy in 1989, with Canada starting the subsequent year and the UK doing so under Gordon Brown in 1998. The European Central Bank and Federal Reserve in the USA are both a little coy about whether they really target inflation (central banks are of course known for being mischievous boxes of fun), even though everyone knows they have targeted inflation for a similar amount of time. Over the years many other countries have followed suit including Japan, Switzerland, Australia and more recently India.[25] Independent central banks take away the power of meddling politicians to change interest rates as they see fit – say, lowering them with an upcoming election to get votes. It seemed that prior to this, inflation had been too high precisely because of the electoral gains from low interest rates.[26]

THE CRASH

For a long time, inflation targeting was believed to be a clear victory for economic policy. However, when the financial crisis of 2007–9 hit, it forced a lot of soul-searching – after all, central banks were among those who failed to see it coming. One of its limitations was quite subtle: a lack of appreciation of the role of asset bubbles in the macroeconomy. It was thought that what went on in the financial sector, though important, may not have systemic consequences for the rest of the economy. For this reason, central banks tended to be focused on managing interest rates to ensure stable inflation – with one eye on growth and unemployment – because a bubble bursting would affect these things.[27] The bursting of the dot-com bubble in 2001, which did not lead to a serious recession, seemed to support this notion. In such an eventuality, the central bank would simply respond as it always had, lowering interest rates to boost the economy.

Finance was not the only problem raised by The Great Recession; the most immediate problem was the crash itself. The economy plummeted to such depths that central banks quickly encountered a simple problem: interest rates cannot go below 0 per cent. Naturally, if you start charging people to hold onto their money, they'll generally prefer just to keep it themselves.* With rates stuck near 0 per cent and the economy tanking, central banks were worried about a deflationary spiral mirroring the 1930s. This was one of the rationales behind the modern policy of quantitative easing (QE), which saw central banks stretch beyond buying government bonds and into other assets such as corporate bonds to combat the recession. The hope was that this would affect a wider range of interest rates than normal OMOs that we detailed above, and it did. It is commonly believed that QE helped

---

* The zero lower bound may be less strict than this, since holding cash can itself be costly and risky, but even when interest rates go slightly negative, they won't go much lower.

avoid the economy falling off a cliff by reducing these borrowing costs, though whether it gave growth a sizable boost is less clear.[28]

When central banks took aggressive action with QE, they probably did not foresee that they'd create another long-term, fundamental change in the money system. Ever since then, private banks have been awash in reserves. This means that managing the level of reserves in the system – as we detailed above – isn't really possible; it's a bit like managing the level of water in the ocean. The result is that central banks in rich countries, most notably the Federal Reserve in the USA, rely on other channels than OMOs where they buy and sell bonds. Do not be alarmed: this doesn't mean everything I've told you so far is a lie. The basic dynamic is the same as we've discussed: the central bank engages in activity to increase or reduce the lending and borrowing of reserves. However, there are subtle differences in how that is done.

Nowadays, the Fed in the USA mostly operates by paying banks interest on their reserve accounts. The higher the interest rate banks get on these accounts – their 'deposits' at the Fed, remember – the more likely they are to hold onto them and the fewer reserves circulate throughout the system. The new mechanism does an equally nice job of controlling the interest rate, because why would a bank lend reserves if they can get more just by holding them in their Fed accounts? The higher the interest rate there, the higher the interest rate in the rest of the economy as banks pass it on. However, this does change our focus somewhat – the total money supply becomes even less relevant under this system.[29]

In one sense, the history of central banking reads like a history of them repeatedly throwing off the fetters of an era and surrendering to the reality that money creation has to be dynamic and respond to the times. Originally, the idea of central banks existing at all was thought irresponsible as they'd fund spendthrift governments; once established, they were often chained down by metallic standards, until this brought the economy down with it in the Great Depression; then strict rules like money supply or inflation targeting, coupled with independence from governments, promised to create clear rules with sufficient flexibility. Following 2008 and 2020, central banks have become aggressively involved in more and more action, and the system is barely constrained by a lack of money any longer. However, central banks still officially target inflation.

You should now be able to see that, although economists have settled on a 2 per cent inflation target for understandable reasons, no such target is beyond question. For a start, there are other things in the world to worry about than inflation. If low inflation means high unemployment, low growth, or has otherwise undesirable consequences, we may agree to tolerate inflation above 2 per cent. Central banks have been criticised in recent decades for not paying enough attention to unemployment, keeping it higher than is necessary for low inflation. Some economists have therefore called for a 3 to 4 per cent target to loosen the grip of monetary policy.[30]

Many go further in criticising our limited approach to central banking. In buying assets disproportionately owned by the wealthy, it may well have increased inequality.[31] Others have called for central banks to have green aims in their policies, for instance by buying assets owned by companies investing in renewable energy.[32] And while our earlier, fanciful example of unlimited money from central banks might be taking things too far, the idea that citizens could each have an account with a central bank which was credited with a bare minimum income to survive every month is more moderate. You might recognise this as one way of enacting the Universal Basic Income (UBI) that we saw in Chapter 4. Dubbed 'The People's QE', this has been advocated by the economist Frances Coppola as a way of alleviating the worst of poverty and keeping spending (and therefore employment) up, while being too little and too predictable to lead to massive, uncontrollable inflation.[33]

COLONIAL CURRENCIES

It may surprise you to learn that the Franc still exists. Although France officially abolished it in 1999 to adopt the Euro, a version of it is still used by over 160 million people. Owing to the country's colonial legacy, 15 West African countries are obliged to use a currency called the CFA Franc.[34] This means that many of their decisions have to go through the French Treasury and they are required to maintain a fixed exchange rate between the CFA Franc and the Euro. In regions such as West Africa – as well as Latin America, which has a similar relationship with the dollar – central banks have to pay more attention to foreign currencies than in wealthier nations. We have excluded these countries from the discussion up until now, largely because monetary policy requires a whole new set of considerations, top among them being exchange rates.

Imagine that the exchange rate of the CFA Franc to the Euro is at 1,000 to 1, which means 1,000 CFA Francs can buy one Euro. If you're the central bank of the Ivory Coast, how do you ensure this exchange rate is maintained? The answer is kind of similar to the other monetary policy we've seen: you raise and lower interest rates. Higher interest rates in the Ivory Coast mean that their currency is a better investment so more people will buy it, which will increase its value. The ratio of Francs to Euros might now be 500 to 1, so Ivorians only need 500 Francs when they previously needed 1,000. The consequence of a stronger currency is that when citizens of the Ivory Coast look abroad, they'll be able to buy more with their money.

This matters for a couple of big reasons. Firstly, it is difficult – if not impossible – for a country to maintain a fixed exchange rate while also ensuring stable inflation, employment and growth. This is a simple matter of not being able to balance too many plates at once: unemployment could be high, but international market conditions mean that the interest rate has to increase to maintain the exchange rate. In this case, interest rates will have to rise even though that means unemployment has to go up even further. As a result, these countries have a lot less scope over what their own policies can be than richer countries. While they may try to manage their economies effectively, their hands are tied by the fact that their currency is not truly their own.

Secondly, the colonial legacy in West Africa means that these countries' relationships with France generally serve – you guessed it – France. It is possible for a system of fixed exchange rates to be managed fruitfully and fairly with enough international cooperation, but France has dominated this arrangement. They valued the currencies of West African countries far too highly – think 100 CFA Francs to 1 Euro. A high-value currency might sound like a good thing, but it meant that West African exports were way too expensive for international markets. Nobody wanted to buy their manufacturing goods because the CFA Franc was too expensive, while simultaneously buying abroad became cheaper for West Africans themselves. Naturally, this was a boon for France, since it was the first country these countries would import from instead due to historical linkages. Although West Africa had started to orient its economies away from France by the end of World War II, after the CFA Franc was established, imports and exports rebounded back towards their coloniser. Although colonialism ended over the next couple of decades, the CFA remains to this day.[35]

Even if their links to the USA are not quite as explicit as West Africa's links to France, Latin American countries rely heavily on the dollar. As so many of the continent's transactions have to use dollars, from businesses to financial institutions to governments, they also find themselves extremely dependent on a currency they cannot control. This has tied their hands, especially in terms of managing inflation, and there are many horror stories of hyperinflation from Latin America for just this reason. You can trace the decline of manufacturing in Brazil or Argentina back to this problem: as the global economy changed in the 1970s and 1980s, interest rates rose. Both the public and private sectors found themselves scrambling for dollars, which led to waves of bankruptcies and drops in GDP.[36]

MONETARY SOVEREIGNTY

It is not just Latin America that is affected by the US dollar. It is the worst-kept secret of the global economy that for a long time the dollar has been the de facto reserve currency of the entire world. Most countries are limited in how much currency they can issue and in how freely they can spend, since international markets will be spooked if they spend too much or spend on the 'wrong' kind of thing. But as the dollar is used by financial institutions across the world, rather than just in the USA, the globe has so much demand for it that the US Government can issue as many dollars and as much government debt as it wants with few consequences. This has been referred to as the 'exorbitant privilege' of the USA.[37]

Investor Palak N. Patel has detailed that history shows the top dog changes over time: 500 years ago it was the Dutch, then Britain, and now it is the USA. All three countries enjoyed extremely low interest rates and a large amount of control over the international monetary system in their respective heydays.[38] They were at the technological frontier and this often came with military dominance, too. In the case of the Netherlands and Britain, they tended to benefit from being the 'workshops of the world', importing cheap from colonies and selling expensive, high-tech (for the time) exports – a pattern France has managed to emulate with its former colonies in West Africa. The USA is unique here since it actually imports far more than it exports, meaning it is 'leaking' money abroad. The fact that this money is desired by the entire globe means that, unlike most other countries, the USA can get away with leaking money without fear of investor panic.

The idea of 'monetary sovereignty' refers to the hierarchy imposed on countries by their position in the global monetary system. At the top, you have the US dollar, and this is followed by other major currencies like the British Pound, the Swiss Franc, the Euro, the Japanese Yen, and the Chinese Renminbi.* After this you have the currencies of countries like India, South Africa, Russia, Iran, as well as many in Eastern Europe and Southeast Asia, who have a degree of autonomy but are constrained in important ways by those further up the hierarchy. Countries in West Africa and

---

* An additional complication is that although the Euro overall is itself considered a sound currency, countries within the Eurozone do not have monetary sovereignty over the currency themselves, which, as we saw in the introduction, has especially been a problem for poorer countries such as Greece and Italy.

Latin America are next as they are so directly dependent on the dominant currencies for historical reasons. Finally, economies such as Madagascar, Sudan or the Democratic Republic of Congo have limited capability to enforce their currencies even within their own territories, and many citizens may just use currencies further up the hierarchy – or revert to precious metals.

In 2020, when the Covid-19 pandemic shook the world, there was initial panic which threatened even the dollar, but markets stabilised thanks to aggressive intervention from the US Government and the Federal Reserve. It became clear that financial markets were at risk of destabilising even in richer countries and that central banks across the world needed dollars.[39] After 2008, the Fed had decided to extend free 'swap lines' to countries across Europe and the English-speaking world when necessary. In 2020, these were extended to South Korea, Mexico and Brazil and the whole process was massively streamlined and expanded. Many countries can now freely swap their own currencies for dollars: essentially, this gives them the de facto ability to 'print' dollars by creating their own currency and trading it in. We've spoken about central banks as the 'bank of banks'. Increasingly, it seems like the Federal Reserve is the 'central bank of central banks' across the globe, with the caveat that this privilege only applies to a select few.[40]

There have been numerous attempts to manage the international financial system throughout history. Before World War I, most Western countries were bound by a shared metallic standard which meant to facilitate trade. In practice, it was far too rigid and collapsed with the advent of the war. After World War II, the Bretton Woods system of fixed exchange rates was established to manage currencies in everyone's interest. This was not only meant to engender economic growth across the world, but to prevent another political catastrophe.

John Maynard Keynes wanted a global reserve currency which did not belong to any country, which he called the Bancor. The US prevailed, though, and the Bretton Woods system was centred around the dollar, which at the time was still linked to gold. Unfortunately, it also struggled with its numerous rigidities, plus an unhappy financial sector which sought ways around it, until it collapsed outright in 1973. Economic historian Adam Tooze has argued that we should not idealise any past system, but should look at them as part of an ongoing struggle to design a financial system which is properly regulated and managed in the interests of everyone in the globe, rather than those of Wall Street.[41] Ultimately, the first step is recognising the imbalances and absurdities in the system we already have.

THE ROLE OF TRUST

In the previous chapter, we learned about housing, which everyone recognises as one of the most impactful sectors of our economy. In this chapter, we have turned to an equally impactful topic: money. You might have noticed that this chapter has been a bit more involved than the others, but these debates are extremely important in the real world. It is pretty much impossible to have a good understanding of how contemporary economies work without knowing a bit about balance sheets and monetary policy. Because integrating money into economic analysis leads us to some very different conclusions to the ones we are typically fed.

As David Graeber reminded us, all money is essentially debt.[42] Most of the money created in a modern economy is done so as credit by private banks. It is therefore an automatic IOU, both from the bank to the depositor (the loan), but also from the depositor back to the bank (the deposit). When credit is granted, it is a way of giving bringing resources from the future into the present, so that somebody can buy or invest now and pay back at a later date. The entire financial system depends on the trust of participants to honour their future obligations to keep it going. Even the hard cash or reserves that underpin this whole process are essentially promises from central banks and governments to banks and citizens that they will honour their obligations.

When the monetary system breaks down, it is a sign that trust has broken down. This manifests in its worst form in hyperinflation, when people completely lose faith in a currency due to economic, social and political breakdown. It can also manifest more subtly: many people reasonably feel that private banks and corporations benefit more from existing monetary policy, not to mention direct bailouts. Citizens either rebel politically – by voting or protesting – or else economically, by looking for alternatives like gold or cryptocurrency. Wherever you stand on these alternatives, they are completely understandable when a system based on trust has repeatedly violated that trust. Many people feel that the existing monetary arrangements have made them poorer.

Money is the lifeblood of the market economy, so everybody who participates in the market economy needs to be able to rely on it. Our valuable IOUs that we use in increasing areas of our life need to retain their value. Yet since the pandemic, many people have experienced the exact opposite, as costs rise across the board. People need to have a better understanding of inflation and to participate in how to manage it, instead of leaving it to arms-length authorities. We will now turn from the abstract operations of money to the more practical problem of how the cost of living got so damn high.

CHAPTER 7

WHY DOES INFLATION HIT US SO HARD?

The surprising truth about how we deal with rising prices

In my home country of the UK, the humble Freddo chocolate bar has long stood stalwart against the tides of change. The small, frog-shaped bar was known for being priced at 10 pence and was effectively one of the only things you could buy with a 10p coin. Certainly, the most satisfying. It is not an exaggeration to say that the Freddo has become something of an institution in Britain. Armed with my 50p on 'sweety day' (I'm not sure if this was just a British thing), I could purchase five whole Freddos if I pleased.

Yet even the Freddo has proven unable to resist modern inflation. Launched in 1994, it wasn't until 2007 – around the onset of the global financial crisis – that Cadbury's finally gave in and raised the price to 15p. This naturally caused a lot of outrage, but there was more when just three years later, the price went up to the frankly unnerving choice of 17p. This upset people for reasons other than the increase itself: nobody carries 17p around, so the chocolate's significance as a trademark of simple and affordable pricing had come to an end. One year later, the price rose again to the rounded 20p, then 30p in

2017, before more outrage forced Cadbury's to lower it back to 25p just ahead of the coronavirus pandemic.

The Freddo's price has become something of a national obsession, with newspapers diligently documenting any and all price changes. In 2018, the *Daily Mail* gave us their 'Timeline' of the 'Rising Cost of a Freddo' which led the *Sun to* report that 'Freddo bar prices have surged 200 per cent since 2000'. One year later, polling website YouGov noted that Britons had 'lost track' of how much Freddos cost, with only 1 in 9 knowing the 25p retail price tag. In 2022, as the cost-of-living crisis really started to bite, the *Liverpool Echo* noted their reporter Eleanor Dye's horror when she found a Freddo for 49p at WHSmith. This was picked up by many others: the *Mirror* reported 'Freddo bar soars to nearly 50p as chocolate fans hit by cost-of-living crisis', while *LADBible* went with the click-bait title 'Newspaper Investigates Cost Of Freddo And Most Expensive One Is Baffling'.

If the Freddo is interesting, it isn't just because it confirms that British people are uncomfortably obsessed with slightly crap food. Instead, this humble chocolate bar demonstrates quite how much our experience of everyday price changes can differ from official measures of price inflation. Price inflation is defined as the general change in the price of goods and services in a given country over a given period of time. Between 1994 and 2019, the official statistics show that prices in the UK rose by 66 per cent, while even if we include Cadbury's lowering of the price from 30p to 25p, the corresponding inflation rate for the Freddo was 150 per cent. Before Covid-19, the bar's price had increased by more than twice as much as the official statistics would imply. UK-wide inflation then rose by 12 per cent over four years, while even if we take the lowest individual price from Eleanor Dye's investigation, Freddo prices rose by 20 per cent. If we take the high WHSmith price, the cost of a Freddo rose by almost 100 per cent, just over the pandemic.[1]

The British chef, author and campaigner Jack Monroe has documented that the Freddo is not alone. Many of the cheapest food staples have increased massively in price over the past few years. Between 2021 and 2022, the cheapest pasta at Monroe's local Asda supermarket went from 29p to 70p, a 141 per cent price increase which contrasted starkly with the apparent 5 per cent 'rise in the cost of living' reported by the media at the time. Baked beans went up 45 per cent; canned spaghetti went up 169 per cent; bread went up 29 per cent. A one-kilogram bag of the cheapest rice had been 45p; it was now £1 for only 500g, which was a 344 per cent price increase. Everywhere she looked, Monroe could see that cost-of-living increases for the poorest were orders of magnitude higher than the official statistics suggested.[2]

So where do these differences come from? While the price of Freddos and Asda staples has jumped massively, the price of many other things has changed far more slowly or even gone down. Clothing in the UK has dropped in price over the past few decades, owing largely to the fact that clothes production has moved to countries where wages are low, like China and Bangladesh. The prices of relatively new technologies such as flat-screen TVs, mobile phones and computers have dropped even more precipitously. I am old enough to remember a time when flat-screen TVs were a luxury worth thousands of pounds; now you can pick up a decent one for less than £200.

Another reason that our perceptions differ from official economy-wide inflation is that the statistics are not gathered from just one shop. It is entirely possible that Monroe's experience at Asda was particularly bad. According to retail analyst Steve Dresser, Asda's value range is on its way out: 'Asda have been cutting value tier products for a while . . . it's not indicative of the wider market.' This is of course of no solace to those who live closest to an Asda, but we need to make sure prices from a variety of shops are included to be representative of the country as a whole, including those who shop at different places.[3] A key challenge for inflation measurers is trying to account for the diverse range of shopping experiences across the nation.

The Office for National Statistics (ONS) measures inflation averages by looking at price changes across 600 or so goods and services. This 'basket' of goods is chosen to represent the spending of the 'typical' household. You will find everyday items like milk, meat and fruit in the food category; garments and footwear in the clothing category; as well as water, gas and rentals in the 'bills' category. The mysterious 'miscellaneous' category includes personal care (hairdressers, grooming) and personal effects (jewellery, watches). Naturally, public services are tricky to include in inflation because price indexes concern private expenditure only. Healthcare is largely measured by the cost of equipment and medicine, plus the fees charged by doctors, dentists and nurses. Education is often measured by fees charged by universities and private schools. The aim is to track how much people are spending out-of-pocket.[4]

As the basket changes every year, examining which products are in and which are out is actually a neat way of documenting economic and cultural change. Additions in 2022 included meat-free sausages, antibacterial surface wipes and electric and hybrid cars, while they binned men's suits, coal and camcorders.[5] Using ONS data, it seems that between 1990 and 2019, the biggest fall in price was audio-visual equipment, which is almost twenty times less expensive than it used to be despite modern equipment being far superior in quality. The largest increase in inflation was for higher education, whose price has tripled – as people of my generation know all too well.

ZOOMING IN ON INFLATION

The way I imagine all of this is analogous to playing around on Google Earth (does anyone still do that? Let's assume they do). Looking at an individual Freddo has us zoomed in closely on one area of the map, as if we were looking at a single river. Anyone who is close to that river needs to know that it's there, what it looks like, how wide and rapid it is, and so on. At the same time, we're all aware that there is much more going on in the landscape. We can't conclude that the whole world is a river from looking at this one part of it, any more than we can measure inflation purely from the price of Freddos. We need to zoom out a little and see the surrounding area to get a better idea of the whole.

With an enlarged vista we might catch grass, trees, a bench and some wildlife in our section of the map. Now we are at Jack Monroe's visit to her local Asda to see the price of various staples, learning a bit more about the pasta, beans and bread bought by your average low-income shopper. Still, we may only be seeing a partial picture. On Google Earth, it's possible that the area we're looking at is quite elevated: say, at the top of a hill. But when we zoom out even further, we can see the whole locale. This has our river running down our hill as well as lower-lying lands featuring marshes, long grass and lakes; plus roads and railways snaking through the landscape; and humans residing in towns and villages. This is the equivalent of observing prices for a wide variety of products: pasta and rice, staples and luxuries, products from Asda and products from Tesco.

As we zoom out even further, we can see the whole country. Now we can see that it features both countryside and built-up areas. It has vast tracts of farmland as well as skyscrapers. There are roving coastlines, which contrast with the towering mountains further inland. This is getting closer to the full basket gathered by the ONS, which should ideally measure prices for a wide variety of products – just as our vista now captures a wide variety of features of the landscape. We have hopefully acquired the knowledge we need to understand what is happening to inflation across the whole economy.

But now we have a new problem. The breadth of our view may cause it to obscure some of the details and flatten interesting features of the landscape. Looking at the whole country on Google Earth is interesting to cartographers but actually fairly useless to travellers in practice. Just as working families routinely have to navigate their local Asda, a group of hikers will have to walk up our original hill. Telling them not to worry about the hill because, on average, the local landscape is nowhere near as high as the hill is likely to result in some hiking-stick-shaped marks on your legs.

THE MANY-FACED INFLATION

The facts raised by Monroe and by the Freddo bar give us pause to reflect on how we think about inflation and the cost of living in economics. The key lesson is that inflation is not simply one thing: the headline number hides so many important distinctions that we may even want to reconsider using it altogether. As the British economist Tim Harford put it at the time, 'What colour is a rainbow? On average, white. And what is the current level of UK inflation? On average, 5.4 per cent. Both answers are true. Both are missing something important.'[6]

Our measures have failed to grapple with the realities of inflation and left us unprepared to deal with the lingering cost-of-living crisis. And as with so many cases we've seen, it seems the poor are hit hardest by economic volatility. When the newspapers report that inflation is 5 per cent, they are taking the average from the ONS basket of 600 goods and services consumed across the country. But averages can be misleading if they hide big differences: between different goods and services;

between North and South; between Asda and Tesco; or between rich and poor.

To take an extreme case of the latter, imagine that the population is split into richer people and poorer people. The rich only eat cake, while the poor only eat bread, and the same total amount is spent on both. The price of cake has stayed the same for 10 years while the price of bread has risen by 10 per cent over that same period. In this case, official inflation measures would report inflation at 5 per cent – the average of 0 and 10 – even though this number applied to absolutely no-one. The rich would have experienced 0 per cent inflation while the poor would have experienced 10 per cent, so neither group would be accurately represented by the official statistic of 5 per cent – though this situation is obviously more harmful for the poor.

The reality of inflation measurement is not quite this stark, since there is so much overlap in the prices that different groups of people face. Much of the population will buy both cakes and bread, among other common goods like cars, housing and electricity. Some groups may buy small amounts of one brand, others large amounts of another, but the overlap is enough that the inflation rate is a decent benchmark for a vast demographic. Yet this benchmark can only be our starting point if we want to understand how inflation really works and what to do about it. To get a better picture of things, we must do the equivalent of zooming in on Google Earth and taking a good look at the different groups affected by inflation.

There is an increasing recognition among economists that our measures of inflation have neglected the poorest. For a long time, statisticians in the UK and across the world calculated inflation based on a seemingly sensible idea: every pound, dollar, yen, or real counted for the same as every other. This 'one dollar, one vote' principle meant that the ONS basket of goods accurately reflected how the UK, taken as a whole, was spending its collective income. To return to the example, if we as a country were spending £100 on bread and £100 on cake, then the basket would be half bread and half cake. If we instead collectively decided we loved cake and spent £150 on it instead of £100, then the basket would change accordingly. The idea is that this gives us inflation measures that represent how the country is choosing to spend its money.

This all seems eminently reasonable – until you start to think about *who* is buying the bread and *who* is buying the cake. Imagine that there are 100 poor people who each spend £1 on bread to give our £100 total. Meanwhile, there are 10 rich people who each spend £10 on cake to give the other £100 total. It is clear that the 10 rich people count for the same as the 100 poor people in our inflation basket, which seems a little unfair. Owing purely to their higher income, each rich person has a bigger say in the inflation statistics. This type of inflation measurement has been called 'plutocratic' by the ONS because it is dominated by richer households. Alternative measures, which weight every household equally, are accordingly known as 'democratic' measures.

When the ONS tried to account for poorer households with these democratic measures, they found inflation was slightly higher than the official statistics. The difference was only 0.1 per cent a year, which may seem small, but as we know from the case of Freddos, a small change in the average can mean big differences for individual items.[7] Food and housing, two notable expenditures for poorer households, are generally more than just 0.1 per cent higher for those households. You can think of these as the 'bread' in our previous example, and the democratic approach to inflation gives them more weight in its calculations. This is one example of how the poor may be facing higher inflation than the official measures suggest, but it's far from the only one.

As Harford points out, the official data for inflation leave a lot to be desired. In many cases they do not even measure the type of goods bought by the poorest – the equivalent of leaving bread out of our example altogether.[8] The ONS tends to target the most popular products, but it simply has not done the leg-work to know how representative this is of, for example, Jack Monroe's low-income staples. I wish I could say the UK was alone in this regard; sadly, inflation statistics across the world share similar features. Information gathering is costly and diffi-cult: when it comes down to it, price collection is often little more than someone taking a visit to their local supermarket. That person has to deal with the fact that certain items may have sold out on the day, which is actually why 'lamb shoul-ders on the bone' were taken out of the basket in the UK in 2021 – they simply weren't on sale when the statistician went to visit![9]

An approach that is growing in popularity is to eschew the dated practice of sending an ONS statistician on a trip to Asda to gather prices (presumably after drawing the short straw in the office). Modern studies try to better track how different households spend their money, for instance by asking them to keep diaries. This matters more than you might think because it means that the ONS will no longer have huge black holes in its calculations, especially for the poor. Unfortunately, although the ONS are working on this kind of thing they are not quite there yet, so we will have to look across the Atlantic Ocean to see what this does to inflation measures.[10]

The more we consider the fact that the rich and the poor buy different products, the higher inflation seems for the latter (and the lower it seems for the former). Evidence using data which is more reflective of the typical spending of poor households shows that inflation is usually higher for poorer households than for richer households, with a difference of 0.4 per cent between the haves and the have-nots.[11] Again, these may seem like negligible differences, but they start to add up, especially when you compound them over decades. We saw that with democratic weighting, inflation was 0.1 per cent higher, so let's (admittedly crudely) add this to our 0.4 per cent. Together, this means 0.5 per cent extra inflation for poorer households, which culminates in prices that are 16 per cent higher after three decades.

Modern inflation research in the USA uses data directly from the scanners of supermarkets, which gives us access to a much wider variety of goods and continuous updating as the products are scanned. The phrase 'scanner data' may not make the hairs on the back of your neck stand up, but the results from using it are so striking that they may well do. Studies generally show that using this data only increases the measured gap between inflation for the rich and the poor. In the USA, a 2017 study which used scanner data showed inflation was 8 to 9 per cent higher over a nine-year period for the poor than for the rich, or around 1 per cent higher every year.[12]

We have already seen in Chapter 4 how the rich and the poor often inhabit different universes. The world of prices is a case in point. The rich and poor may both be residents in the same city, but because they live in different areas, shop at different stores and buy different things, their experiences of inflation are markedly different. In addition, shops in wealthier places tend to cater

to the wealthy, which means that value products fall by the wayside and the poor who inhabit those areas must cough up for
expensive products that wouldn't be their first choice if value
ones were available. This kind of economic segregation – invisible to the naked eye – is perhaps one reason people have become
so disbelieving of official inflation measures.[13]

All of this is to say that the puzzle raised by Jack Monroe at
the start of the chapter reflects genuine problems with how
economists measure inflation. We had gathered data on what
we considered 'usual' goods and services without considering
whether it reflected the spending of poorer families. We had
relied too much on averages, neglecting the important inequalities in how inflation is experienced by the rich and the poor,
and differences between different areas of the economy. All of
this has conspired to make us underestimate the price increases
faced by the worst off: in some cases, inflation is notably higher
for poorer people than in official measures. They are gradually
losing ground to rich people as inflation erodes their incomes
slightly every year. [14]

On the other hand, the simple view-from-Freddo raises clear
problems about myopically focusing on too small an area of the
economy without considering others, whether those others take
the form of different chocolate bars or completely different sectors
of the economy. Monroe's experience of inflation in low-priced
goods at Asda is important for many actual families, just as
the landscape of a small area of Google Earth is important for
the hikers at that location. But as with that small feature of the
landscape, it neglects many other people and will end up giving
a biased picture if we pay it too much heed. The hope is that the
future of inflation management will consist of a continual conversation between top-down experts and bottom-up observers.

THE CUSTARD THEORY OF INFLATION

The world is full of interesting little complexities. Custard, for example, is what's called a non-Newtonian liquid, which means that it acts like a normal liquid with one important caveat: if it is subjected to enough pressure, it effectively transforms into a solid. If you have some custard at home, you can experiment with this by making custard then rolling it into balls – *after* letting it cool down, I should add, so I don't get sued – and seeing how it transforms in your hands. You will see that the custard's state changes depending on the world around it – in this case, whether or not it is being squished together by a pair of hands.

As we've seen, the inflation statistic you see in the news hides a whole world of prices, each moving stubbornly in whichever direction they so choose. But as with custard, there is an important caveat. When inflation is high, it stops being lots of different things and starts being just one thing. In many rich countries during the 1970s and 1980s, inflation was well into the double digits, and it began to take on a life of its own. At that stage, we really were talking about a singular 'inflation' driven by a simultaneous rise in the vast majority of prices and wages, and propelled by the expectations of workers, consumers and governments that these rises would continue.[15] Just like the custard changing its state in response to pressure, inflation changes in response to widespread pressure in the economy.

It was during the 1970s and 1980s that our current approach to taming inflation was born. We discussed inflation targeting briefly in the last chapter, but now I want to go over it with a fine-tooth comb. As you may remember, interest rates are the main lever the central bank uses to try to control inflation.

When prices were spiralling upwards in the 1980s, central banks decided that they needed to increase rates to bring them down. The idea was that higher interest rates meant that saving your money became a more attractive prospect, while borrowing more money became less attractive. The new reality of high interest rates would generally dampen the spending of families and businesses while making them save more, so it would put the brakes on the economy. In the 1980s, central banks in the USA and UK increased interest rates to almost 20 per cent in some cases, to stop the spiral and bring inflation down.

Conversely, once inflation is no longer a problem – when it is down to a few per cent a year – central banks will be comfortable reducing rates. This will stimulate spending in the economy, which can be good for economic growth and reduce unemployment; the mirror image of what happens when rates go up. Central banks ideally want to keep rates low enough that the economy is functioning well, which was not the case in the 1980s but was so during the 2000s, when inflation averaged roughly its 2 per cent target in most rich countries. Interest rate management has thus been the policy for as long as I've been alive, and I have fond memories of being read bedtime stories about the heroic Bank of England coming to the rescue of the British economy as a child.*

WHO PAYS FOR INFLATION?

Inflation targeting seemed successful for most of its lifetime, with inflation usually remaining around 2 per cent in most rich

---

* To be clear, this didn't happen.

countries. There were temporary fluctuations – after the 2007–9 financial crisis, inflation peaked at around 5 per cent in the UK (oh, innocent days) – but it always came back down again. Despite former Bank of England Governor Mervyn King's warning that inflation targeting would turn central banks into 'inflation nutters' – sacrificing growth, unemployment and baby goats to bring inflation down – they largely tolerated these short-term fluctuations. Economists everywhere were happy with our perceived ability to keep a lid on inflation while ensuring relatively high levels of growth and employment.[16] Yet post-pandemic, inflation started to seem like more of a problem than central banks could handle, which raised important questions about their approach.

If our measures of inflation neglect working people, there's a case that our policies for dealing with inflation actively target them. The big secret about interest rates is that they operate mostly through some unsavoury channels. As many readers will be acutely aware, higher interest rates mean higher mortgage costs. Paying more on mortgages reduces the disposable income of households, which reduces consumer spending, which contracts economic activity. In English, this means taking money away from homeowners (and renters, to whom the cost is passed on) so they can't buy things, which has knock-on effects on business and the rest of the economy. Ultimately, the aim of the central bank is to increase unemployment so that workers are forced to accept lower wages, which should 'hopefully' filter through to lower prices.

Even more unsavoury is that the unemployment channel may only have worked because over the past few decades, workers have been weak, especially in Anglo-American countries. Union membership has declined precipitously in these countries;

technology has changed to make work more precarious; and labour rights have been eroded. Many Western countries have outsourced work to countries who have had virtually non-existent labour rights, pitting rich country workers in competition with far lower-paid workers across the globe. In the two to three decades following World War II, unemployment was frequently as low as 2 per cent; from the 1980s, it was more likely to be 6 to 7 per cent. A situation of low unemployment is described as a 'tight labour market' by central bankers. This language obscures the reality that they do not like it when employment is easy to find because it gives workers more bargaining power.[17]

In case this sounds conspiratorial, know that none of the above is lost on the people making the decisions. During the 1980s, then-chair of the Federal Reserve Paul Volcker was obsessed with union meeting notes and paid at least as much attention to organised labour as to financial markets. When the air traffic controllers in the USA went on strike, President Ronald Reagan famously fired *all of them* by executive decree. Volcker described this as 'the single most important action of the administration in helping the anti-inflation fight'. A decade later, the new chair Alan Greenspan praised the 'subdued wages' that resulted from a 'heightened sense of job insecurity', which he thought was responsible for the economic boom in the 1990s. Jerome Powell, the current head of the Federal Reserve, justified the 2022–23 interest rate increases by saying 'there is a very, very tight labor market, tight to an unhealthy level. Our tools work as you describe . . . if you were moving down the number of job openings, you would have less upward pressure on wages, less of a labor shortage.'[18]

I wouldn't want you to go away thinking interest rates are useless as a way of controlling inflation – they definitively have an impact. The trouble is that they tend to solve the disease of inflation by killing the patient. Interest rates can be made to 'work' because if they are high enough, they engineer a reduction in growth and bring inflation down. They can increase borrowing costs, reducing demand and therefore increasing unemployment. They can prick financial bubbles and cause a cascade of bankruptcies. This is why extensive evidence shows interest rates are better at bringing employment and growth down than at pushing it up. They can hurt the economy, but they're less effective at helping it.[19]

If interest rate increases in rich countries harm the poor within those countries, their impact on the poorest countries can be catastrophic. As Latin American countries have to borrow dollars – being unable to print them themselves – higher interest rates mean higher borrowing costs for governments. Increases in interest rates like those in the 1980s do not just cause hardship; they can trigger outright crisis, which is exactly what happened at the time. Investors fled, credit contracted and growth nosedived. Contemporary interest rate rises could once more lead to serious problems in countries in Latin America, which is especially galling given their relative poverty and the fact that they have no democratic input into these decisions whatsoever.[20]

A BALANCING ACT

There is certainly a delicate balancing act to be done when managing inflation; it should not be considered an easy job. Out-of-control wage demands combined with militant unions can cause what's called a wage-price spiral, as occurred in the 1970s. Wages go up, then prices go up to compensate, then wages go up again, and ultimately everybody loses. You as a worker cannot gain from an increase in your wages when prices just rise in a tit-for-tat, since the extra money you secured can now buy less than it could before. Similarly, businesses cannot increase or uphold their profits in a situation where they are paying more and more in wages. A wage-price spiral is ultimately a fruit-less endeavour for all involved, while spiralling inflation itself makes things more unstable across the economy as a whole.

When inflation does get out of control, it becomes tempting for people to moralise and play the blame game. For left wing-ers, the issue will generally be the greedy businesses who are raising their prices, an issue that has become known as sellers' inflation or even 'greedflation' (because apparently, there aren't enough horrible portmanteaus floating around). For right wing-ers, the issue is workers who refuse to accept reality and demand wages above their station. For decades, central banks have aligned more closely with the latter group despite their purported independence, and the Bank of England's Chief Economist Huw Pill caused quite a stir when he claimed in 2023 that Brit-ish workers needed to 'accept' that they were poorer and to stop seeking pay increases.[21] As you may have realised, it is the pri-mary message of this book that we do not need to accept that.

A policy that bluntly limits the power of workers to demand pay rises is not the right tool for dealing with such a complex process. For a start, spiralling inflation takes more than work-ers demanding higher wages. The observant among you will have noticed that the very term 'wage-price spiral' mentions prices, too. For inflation to take off, businesses have to play their part. They increase prices following a wage increase to maintain profitability, which is why some have taken to calling it a 'profit-price spiral' instead.[22] Such a term is no more or less valid than wage-price spiral, though I stress that such subtle changes in language are not of too much concern to me; what matters are the lessons we draw from this debate.

To put it bluntly, central bankers are too obsessed with wages, specifically with when they go up, which is often assumed prima facie to be a bad thing. This is a political choice that we do not talk about nearly enough. Instead of playing the blame game like Huw Pill, we can think of inflation as a problem of coordination to be solved. It is completely natural for workers and especially for unions to demand what is best for their members – that is, after all, their job. It is also understandable that businesses will raise their price in the face of inflation – any business that failed to do so would be punished by its shareholders, or even go bust. Sustained inflation arises because of a battle between workers and businesses over the spoils of economic output, and when that fight goes badly is when inflation becomes impossible to control. Imagine a bunch of cats fighting in a bag and you have approximately the right image of what an uncoordinated inflation policy looks like.

The only way to stop this tit-for-tat is to put in place ways for large groups of workers and businesses to coordinate with each other better. And this type of negotiation policy is not as unrealistic as it might appear at first glance. In Germany, for instance, unions have a seat in labour relations at the national level and historically they have been quite conservative in their wage demands to maintain price stability and export competitiveness, since Germany relies so much on its renowned high-quality industries like its famous BMW and VW cars. Germany has been able to manage inflation and wages through such coordinated mechanisms for decades. Scandinavian countries have similar mechanisms, where unions are able to negotiate at the regional or even national level to coordinate wage demands with businesses.[23] In fact, most of continental Europe has some version of this setup.

The economist Olivier Blanchard has acknowledged that the best solution to inflation would be to get all major players around the table to negotiate over the appropriate deal. If workers could accept a certain amount of wage increases, while businesses agreed to a certain amount of price increases, while central banks and governments agreed to a set of policies surrounding the relevant interest rates, taxes and spending, then the conflict would cease. Any potential spirals would be averted and although most parties would presumably walk away only partially happy, none of them would be completely thrown under the bus.[24]

INFLATION WARS

For most of us, a readily available memory of high inflation is the energy price crisis following the Russian invasion of the Ukraine. There is no doubt that the energy crisis was a situation of genuine scarcity: there was more oil and gas to go around before the war. We saw what were previously unimaginably large price increases, with energy prices around doubling for the average household in the UK.[25] Most people had to reduce their energy use in the short term, with money-saving tips circulated around the country. Reduce your thermostat by 1 degree C, have colder showers, fill the kettle up only as much as you need it, invest in an electric blanket – these are all examples of the kind of advice that money-saving experts like Martin Lewis have given in the UK over the past couple of years.[26]

This is all sound advice for individual families, but taking a bird's-eye view we can ask the question of who should have to cut down and how. Firstly, how do we make sure the cuts don't disproportionately impact those who are most vulnerable? Secondly, how do we make sure that this whole thing doesn't result in an inflationary spiral?

The first question was answered adequately, even if imperfectly, by governments the world over. Through their subsidies to families, which gave more money to low-income people, they have alleviated the immediate financial burden of higher energy prices. This ensured that although everyone was paying more, assistance went to people who were least able to bear the burden. The assistance actually helps to address the second question, too, since households who got the subsidies were less likely to demand higher wages to make up the difference. Wage pressure was relatively subdued after the war broke out, and this may have been one reason why.[27]

Turning to the profits side of the equation, in the UK we are all too familiar with people fairly complaining about the high energy prices charged to them by companies like British Gas. However, these retail energy companies actually have relatively small profit margins, usually of around 5 per cent. The profit margins of the grid companies that distribute the gas around the country, on the other hand, are over 40 per cent and that industry is one of the most concentrated in the UK.[28] When energy prices rise and these companies pass the rise on to the retail companies and to consumers, it is fair to ask whether they could instead have absorbed some of the cost through lowering their substantial profits. As they are unlikely to do so voluntarily, this is a good example of where the state would have to step in.

It is not reasonable to place all of the burden on these

companies, though – or any one player in the system – not least because even if profits were reduced to 0 per cent, the sheer magnitude of the shock from Russia's invasion would still mean higher energy prices. This is where Blanchard's idea of having all major players negotiate comes in. Every one of them would have to make sacrifices, but it is key to make sure that the burden is shared fairly so that richer households and more profitable businesses do more. Just as importantly, if every single player can reach an agreement then this creates exactly the kind of stability needed to tame inflation, and avoids creating the dreaded tit-for-tat wage-price spiral.

These European-style bargaining policies are great for managing inflation on an ongoing basis, but they are still not quite enough. The cost-of-living crisis was driven by big price increases in certain areas like energy, microchips and food, not by a generalised rise in prices and wages across the board. In other words, we had liquid custard but were acting like it was solid.[29] A policy which deals with both kinds of custard – sorry, inflation – means more than just managing a wage-profit-price spiral. A comprehensive inflation management policy, which takes into account everything we've discussed so far, means clever, forward-looking policies. To illustrate what the exact opposite of those might look like, I present to you the 2010s UK Government.

AUSTERITY AND INFLATION

In 2010, David Cameron assumed office as head of a Conservative-led Coalition in the UK. At the age of nineteen I had voted for the junior partner, the Liberal Democrats, which resulted in a swift end to my enthusiasm for British politics when they joined the Coalition. As the Conservatives had promised, they immediately began implementing harsh austerity measures, cutting public services across the board from education to health to transport and especially local services. Owing partly to my A-level in economics but more so to my ability to engage in basic reasoning, I was sceptical that austerity would achieve its aims. It was promised to bring down the national debt, streamline public services and boost the economy. It did none of these things.[30]

As I write this in 2023, I have just returned from attending a strike by over 100,000 education sector workers, including schoolteachers and academics. Doctors and nurses, rail unions and assorted civil servants also participated in this strike, as well as other strikes before and since. Many of the striking professions have endured real-terms pay cuts since 2010, which have become impossible to bear given the cost-of-living crisis.[31] This has made inflation difficult for these groups, which has resulted in the political tumult that we see now. These groups were not experiencing 'inflation' as a generalised phenomenon; they had simply not been paid enough and were losing the battle over the spoils of economic output.

The reason I bring up austerity in the UK is because it's a perfect example of how managing inflation requires forward thinking and a multifaceted approach. Generalised pay cuts aside, one of Cameron's most revealing direct interventions – which were few and far between, given the amount of time he seemed to spend watching TV during his premiership[32] – was in 2013. He ordered the civil service to 'get rid of all the green crap', which meant cutting programmes that aimed to insulate homes, subsidise solar panels and build wind farms. The idea was that energy bills, which were thought of as high even back then, would be reduced by getting rid of this superfluous spending and opting for cheaper and better-established fossil fuels.

In January 2022, the thinktank Carbon Brief estimated that this underinvestment in green energy now cost UK households £50 a year in higher energy bills, which amounts to £2.5 billion in total.[33] Houses were less well designed and had access to a lower variety of sources of energy, which had led to higher costs. Far from reducing fuel costs, Cameron's intervention had increased them – but things only got worse from there. Shortly after the Carbon Brief report was released, Russia invaded the Ukraine. Carbon Brief subsequently tripled their estimate of the annual cost of cutting the 'green crap' a decade earlier: households were now spending £150 more on gas and electric than they would have been otherwise, costing the country £7.5 billion in total.[34] Had investment instead been accelerated so the majority of our power came from renewables, who's to say where inflation would have been at the time of the strikes?

You can contrast the UK's haphazard approach with that of Spain. By 2023, Spanish inflation has settled down to recognisable levels: between 2 and 4 per cent, much lower than other European countries at the time. Like most governments, the Spanish authorities subsidised electricity and gas use, but they went further. They put a cap on gas prices, known as the Iberian Exception, so that no Spanish household would have to pay more than a certain amount. They introduced a raft of additional measures including raising the minimum wage, controls on rent increases and free public transport. These measures stopped both families and businesses from facing serious hardship that would be economically counterproductive in the long term as it would increase bankruptcies, reduce employment and increase poverty. For Spain, reducing overall inflation and helping individuals with the cost of living went hand in hand.[35]

In mid-2023, my godfather asked me with puzzlement why, at a time when households were struggling, the accepted solution was to increase interest rates and make things harder for people. It is a marker of how absurd things have become that our number one tool for addressing a cost-of-living crisis is to push housing costs upwards, even though this is the number one cost faced by most people and businesses. Echoing my godfather, a group of economists argued in 2024 that contemporary measures of inflation in the USA neglect these mortgage costs, and that inflation is much higher if you include them.[36]

INFLATION VS COST OF LIVING

The relationship between overall inflation and the cost of living is not as straightforward as it might seem. If inflation is high but wages rise with it, this does not lead to a cost-of-living crisis because people can afford the higher prices. The problem is that we have confused 1970s- and 1980s-style inflation, which was one generalised rise in prices and wages, with the messy web of idiosyncratic price changes that created a crisis in the cost of living from 2022 and beyond. In fact, they were two distinct crises which required two distinct sets of tools. Identifying which areas of the economy are the most important for inflation, which respond most to interest rates, and how else to manage those that don't, is an open challenge and requires a larger set of tools.

Since interest rates only operate through specific channels, they will have an outsized effect on the areas of the economy most connected to those channels. The clearest example is construction, which is far more responsive to mortgage rates since so much residential construction is financed through them. Housing is what's known as a 'pro-cyclical' sector, which means that as the economy goes up, housing goes up; and as the economy goes down, housing goes down with it. Procyclical sectors are generally more responsive to interest rates – other examples are eating out or going to sports games, activities people are more likely to engage in when times are good.[37] Sure enough, house prices in the USA plateaued as interest rates rose in early 2023.[38] The consumer group *Which?* reported that the UK saw an immediate spike in non-payments of rent, mortgages and other bills over the same period.[39]

The natural question is whether the sectors most affected by interest rates are those that are the most important for managing inflation. In case you hadn't spotted the theme of this chapter, the answer is 'not really'. German economist Isabella Weber and her co-authors investigated which sectors were 'systemically significant' for inflation in the US economy.[40] They defined systemically significant according to what they call direct and indirect impacts. Direct impacts are straightforward: how much does this particular price count towards inflation? Housing contributes directly to inflation because it is such a large outlay for so many people, so it is counted for a lot (14 per cent of the total) in inflation calculations. There is nothing mysterious here: saying housing matters for inflation is like saying flour matters for a cake. If you put a lot of X into Y, then what happens to X is going to matter for Y.

The second part of Weber and her co-authors' analysis is more tricky. They investigate what they call 'forward linkages' in the economy: the way that the inflation of a given commodity will affect others downstream. When the price of wool changes, the price of my grandma's knitted hats is going to rise because her costs have gone up (though Judith may just be exploiting her monopoly power). In contrast to the housing example in the last paragraph, oil and gas extraction does not feature in consumer's prices directly.* The entire effect of this extraction on inflation is through its effects on other industries, which includes those that use fossil fuels. This is essentially every industry, given the necessity of fossil fuels for energy and for travel, so when the costs of fossil fuel extraction go up, the costs of these industries will, too.

These so-called indirect effects show how interlinked inflation is across the economy and how much one sector can matter for all the others. In fact, the indirect effect of oil and gas extraction on inflation was large enough to earn it second place among the most 'systemically important' commodities. Despite having almost no forward linkages, housing managed to get seventh place out of seventy-one commodities in total. In first place was the category 'petrol and coal', which combined large direct and indirect effects, being a huge outlay for many households while also being used in many industries. Other high-ranking sectors included farms, utilities and 'food, beverage and tobacco products'. Weber and co. split the top nine systemically important sectors into three categories: energy, basic necessities (like Freddos) and basic production inputs. If you think about these industries, then this makes perfect sense. Everything uses energy, everyone needs necessities, and every industry relies on basic inputs such as metals and other raw materials.

---

* *Extraction* of fossil fuels, as in drilling for oil, is a separate category to things like petrol sales.

The Weber study was completed in 2022, but the authors undertook the exercise using data only up until 2019. This led to the striking finding that if the study had been done before the coronavirus pandemic, it would have correctly identified the most significant sectors before the crisis started. This could have led to policy which shored up these sectors, ultimately reducing shortages and inflation. By cutting our capacity to produce energy, David Cameron's cuts did exactly the opposite of what was needed. In the future, we need more investment into systemically important areas to ensure that their costs fall. Long-term funding into green energy, transportation and housing will help to alleviate these costs, which will have a knock-on effect on other upstream goods and services.

SPENDING OUR WAY OUT

Economists Josh Mason and Arjun Jayadev have argued that we need much more proactive thinking around solving inflation issues, which are really two sides of the same coin. Inflation is often thought of as one thing when it is actually many things, but we can go further than this.[41] Inflation is a *symptom* of a problem, when there is a mismatch between what people want and our economy's ability to fulfil that want. Our current approach is austere: when we want too much, we have to raise interest rates so that we demand less. But another approach is to invest in the areas where there is not enough capacity, both in terms of building capacity and in terms of better coordination across the economy. In the USA, the approach was closer to that of Spain's – albeit more focused on investment and innovation – and they also experienced a rapid fall in inflation, alongside a booming economy.[42]

It is tempting to dismiss this kind of thing as just throwing money at the problem, but over the long term we are looking at a more broadscale shift in how we monitor and manage inflation: organisations which are responsible for systemically important goods and services, and which are given the power to intervene to stabilise their prices. This is just what central banks do now with the money system, but it could be expanded to other key commodities. Examples of these policies already exist as governments do hold stocks of oil, food and more, but these approaches are currently ad hoc. Were they institutionalised, we could create and monitor capacity in the system more closely, which would help us when our system is shaken by something like the pandemic. International coordination would bring in long-neglected countries such as those in Latin America and West Africa.

At the time this book is going to press, inflation has fallen across the world. But even as the cost-of-living crisis recedes from memory, we should remember how ill-equipped we were and how much damage was done. After all, inflation falling doesn't mean prices are going back down; it means they've stopped going up so fast. Many families across the world will continue to feel the pinch because of the impact the massive rise in the cost of living had from 2022 to 2024. And as the global economy becomes more volatile over the next few years owing to climate change, war, or even another pandemic, we will be vulnerable to even worse if we fail to act.

The kind of approach outlined in this chapter would have helped to create the capacity in the system to handle the pandemic and lockdowns, which exposed so many fragilities in our economies. As Mason and Jayadev highlight, inflation was just a symptom of a bigger problem. For a long time, we had pursued narrow ideas of efficiency and free trade while neglecting the resilience of the system. Many global supply chains are stretched or overly dependent on isolated locations, which means they can easily fail in the face of health, political, environmental and financial crises. It is with these fragilities in mind that we turn to the next and final chapter.

CHAPTER 8

WHY DID THE GLOBAL ECONOMY BREAK?

Our vast, marvellous, efficient, fragile, exploitative economic factory

In *The Simpsons*, the students at Springfield Elementary School are taking their standardised national tests. Upon completion, two armed guards enter the room stating that they are 'here for the tests'. They fly the batch of tests across the country to Iowa and from the airport the tests are thrown haphazardly into the back of a delivery van, despite the sign on the bag that states 'handle with care'. The tests are then taken to the national test centre and sorted onto a conveyor belt where they are processed through a big machine. When Bart's test scores go through the machine, it breaks down and the whole thing shuts off. The scene then pans to an old man sitting on a rocking chair next to the machine, who pulls a face and hits it with his broom, exclaiming 'C'mon, Emma!' The machine starts running again and the old man sits back in his rocking chair, looking contented.

This sketch accurately reflects how we organise our global supply chains today. These bring together technologies, materials and workers from across the globe to produce millions of goods and services that we use every day. They seem to work quite well on the surface and in 'normal' times. But on closer inspection, they display worrying fragilities and design flaws which threaten to upend the whole system. Much like the children's test scores, the average product will go through some intensely sophisticated and formal processes to get to one place, only to rely on a metaphorical old man hitting a machine with a broom to get to another.

It is remarkable how well many of these arrangements have worked for so long, but this has hidden two major problems which have come to the fore since the pandemic. Firstly, this kind of haphazard system falls apart easily when tested. Secondly, it has taken for granted those who work so hard to keep the whole thing running. Over the past few decades, we have stretched our production across the globe, with supply chains moving key goods – from food to clothes to electronics – across national boundaries and multiple oceans before they reach their destination. Following numerous shocks we have seen that this system is astonishingly fragile, exploitative and unreliable.

When Covid-19 hit, the world went into lockdown and businesses around the world shuttered their windows and trade seized up. This needn't have been anything but a temporary slowdown that lasted as long as the lockdown measures themselves, but the economic machine proved difficult to restart. Countries such as China, on which we have relied so much, tended to have stricter lockdowns, so production of key goods, most famously microchips, was shut down for a long time. As the world came out of lockdown unevenly, the different parts of the global economy found themselves out of sync. When everyone is performing a tightly choreographed economic dance, the misstep of just one person can ruin it for all of us. We need a better understanding of how the global economy works if we are to prevent these upheavals from happening again.

REAL VERSUS IMAGINARY ECONOMIES

> For want of a nail the shoe was lost.
> For want of a shoe the horse was lost.
> For want of a horse the rider was lost.
> For want of a rider the message was lost.
> For want of a message the battle was lost.
> For want of a battle the kingdom was lost.
> And all for the want of a horseshoe nail.
>
> Ancient Proverb[1]

In a famous lecture, the free-market economist Milton Friedman contemplates the journey of the pencil he is holding. 'There's not a single person in the world who knows how to make this pencil,' he exclaims. 'Literally thousands of people cooperated to make this pencil, people who don't speak the same language, who practice different religions, who might hate one another if they ever met.' He notes that the pencil and its raw materials were produced in places as varied as the USA, Latin America, British Malaya (now split into Malaysia and Singapore) and likely many other countries. As Friedman states, it is a marvel of modern capitalism that this was all done without any 'commissar sending out orders from some central office'.[2]

Friedman was a great orator, and his fascination with something as simple as a pencil shines through in his lecture. But I've always found he raises more questions than he answers. According to him, the wood is 'for all I know' from the State of Washington, while the graphite 'probably' from mines in South America. He concludes that he hasn't the 'slightest idea' where a number of other components of the pencil came from, including the paint for the famous black and yellow stripes. Now, it's true that this lack of understanding is part of Friedman's point. Capitalism and global markets are so complex that we don't fully grasp their inner workings, even though we buy products with supply chains at least as complex as the pencil every single day. We could charitably conclude that Friedman's approach is to play the fool as a rhetorical device to enamour his audience.

Nevertheless, it has always seemed curious to me that such a famous lecture about the economics of pencils, given by one of the most famous economists who has ever existed, does not communicate more information about how the pencil was made. As economists, we should collectively have a solid understanding of each step of the supply chain. We may regard the whole process with a degree of awe, as Friedman illustrates through wood and graphite, but doing so also leaves us open to mysticising globalisation, markets and capitalism, accepting that they are in some way unknowable and uncontrollable.

The supply chain of the pencil illustrates an old idea in economics known as specialisation. We can split up the production of goods into discrete tasks so that each task is carried out with maximum efficiency, or so the thinking goes. You probably practise specialisation in the home: it is both easier and faster to have one person wash the dishes and another dry them and put them away. If you had two people washing, drying and putting away at the same time, there would be all sorts of problems: switching between tasks would take time; people would get in each other's way; and you would need twice the number of sinks, tea towels, sponges, and so on. Splitting up the task of doing the dishes makes it both easier and more efficient.

Our obsession with specialisation dates back to Adam Smith and his famous example of not pencils but pins. Smith observed that one person, working alone, could 'scarce, with his utmost industry, make one pin a day', whereas in the factories of his time the task was split up into up to 'eighteen distinct operations'. This is the division of labour we saw at the very start of the book: 'one man draws out the wire, another straightens it, a third cuts it . . .' and so on. Smith claimed that 10 men working in a factory could make 48,000 pins or 4,800 pins each, a number that dwarfs the single pin one man could make in a day. According to Smith, the efficiency gains from splitting up a task are enormous: going from a small factory to a large one might multiply the number of pins produced by a couple of hundred times.[3]

In our global economy, we have pursued this insight ad absurdum. If we can achieve gains from specialisation at the level of an individual pin factory, the logic goes, we can stretch that all the way across the globe. An increasing number of links in the supply chain have gone hand in hand with increasingly specialised tasks at each link. Whereas car companies used to source materials, build individual car parts, assemble the cars, distribute the cars and sell the cars themselves, now most of those steps are done by separate companies. These companies are generally extremely good at doing what they do, to the extent that they are literally the only companies in the world that can do them. As both Friedman and Smith attested, the variety and volume of goods produced by these specialised supply chains is nothing short of remarkable.

At the same time, these insights are often taken too far. An investigation into Smith's example by Jean-Louis Peaucelle and Cameron Guthrie found that Smith's numbers were, well, made up.[4] Pin factories did not have up to 18 separate operations; they maxed out at 8 or 9. A single person could not make merely 1 pin per day but up to 2,000. The result was that pin-making workshops of various sizes, from those that employed fewer than 6 labourers to those that employed up to 20, would have competed on a roughly level footing with each other despite their different degrees of specialisation. As Peaucelle and Guthrie put it: 'Productivity improvements would not have been as spectacular as Adam Smith imagined. They would have been closer to a factor of 2.4 rather than 240.' The fact that such a famous example seems to be completely out of line with the facts on the ground should give us pause for thought when mysticising about specialisation.

What's even more concerning is that specialisation comes at the cost of vulnerability. Writing in 2007, thirteen years before the pandemic, the journalist Barry C. Lynn produced the following summary of globalisation, which in hindsight is uncomfortably prescient:[5]

Our brand-new global factory does look awfully efficient. But it is an efficiency purchased through the destruction of all flexibility, and hence sustainability. What we should be fretting about now is what happens when, one day soon, we awake to find that war, revolution, disease, or natural disaster has cut us off from some of the increasingly scattered pockets of workers we rely on to produce keystone industrial components or to process vital back-office information; what happens when, for want of access to one or a few of the links that make up the global assembly line as a whole, our entire industrial system breaks – pins, electronics, pharmaceuticals, food, and all.

Should one link in the chain be broken, there are no alternatives, and the only choice is to shut down production. For example, there is a pigment called Xirallic which gives cars a modern, shimmery black hue and is used by General Motors, Ford, Chrysler, BMW and Volkswagen. Xirallic is produced by a solitary Japanese company called Merck; nobody else in the world can make it. So when the simultaneous disasters of an earthquake, tsunami and radioactive release in 2011 Japan caused the supply to dry up from Merck, the companies had to do without as they simply could not get Xirallic anywhere else.[6] Production of shiny black cars halted entirely. While it may not be of concern to anyone but a few well-off car owners that they can't get a fancy car that shimmers in the sun, the degree of specialisation epitomised by Merck makes our economies vulnerable in ways that affect everyone.

EFFICIENCY VERSUS RESILIENCE

The human body is a remarkable thing. It is also remarkably inefficient. For example, we have two kidneys to remove excess fluids and waste from our bodies, even though medical professionals know that we can survive pretty well with only one. When one kidney ceases to work, we can place extra demands on the remaining one, which is capable of handling our bodily functions all on its own. If our bodies were purely focused on efficiency, then they would eject our second kidney: it takes up unnecessary space despite us barely using it most of the time.* As with every part of our body, it demands sustenance as its

---

* For the pedants, what I mean is that we do not use anywhere near the full capacity of two kidneys, usually running at about 30 per cent of each, which increases to 60 or 70 per cent even with only one kidney. That is still quite a bit of spare capacity.

tissue must be nourished and replaced continuously. So why even bother having it?

The answer is something known as robustness or resilience. The extra kidney serves as a cushion (not literally – please don't try this) for us so that we have spare capacity in our bodies, should we find the other kidney temporarily or permanently disabled. This is why people with one kidney must take extra care with their diets and the type of activity they do: they risk harming their one remaining kidney, which would put them in real trouble. If you could guarantee a life with a healthy diet, free from injury, free from illness and operating at exactly the right level of physical strain, then one kidney would be the optimal choice. But as anyone knows who has, well, been alive, this is a far cry from reality. Evolution has determined that our bodies must have the extra kidney because these ideal conditions are rarely achieved, and we need the resilience to deal with it when they aren't.

Resilience is not something we have consciously embedded into our economies. In fact, we have often celebrated specialisation and efficiency at the cost of resilience. One of the most telling trends in global production over the past few decades has been the rise of 'just-in-time' production. Invented by the Japanese car company Toyota, this approach orders materials only as and when cars are bought by consumers. This means lower inventory, which means lower storage costs, and hopefully a more accurate match between the raw materials ordered and the cars eventually sold. Companies using just-in-time will not find themselves holding onto useless inventory, having incorrectly predicted the amount they'll sell in the future. Just-in-time production is a kind of hyper specialisation which requires not only unique links in the chain but that those links be in a specific place at a specific time.[7]

There's no doubt that just-in-time production has been highly profitable for Toyota and other companies who have adopted it, but, once again, balancing production on a knife-edge has made it vulnerable to shocks. When demand for cars rebounded unexpectedly fast in the latter half of 2020, companies like Toyota found themselves with a shortage of microchips. Thanks to just-in-time production, they were used to securing them instantaneously. But following the pandemic, microchip companies wanted chips to be ordered six months in advance and they were already at capacity because of the broader issues with the supply chain. Despite demand being there, the automobile companies let plants sit idle and had to furlough workers. The whole episode has been estimated to have cost the automobile industry $110 billion in 2021 and resulted in four million fewer vehicles being produced than they had originally planned.[8]

Our economies today could be likened to one-kidney human bodies. Many of the goods we rely on, from microchips to cars to pharmaceuticals, are often produced almost entirely in one country, one region, or even by one business. You may have heard that Taiwan produces most of the world's microchips, but it goes further than that. Most Taiwanese microchips are produced by a single company: the Taiwan Semiconductor Manufacturing Company (TSMC).[9] These microchips are the basis for a wide range of technologies, from smart phones and televisions to missiles and military software. This means that everyone in the world relies on a single business in a single country to produce something that we depend on every single day.

Taiwan is an island just off the coast of China, south of Japan but north of the Philippines, a country which, like many of its neighbours, has enjoyed rapid industrialisation since World War II. It went from an agricultural economy to leading manufacturing hub in a matter of decades thanks to smart policy.[10] But it is hardly an island without its fair share of hardships. It is deemed 'strategically important' for both the USA and China, which has led to geopolitical posturing that constantly puts the fate of the nation at stake, particularly as China denies Taiwan's sovereignty altogether and feels that it rightfully belongs with the People's Republic.

On top of this, Taiwan sits at the intersection of two tectonic plates and is therefore prone to earthquakes (there's my GCSE in geography kicking in again, thanks Mr Howlett). When a devastating earthquake hit Taiwan in 1999, it killed 2,500 people and destroyed large parts of the country. This was a local tragedy, but it also became a global crisis because it cut off the supply of microchips. An earthquake in East Asia led to factories shutting down and people losing their jobs on the other side of the world, in car factories in the USA.[11] And our dependence on microchips has only grown over the past 25 years.

Though they are the thing people most often focus on, our supply chain issues extend far beyond microchips. The growth of China's role in the world economy has been so noticeable it became a cultural phenomenon: the phrase 'Made in China' was the punchline of jokes when I was growing up (albeit not funny ones). China is known for making toys and clothes, but they have kept up with the changing modern economy, too. The country refines most of the world's lithium and cobalt and mines most of its graphite. Graphite is a key ingredient in Friedman's pencils, while all three materials are necessary for electric car batteries. China already produces millions more electric cars than anywhere else, a gap that it is looking to expand. It is also responsible for 80 per cent of the world's solar panels and about half of all printed circuit boards.[12]

China has been a reliable economic powerhouse over the past few decades, but the coronavirus pandemic illustrates the challenges of relying too much on any country, however large and productive it may be. Wuhan, the epicentre of the Covid-19 outbreak, is a manufacturing hub and a crucial port through which Chinese goods must pass. In a twist of fate, Xiantao, just west of Wuhan, was a key producer of the Personal Protective Equipment (PPE) the world so sorely needed to fight the coronavirus. Xiantao's PPE had to pass through Wuhan to get to the rest of the world just at the time it was locking down, leading to difficulties securing PPE for countries across the world.[13]

Nor are our supply chain issues limited to East Asia. We have already discussed the effect of the Russian invasion of Ukraine on energy prices, but the consequences go beyond this. Firstly, Ukraine is a major exporter of neon gas, which is a crucial ingredient for the process of making – you guessed it – the semiconductors used for microchips. Secondly and more worryingly, the Ukraine is a major exporter of wheat – its yellow and blue flag actually depicts a wheat field – and the war threatens the grain supplies of the Middle East and Africa, regions where food stability cannot be taken for granted.[14] This threat was exacerbated by the fact that many exports pass through the ports in the Black Sea, a contentious zone even during peacetime. The world has been watching with trepidation as the trade agreements between Russia and Ukraine, which allow the latter to export wheat across the Black Sea, have been teetering with every major twist and turn of the war.

The notions of resilience and security will not be news for countries in the Middle East and Africa, since unlike many Western countries they have not been able to rely on the supply of anything, whether food or pencils or semiconductors, throughout their history. These countries have long struggled to maintain food security, to the point of starvation for many millions of their people, so it probably seems a bit fresh for the West to suddenly discover that we don't like it when the supply of our (less necessary) goods is disrupted. This is compounded by the institutions which inhibit these countries in their quest for food security, including their financial reliance on our currencies. Poorer countries are also typically prevented from subsidising their own food, even as the USA and EU do exactly that with massive subsidies to agriculture. In one sense, then, establishing reliable supplies for everyone means dismantling these lopsided systems before we do anything else.

REDUNDANCY AND COMPARTMENTALISATION

Barry C. Lynn castigates economists such as Smith and Friedman for choosing to proselytise about markets and globalisation instead of doing their due diligence as economists and ruthlessly interrogating the system's vulnerabilities. Systems which are as specialised as our global economy are inherently vulnerable: these are two sides of the same coin. When each node in a network is necessary and unique, the failure of any one node can cascade throughout the whole system, as we saw with the Xirallic paint from Japan, then more consequentially with PPE equipment from China. To build a more robust system, we may well be content to sacrifice some short-term efficiency. Lynn describes two key principles in the design of a resilient system, both of which are made more possible by a globally connected economy.[15]

The first key principle is redundancy, where there are several ways of doing the same thing, so that at any one time many of them seem redundant. To give you an example, the internet has so many such redundancies that the notion the whole thing could 'go down' is inconceivable. The internet does not really exist as one thing: it is located on countless servers held by countless companies, governments and households. Localised problems can be overcome because the internet will simply reroute around the problem so that information can reach its destination. As any decent engineer knows, building in redundancies – an extra kidney, an extra computer server, another business capable of producing Xirallic – is essential to ensuring reliability and resilience in the face of disruption.

The second key principle engineers use is compartmentalisation: demarcating different parts of the system so that if they experience problems, those problems do not spread much further. The internet builds in compartmentalisation as well: if my home broadband router goes down, it doesn't directly affect next door's. We each have our own home internet zones which can work or fail independently of other parts of the system.

It is easy to forget that in the past, economies were organised with both redundancy and compartmentalisation in mind. For instance, twentieth-century car companies did almost everything in-house, which meant they could fail without bringing down the industry in other parts of the country. Each company sourced their own materials and manufactured their own parts, which meant that if one source of materials suddenly dried up and the company that used it suffered, others would be less affected because they'd have another option. If there was a backlog of orders for one of the component parts of a General Motors car, it wouldn't cascade throughout the economy; it would only affect General Motors.[16]

Ironically, as our economy has become more globalised the potential for both compartmentalisation and redundancy has *increased*; we've just chosen not to take that route. Helpfully, compartmentalisation and redundancy can both be achieved by similar policies. The clearest examples come from the recent efforts to expand microchip production across the globe. The CHIPS and Science Act in the USA put $280 billion into research and manufacturing of semiconductors; Japan's government sponsored TSMC to build a new factory in Japan; the EU subsidies aim to increase the EU's semiconductor market share from 9 per cent to 20 per cent by 2030; India have launched their Semiconductor Mission; China have launched the China Integrated Circuit Industry Investment Fund; and Taiwan and South Korea have expanded their existing subsidies.

There are various accompanying trends which are already pushing us towards greater compartmentalisation, all with their own irritating buzzword names. There's onshoring (bringing previously offshored jobs back to the home country); reshoring (the same), nearshoring (locating in neighbouring countries instead of halfway across the globe); and the especially embarrassing 'friendshoring' (locating in countries which we aren't going to fall out with – a tough find for my own country).[17] Again, there have been plenty of moves to do this in the semiconductor industry, but it has been happening more generally – and not always as a result of government subsidies or regulation. Companies have begun to realise the dangers of overstretched supply chains and 2021 saw 160,000 jobs added in the USA from reshoring, a number that has only increased.[18]

My point is not that we need to return to the so-called glory days of cars produced in one country – we don't need the old three-wheeled Reliant Robin back here in the UK, cute as it was. Nor is it that we need to pursue a situation where every single country can handle the entire supply chain of microchips: the Dutch firm ASML's ultraviolet light mirrors can hit a ping pong ball on the moon, and others aren't going to emulate that any time soon.[19] Such a situation is impossible, and more generally it may be that the cat is out of the bag as far as modern supply chains go. We need to harness the benefits of globalisation while ensuring that there is enough resilience in the system to deal with pandemics, climate change, war, political upheaval and financial crises. As the twenty-first century has taught us, these events are far from a relic of the past.

TAKEN FOR GRANTED

On the sunny but busy shores of Los Angeles, the Mexican truck driver Omar Alvarez spends much of his day waiting. He drives his truck down the slow-moving highways to the ports, where he is responsible for taking the produce that comes off the ships to nearby warehouses or to train yards, after which it will be shipped across the rest of the USA. But the waiting is far from over when Alvarez gets to the ports. It can take hours just to drop off his empty container from the previous day, and more to pick up his new container for today. Alvarez calls these unpaid and unpredictable waits 'a direct threat' to his ability to earn enough money to put food on the table. He is one of 12,000 port truck drivers in a similar situation in LA, who ensure that goods get to where they need to be, yet are grotesquely underappreciated for their efforts.[20]

These drivers, many of whom are immigrants like Alvarez, are classified by the logistics companies as independent contractors.

This means they are not subject to minimum wage laws, get no health insurance and their annual income before taxes (but after trucking-related costs) is a paltry $28,000 a year. They lease the trucks they drive from XPO, the same company they work for. As drivers are paid based on the amount of cargo they move, the time they spend queuing to collect the cargo is not reimbursed. It can be a long wait and during Covid-19 the whole system became orders of magnitude slower, with some drivers waiting up to six hours.[21] There are no bathrooms provided and it is quite easy to get stuck in the wrong queue, wasting hours for nothing while, to add insult to injury, you're also bursting to go to the toilet.

According to economic sociologist Steve Viscelli, 'the port truck driver, for decades now, has basically been the slack adjuster in the whole system'. Viscelli has gone so far as to claim that the entire distribution system is 'built around free labor from truck drivers as they wait for containers', a precarious situation for both the drivers and the supply chains that depend on them.[22] Many are having second thoughts: around 30 per cent have stopped showing up on weekdays, which rises to 50 per cent on weekends. During the Covid-19 supply-chain crisis, newspapers were writing about the shortage of truckers, but as Alvarez puts it 'the real shortage is a shortage of good, union jobs that fairly compensate workers and treat us with the dignity and respect we deserve'.[23]

Long-haul truck driving – which is distinct from those who work solely in and near the ports – has long been a staple of life in the USA and a symbol of the working class. Driving on the open road (a topic of yet another *Simpsons* episode, but at the request of my editor I will not discuss this one in more detail) is often depicted as a tough but rewarding job. Transporting large quantities of goods is crucial to keeping the economy running in a country with high consumption levels yet such a large, varied geography. Given the size of the US economy and the amount it imports from across the world, the industry is of global importance. And despite our reliance on long-haul truck drivers, like their port-based brothers they have long been overworked, underpaid and underappreciated.

In 2021, the American Trucking Association (ATA) estimated that the USA was short 80,000 truckers and that this number would only increase in the future. Even before the pandemic, an astonishing 94 per cent of truckers quit every year.[24] And who's to blame them – the job does not pay especially well when compared to similar jobs such as construction or warehouse work. It also puts strain on families as it requires working long hours, as well as travelling and staying around the country. Sitting down and eating on the move does not lend itself to good health and truck drivers have a high incidence of obesity and diabetes. When you disregard such difficult yet crucial professions, you can't be surprised when people opt out and the whole thing crumbles.

It was not always thus. When President Franklin D. Roosevelt enacted the progressive New Deal in the 1930s, trucking was an industry that benefitted majorly from the new support for labour. Truckers were able to unionise and bargain for better wages and conditions, banding together across large geographic areas. This was important for such a mobile profession: negotiating with individual businesses or cities was tricky given how often truckers would move from one area to another.[25] Truckers as a group could demand more in terms of pay, pensions and health insurance because their cohesion as a group stopped employers from pitting them against one another. Truckers ended up with nationwide minimum standards, which made it a classic example of the steady, lifelong, blue-collar job enjoyed by so many in the post-World War II era.

Things changed when President Jimmy Carter began to deregulate the industry in 1980. The Motor Carrier Act essentially abolished the minimum standards that truckers had grown used to. Owing to the 1970s economic crisis, which saw recession and rising inflation, there was an appetite for change in economic policy. Political winds also meant the truckers were unable to prevent deregulation, with the (not entirely inaccurate) public perception of their union leaders as sexist, racist barons with links to the mafia. Whatever the causes, Carter's deregulation made it much easier for independent truckers and small businesses to enter the market and compete, which led to a reduction in wages and standards across the board.[26]

These problems are not confined to the USA. In 2018, Brazilian truck drivers staged strikes in protest at high diesel fuel prices, creating blockades on federal highways for 11 days. This cost Brazil's agricultural sector $1.75 billion, crippled the industries that depended on transport and emptied out supermarket shelves, leading to rationing. The effects lasted for a long time afterwards, creating a mini-version of the global disruptions we saw during Covid-19.[27] Most transportation in India is done via road, and as the below picture shows, trucks are famously decorated in the style of the region, which serves at least as a cultural marker of respect. Nevertheless, as elsewhere, the trucking sector has long been economically undervalued, and this came to the fore during the pandemic.[28]

In *The West Wing* in the 2000s, political advisor Toby Ziegler confidently claimed 'Food is cheaper. Clothes are cheaper . . . it lowers prices, it raises income . . . free trade stops

wars.' The uncomfortable realities for workers in our modern world are an effective antidote to these kinds of fairy tales. We have overtly pursued specialisation at the cost of resilience, but that doesn't mean the need for resilience has gone away. We have relied on hidden players like truck drivers to be flexible where the rest of the system is rigid. This enormous sector has been invisible to us for so long because we have taken it for granted, assuming it will just 'work'.

Craig Fuller, the CEO of shipping news company Freight-Waves, estimates freight (shipping of goods) makes up about 12 per cent of the global economy, while about 40 per cent of the global economy is dependent on it indirectly.[29] As with the truck drivers of the past, workers in shipping across the globe deserve higher pay, better conditions, permanent positions, healthcare, and limits on their working hours. This is fundamentally a matter of basic rights, but it is also an economic imperative. Unless we treat the people in these sectors as the essential workers they are, we may find they continue to drop out at alarming rates until the system becomes completely dysfunctional.

STRETCHED TO BREAKING POINT

For six long days in March 2021, the super-sized cargo ship *Ever Given* was lodged in the Suez Canal. It became a point of international obsession and the source of a great many memes online. The reason the ship was so difficult to move is because it is literally the size of the Empire State Building, which didn't leave much room left to manoeuvre in the canal. Multiple tugboats and dredgers were needed to dislodge the ship and one unlucky person actually died during the process. There were 369 ships waiting by the time the *Ever Given* got moving again, which translated into holding up about $9.6 billion of trade globally. The blockage raised headaches for companies across the world which lasted for months afterwards and may even have done permanent damage to the global economy.[30]

While the Suez calamity seemed like an unlucky one-off – albeit almost repeated in late 2023[31] – such a size is not abnormal for modern containers and the problems caused by these behemoths are depressingly common across the globe. The rise of the size of the shipping companies has coincided with technological developments which have increased the size of ships themselves. Modern container ships reach colossal magnitudes, to the point that the image conjured up by saying 'ship' doesn't really do them justice. The heavily concentrated shipping industry has relentlessly pursued size to their own benefit, even as the system as a whole has become less effective. In the USA, it can be more profitable for a big ship to unload in LA and head straight back to China empty, than for it to load up to take American exports back across the Pacific Ocean.[32] The situation is good for the monopolies but bad for exporters, smaller shippers, the global economy, local communities and the environment.

The top ten ocean carriers today control over 80 per cent of the market, twice as much as they did in 1998.[33] In early 2022, at a time when supply-chain issues were coming to a head, the world's largest shipping company, the Danish firm Maersk, had its largest profits in 117 years.[34] The industry has become more concentrated, which has spelled problems for potential competitors, workers and the shipping system as a whole. Instead of a steady trickle of goods, the ports found them- selves dealing with occasional massive deliveries from these skyscraper-esque boats. The larger the ship, the larger the port required to dock it. As ships have grown, an increasing number of ports have fallen into relative disuse, with a reliance on larger ones like Los Angeles at the expense of smaller ones like nearby San Diego.

There is a famous notion in chaos theory known as the butter- fly effect, where a butterfly flapping its wings can cause a hurricane on the other side of the world. No area of the global economy illustrates the butterfly effect better than shipping. Although many of the most-circulated images in the media were those of the ports being clogged in the USA, routes from China to Europe, Africa and South America saw larger increases in prices than those in the USA. *Ever Given* is owned by Taiwanese company Evergreen Marine and was heading from Kaohsiung to Rotterdam through the Suez Canal, yet the biggest impact it seems to have had was on routes to the port of Santos in Brazil, which do not go through Suez.[35] It is astonishing how widely these shockwaves emanate across the globe, and an industry which cannot manage them is not fit for purpose.

Economist Joe Weisenthal has commented that problems arise because many key arrangements in global logistics are effectively 'held together with duct tape'. You might reasonably assume that something as significant as shipping thousands of tons worth of goods from China to the USA would always be subject to strict formal arrangements. You'd be wrong. In many cases, no formal contract is signed and there is simply an expectation that the service will be provided once agreed. Weisenthal compares the process to buying a train ticket: once you buy a ticket, there is no guarantee you will actually get a seat on the next train and no way to enforce it should you not. Similarly, a company can arrange to have their goods shipped, but if the ship fills up there is no guarantee the goods will find a place on it.[36]

Once goods arrive in the USA, communication is even more informal and is done using platforms like WhatsApp groups, Facebook or Craigslist. One person will post asking whether anyone is around to take some containers from one state to another, and someone else will reply, 'Sure, I'm in the area, I can do that.'[37] Increasingly, apps are used which resemble Uber or dating apps, and the truckers are told that they will find the most relevant 'matches' for their trucks at any given time. Apparently, US distribution is organised in a similar way to my five-a-side football team. And unlike my five-a-side team, this matters: port congestion was lower in better-regulated Europe and in China, but they still experienced bottlenecks because of the issues in the USA. The butterfly effect reigns supreme.

In the past, shipping was monitored and regulated so that a healthy ecosystem of small, medium and large ships were able to operate simultaneously, slotting into the appropriate ports where necessary. Like the ships themselves, the companies that ran them were numerous and varied in size, and regulation of prices prevented exploitation of smaller operators and workers. The possibility of bottlenecks in specific goods becomes less likely when there are multiple companies and ships delivering each good, since problems with one company can be compensated for by others. Instead of a few big ships arriving erratically to the big ports, each ship can be unloaded in a steady trickle of cargo across both larger and smaller ports. This problem is reminiscent of the game Tetris: only certain ships can fit into certain ports, so losing variety in our ports can quickly lead to calamity, just as a few ill-fitting pieces in a row can quickly lose you a Tetris game.

In 2015, the Federal Maritime Commission warned that developments in the industry had led to queues and congestion, while underinvestment meant a lack of supply of crucial tools and machines needed to keep the ports running.[38] This lack of long-term thinking and coordination was evident to them even five years before Covid-19 hit and no-one listened because no-one reads reports from the Federal Maritime Commission. These days, however, we really have no excuse to ignore them. The dominance of a few big players in shipping, combined with their unwillingness to consider impacts beyond their immediate short-term profit, has led to a system which is not fit for purpose. Their massive, expensive ships mess up the functioning of ports while serving as a costly barrier for anyone looking to enter the monopolised market. Most of us would struggle to start a company with a ship the size of the *Ever Given*.

Fortunately, there exist eminently workable and even inexpensive solutions. As with inflation, the first issue is the lack of formal coordination across the globe. A 2022 report stated that 'value chain actors tend to "optimise" for themselves, which only exacerbates the issues at system level'.[39] The report advocates moving away from an uncoordinated mess of 'first-come, first served' which leaves ports dealing with events as they happen and creates the potential for massive delays when things don't go smoothly. Instead, establishing time slots in which to unload – as simple as it sounds – would be a massive step forward. There are technological solutions like Inspectorio, an information sharing tool from Latin America, which may help this kind of coordination.[40]

Businesses like Flexport similarly aim to 'connect the entire ecosystem of global trade' in what has long been a fragmented and confusing system.[41] CEO Ryan Petersen has characterised the existing process as 'you're just kind of shuffling pdfs around the world trying to make things happen'.[42] Current information systems do track goods as they are produced and transported – it's just that the information is usually kept private by the companies involved. In an ideal world, this technology would be pieced together and made visible, so that the entire system could be connected and capitalised on. European ports share data and coordinate over a centralised database: such efforts could be emulated and scaled up as far as possible to include not just ports but the entire global logistics system.[43] Further integrating the truck drivers, as well as trains and other transportation systems which link up with the ports, would make the whole process even smoother.

Scholar Charmaine Chua has argued that the port has always been central to capitalism, perhaps more than it is given credit for today. Friedrich Engels' *Condition of the Working Class* in 1845 began with a discussion of ports in London and how they inspired awe, juxtaposed alongside the immiseration of the workers. Karl Polanyi, writing one hundred years later, saw the birth of the market economy in the spread of ports and global trade – often at the service of colonialism rather than in the 'myth of barter', which was promoted by Adam Smith and others. Chua argues that these days ports are much less visible but no less important. Unlike nineteenth-century London, modern ports are generally outside city centres, hidden from view. Yet they still physically carry an eye-watering 80 per cent of global trade, so when they stop working, the entire global economy teeters on the precipice.[44]

Series 2 of *The Wire*, set in 1990s Baltimore, depicts ports that are starved of work, with insufficient hours causing individual workers to turn to petty crime, and insufficient revenues causing unions and owners to turn to organised crime. Echoing this picture, ports have become less reliable places to get above-board work over the past few decades. But it's far from just the ports, or even logistics: technological developments, changes in corporate governance and declines in the power of workers have made for erratic and resource-starved industries up and down the USA and, by extension, across the globe. Rethinking our supply chains may mean rethinking the philosophy that has governed our economies for so long.[45]

RESILIENCE IN THE TWENTY-FIRST CENTURY

A 2021 White House report investigated the supply chain problems laid bare by the pandemic. Its verdict was damning in terms of the philosophy that has guided American-led globalisation for the past few decades. It concluded that 'US market structures fail to reward firms for investing in quality, sustainability or long-term productivity', which it attributes to 'misaligned incentives and short-termism in private markets'.[46] Echoing the story of the truck drivers, it adds that 'decades of focusing on labor as a cost to be controlled—not an asset to be invested in—have depressed real wages and driven down union-density for workers, while also contributing to companies' challenges finding and keeping skilled talent'.[47] The verdict was clear: long before the pandemic, our dominant approach was leaving most of us worse off than we should be.

The computing company Intel is an illustrative example. They paved the way for chip technology in the 1970s and 1980s, pioneering the famous 8088 microprocessors which were used in the first personal computers. They enjoyed a monopoly over the computer market for decades and in many ways, they still do. But they have not invested in smartphones and tablets and so have fallen behind. Taiwanese TSMC, as well as South Korean Samsung, were branching out into smartphones and tablets while Intel was happy to sit on its monopoly over personal computers. Intel's strategy has shifted from one of investing in cutting-edge technology to one of abusing their market power, engaging in practices of questionable legality – to put it diplomatically. More recently, Intel has engaged in an impressive number of stock buybacks, spending more than its net income buying its own stocks between 2001 and 2010.[48] That means the company borrowed not to invest, but effectively to speculate on itself.

It is no surprise that Intel has lagged behind in terms of microprocessor technology, too. We typically measure the progress of this technology in nanometres, though this doesn't refer to the chips themselves, which are usually about the size of a thumbnail. What the nanometres measure is the size of the transistors, millions of which make up each chip. The smaller they are, the higher their speed and efficiency. In 2022, TSMC's chips were twice as small as Intel's. TSMC was planning semiconductors that were three nanometres, while at the same time Intel was only just beginning to create ones that came in at seven nanometres. For context, the coronavirus measures ten nanometres across. The issues raised by the pandemic and supply chain crisis may have shaken Intel out of their complacency and there is now a battle to reach two nanometres. At the time of writing, it seems that TMSC is still ahead.[49]

In making these comparisons, I am by no means trying to foment competitive, nationalistic impulses between the West and East Asia. The key issue is that each of these examples represent two distinct philosophies towards globalisation. Southeast Asia has long engaged in active industrial policy, which means governments investing in and otherwise supporting key industries. They have benefited massively from this approach – in the latter half of the twentieth century, countries like Taiwan and South Korea went from dirt-poor to having per-person income comparable to that of Western Europe.[50] Although there is a long history of industrial policy in the West, too, we have nominally abandoned this history in favour of a hands-off approach and a focus on maximising short-term value for shareholders.

Intel and the microchip industry are far from the only examples where short-termism has won out. The same White House report claims that between 2009 and 2018, 91 per cent of the income of the biggest 500 firms in the United States went to stock buybacks. Changes to laws have meant that companies were less likely to get into trouble for manipulating the price of their own stock. CEOs then began to pay themselves in stock, which gave them a new reason to have their companies push up the value of that stock by buying as much as possible. At the same time, investments in capital equipment and research and development have declined.[51]

This raises deep questions about how modern corporations are structured. The dominant idea in the USA has been to keep corporations lean by cutting costs – whether by lowering investment, paying workers less, or outsourcing key functions to other countries. Pressure from investors and Wall Street to increase short-term profits (and therefore payouts to those investors) meant that long-term goals fell by the wayside. This meant that the kind of robust systems needed to cope with serious shocks like a pandemic instead became sclerotic. It meant that the production technologies we needed were increasingly available only in specific places across the globe.

In a sense, this brings us back to the issues raised early in the book surrounding the dominance of the economy by certain firms, plus the failure of laws like anti-trust to curb their influence. The structure of the global economy has favoured large private companies, many of them American or European, who have effectively become vehicles for governing the global economy. Milton Friedman's philosophy generally taught him that market economies would confer on what was best for everyone, producing marvels like the pencil. Yet countless examples have shown that coordinating the economic system so that it is resilient and fair to the people who make it work will require deliberate and sustained efforts which go against the interests of these big companies.

To this end, there is an ongoing attempt to investigate huge shipping companies like Maersk following complaints about the issues we've seen: the inefficiency of their large container ships and the impact their dominance has on drivers like Omar

Alvarez.[52] Shipping companies have long been exempted from anti-trust laws on the grounds that they need to coordinate with one another, but this may have become an excuse to behave anti-competitively. Industry insiders have told me that they are generally thought to be engaging in tacit collusion, fixing prices. As both the USA and EU are currently investigating this behaviour, their exemption from anti-trust could prove short-lived.[53]

The reality may be even more stark than this. Indian economist Jayati Ghosh argues that, contrary to popular perception, wheat prices did not rise after the Russian invasion of Ukraine because of a shortage of wheat itself. Despite an initial drop in production straight after the invasion, the amount of wheat in the world quickly bounced back and global supply is estimated to have exceeded global demand between July 2022 and June 2023. This is because wheat is produced all over the world, so other sources were able to compensate for the fall in Ukraine.[54] Yet prices continued to rise as many of the world's largest grain traders made record profits, as did those speculating on wheat financially. Reining in global fluctuations may well mean reining in these financial excesses.

COOPERATION OVER COMPETITION

In the last chapter, we discussed inflation and how central banks have approached it by increasing interest rates. Hopefully, the discussion of the different factors at play in supply chains has convinced you how absurd this approach is. Increasing lending and mortgage costs, with knock-on effects that will put people out of work, is not going to make ports unclog or semiconductors appear. It may even be counterproductive to building extra capacity over the long term. Central bankers are well aware of this, and the current Governor of the Bank of England stressed that their policy cannot help the problems described.[55] It's not the fault of central banks, exactly, but it shows why we need a better approach to managing not just inflation but the economy as a whole. Designing, monitoring and regulating a resilient and ultimately fair global network is the only way to care for both the economy and the people who make it up.

To answer the question posed at the beginning of this chapter, the reason the global economy broke is because it is so brittle. In the absence of deliberate mechanisms which make sure the system functions well and benefits everyone, powerful private actors have shaped the economy in their own interests, to the detriment of everyone. A lack of investment characterises many Western economies as their companies fall behind the ones that take a more long-term, enlightened view. The workers who are responsible for transporting almost every tangible product we use are treated as an underclass dependent on precarious employment, rather than elevated into roles where they both have a voice in the system and receive a fair share of the pie. Imagine how much know-how Omar Alvarez and his colleagues have about the ports, then ask whether or not the shipping companies are likely to be listening to them.

One possible counterargument is that, despite the supply chain crisis, many companies and industries found workarounds and were able to stabilise their activities. Some might say this is further evidence of the magic of markets, and there's truth in this. But what's important is that the crisis forced both the private and public sectors to rethink their efficiency-oriented approaches and instead centre resilience and coordination. This is true of the investment efforts by many governments and of the new companies which have sprung up to help manage logistics. It is easy to forget the atmosphere of panic in 2021–22 and the damage it caused, even if we fumbled our way through it in the end. We do not want to slip into complacency because the butterfly effect tells us that one day, the system could truly break down beyond repair.

Cooperation over competition is more than a plea to teach the world to sing in perfect harmony; it is an economic necessity. Indeed, this is how I see the economic problem. Bringing together the different actors to make sure that the system functions in everyone's interests is not something markets and capitalism do magically; it is an ongoing governance issue. Those who proselytise and mysticise about markets simply evade this difficult problem and are no better than those who believe we can run an economy based purely on love and vibes. This all raises the question of how to challenge and change the existing system, a question to which we will now turn.

PART III

REDEFINING THE ECONOMIC LANDSCAPE

CONCLUSION

THE POLITICS OF ECONOMICS

A better economy won't come easily

In September 2023 Tim Gurner, a millionaire luxury home developer, made headlines with the following comments:

> We need to see unemployment rise. Unemployment needs to jump 40–50 per cent in my view. We need to see pain in the economy. We need to remind people that they work for the employer, not the other way around. There's been a systematic change where employees feel the employer is extremely lucky to have them, as opposed to the other way around.

This was occasioned by the, at the time, largely buoyant global economy, with the USA in particular seeming to approach full employment. This had led to rising wages at the bottom, with many former hospitality workers quitting and unionisation and strikes on the rise. Clearly, Gurner was not happy with this situation as the workers were getting too many big ideas.[1]

Funnily enough, this was not Gurner's first rodeo. He had previously gained infamy by insisting in 2017 that the reason millennials couldn't afford a house was because they were eating too much avocado toast. As he put it: 'when I was trying to buy my first home, I wasn't buying smashed avocado for $19 and four coffees at $4 each'. As Chapter 5 showed, my generation and younger ones are less able to afford housing than the ones that came before us, and a general lack of housing means many across the world are living in completely unacceptable conditions, so these comments do not pass the laugh test. Numerous people ran the numbers and found that it would take in excess of one hundred years of skimping on avocado toast to afford a down payment on a house, depending on the location.[2]

The reason I bring this up is not just because it's funny that a millionaire's economic analysis consists of 'my employees aren't listening to me' and 'young people shouldn't be allowed to eat fruit on toast'. Nor is it to ask why he is allowed to pontificate to the public as if he is some kind of thoughtful authority. It's because the path to a better economy is by no means easy. Some readers might feel that my analysis has been narrowly focused on economics without enough on politics. To that I can only plead guilty: economics is the subject I am trained in and the one I am passionate about, so I'd rather not do political analysis at all than do it poorly. But it is worth pausing to consider what the path to a better economy might be up against.

A famous essay by Polish economist Michal Kalecki called *The Political Aspects of Full Employment* argued that as employment rose, workers would demand higher wages and this would reduce the power of employers.[3] Even if a fully employed economy was objectively better for everyone, with motivated workers producing happily and spending money, resulting in higher profits for capitalists, it would result in less *relative* power for the latter. It was therefore the case that the richest and the powerful would campaign actively against full employment. In this sense, better policy was often not economically but *politically* impossible.

Gurner later apologised for his remarks about unemployment.[4] However, his demand is basically in line with the actual practices of central banks we discussed in Chapter 7: squeeze the economy to increase unemployment and reduce wage demands. It extends to other economic gains, too: it is precisely the situation we saw in Brazil in Chapter 4, when wealthy families were worried about losing their housemaids to the forces of progress. And it may explain why central banks are more geared towards facilitating the financial sector than providing for their citizens, as seen in Chapter 6. We've also seen countless examples of good economic policy, but the forces acting against them should not be underestimated and may require more fundamental changes to overcome.

A REVIVAL OF DEMOS

Ellen Meiksins Wood has argued that there are two Western approaches to democracy which are often conflated.[5] One stems from the Ancient Greek idea of *demos*, where those who worked were also active participants in decisions about governance. Another concept, which stems from Ancient Rome and has come to supersede *demos*, is the one of 'we, the people' and this has been embraced by the USA, UK and to varying degrees by other Western countries. The crucial difference is that under the latter, economic and political life are generally separated so that the state is run by a distinct class of individuals. Workers and peasants vote for who controls that apparatus, yet the apparatus is not integrated with their everyday lives, such as their towns or places of work. Wood recounts a Chinese philosopher who not only emphasised this distinction but defended it. Eagle-eyed readers may recognise the ancient saying from the beginning of the first chapter:

> Why then should you think . . . that someone who is carrying on the government of a kingdom has time also to till the soil? The truth is, that some kinds of business are proper to the great and others to the small. Even supposing each man could unite in himself all the various kinds of skill required in every craft, if he had to make for himself everything that he used, this would merely lead to everyone being completely prostrate with fatigue. True indeed is the saying, 'Some work with their minds, others with their bodies. Those who work with their minds rule, while those who work with their bodies are ruled. Those who are ruled produce food; those who rule are fed!'[6]

The famous Greek philosopher Plato agreed. He did not believe that the ruled had a right to participate in their own ruling, at least to any major extent. Much to his chagrin, though, there was a widespread culture of *demos* in Ancient Greece. Although their society, as with all ancient societies, was marred by the existence of slavery, full citizens tended to enjoy economic lives free from the tyranny of the state, but also free from the buffeting forces of the market economy that we saw in Chapters 1 and 4. Ancient Greece had a sea of small producers – farmers, artisans, merchants – who generally worked for themselves, absent the huge corporate entities and billionaires who dominate our economy from Chapter 2. Plato argued with his contemporary Protagoras about whether 'blacksmiths and shoemakers' should be allowed to contribute to general assemblies, expressing irritation at their lack of expertise, while Protagoras insisted their knowledge was invaluable.

Wood contrasts *demos* with modern ideas about democracy. Liberal democracy is generally of the representative variety: there is a state which is run by politicians and policymakers who make the decisions, though elected by the people. This is called the idea of 'we, the people' because it creates a separation between the people and the state while allowing the former to act through the latter. Although it has its roots in Ancient Rome, its most notable modern explication is in the US Constitution.[7] Far from being a unifying democratic rallying call, this notion was criticised at the time of its inception for assuming democratic power could be placed in a federal government set above the citizenry.

One of the features of 'we, the people' is that the economy is often considered to be a distinct sphere with its own rules, separate from politics. The process that unfurled in sixteenth-century England has taken on a life of its own, exposing everybody across the world to the trials and tribulations of surviving through the market. It has gone further, though: it has captured our politics. Even if the economy is something of a mysterious entity, we have bought into this idea tenfold. We have turned it into an unchangeable leviathan, issuing edicts to 'leave it alone', often translated to the French *laissez-faire*. Notions of *laissez-faire* or keeping markets free are precisely edicts for the state not to interfere with the economy.

As we have seen time and time again, the notion of a separate economy has always been a fantasy. Politics, the law and society interact with the economy in a multitude of ways and making these ways explicit is the first step to changing them for the better. Intellectual property laws were only invented in the nineteenth century; today they have been expanded and strengthened until they have reshaped the internet to funnel money upwards – and seemingly ruin our experience in the process. Every country in the world has a slightly different approach to managing land and housing, such that it's a stretch to think of the Anglo-centred housing bubbles of the 2000s as simply the natural path of the economy. It is even more absurd to think of West Africa's dependence on the CFA Franc, which is an obvious legacy of colonial rule, as separate from politics.

Everything I've said in this book has been, at its root, a call to move away from 'we, the people' and towards a revival of *demos*. Whether through the increased presence of the public in economic decisions highlighted in Chapters 1, 2 and 7; distributing resources in a more equal manner in Chapters 1 to 4, and 6; giving people control over their land and housing in Chapter 5; or giving every country in the world an equal footing in international institutions in Chapters 4, 6 and 8 – the aim is to bring every facet of the economy under democratic control.

I'm confident in saying that democratic participation is both an intrinsic good and that it usually improves results by better utilising everyone's know-how, especially for those not previously allowed to voice their concerns. One way to make people more grateful and productive is not by threatening them with unemployment but by bringing them into the fold. The political problem of who gets a say is not so distinct from the economic problem of who gets what, since the former, in large part, determines the latter.

GOVERNING THE ECONOMY

The illusion of the economy as a separate sphere may allow those extracting wealth to get away with it. Probably the best example of this is that exemplar of modern capitalism: the corporation. As noted in Chapter 1, the modern corporation is itself a legally granted monopoly and its purpose has changed over time. In fact, the first corporations were more like public projects, rather than the for-profit entities we know and love. Economists Nathan Tankus and Luke Herrine summarise how the corporation has changed over time:[8]

> Before the nineteenth century, incorporation was a highly specific legal privilege, used either for major infrastructure investments (such as mills, roads, or bridges) or for extending networks of global trade and colonialism. In either case, corporations were conceptualized as express public grants of coordination rights – indeed, of monopoly power – over some domain of the social provisioning process. Although they could be (and often were) renewed, these grants were restricted in time, place, and purpose and the corporate form was itself designed as a political institution that accorded to aristocratic republican principles of good governance.

How corporations are run still varies massively across the world today. Economist Ha-Joon Chang notes that when the Swedish car company Volvo set up in South Korea, they were unable to operate because, like German firms, they were used to having strong unions and workers present on the boards. Their way of producing cars happened to include workers in the decision process, whereas a company like Daewoo was much more capital-oriented owing to South Korea's capital-friendly history. Following the 1997 Asian Financial Crisis, Volvo took over a construction arm of Samsung, which has a strict no union policy. Volvo were forced to *ask* the works to unionise so that they could function as usual![9]

One of the first steps to governing the economy using *demos* may be to move towards these more democratic forms of ownership. In recent years, awareness has spread of the idea of a 'cooperative' which is owned by consumers, workers, communities – or some combination of the three. We've already seen credit cooperatives and housing cooperatives in Chapter 5. Cooperatives are not a new idea – they date back at least to the nineteenth century – but they are fast-growing today. Rather than placing the control of companies in the hands of very few people, they try to balance control by giving these groups a vote in the running of the company, including how its resources are managed.

John Logue and Jacquelin Yates, two well-known experts on employee ownership, explained the rationale behind these organisations:[10]

> As democratic member- or worker-controlled enterprises, they try to balance diverse goals such as job and income security, democratic control and participation, safety and health at the work place, profit sharing and patronage dividends, and concern for their communities. The conventional definition of productivity as 'value added per worker' is therefore not fully satisfactory when we examine it in the context of employee-owned firms and cooperatives, because these organizations typically deliver

a combination of economic and social returns to their member-owners and the community at large.

Those in favour of shareholder or owner-run companies might fear that cooperatives are not dynamic and sharp enough to produce the goods and services we all rely on. This fear is almost certainly misplaced. With worker cooperatives, for example, it is difficult to find evidence that they fare any worse on hard metrics like productivity, output and firm survival. For things like job satisfaction, staff retention and pay equality, they appear to do better.[11] One especially interesting study found that giving workers *both* ownership (through shares) *and* control (through votes) paid off in terms of retaining workers while not hurting the company's returns. Workers participated much more in the day-to-day running of the company and everyone seemed better off for it.[12]

Governing a better economy means ensuring that everybody has what they need to continue functioning. This applies to basic requirements like food, shelter and clothing, but it also applies more broadly. The entire economy needs to be reproduced, which means thinking about the rules that govern not just corporations but markets themselves. Consider another flagship of modern capitalism: financial markets. In commodities exchanges, people buy and sell massive quantities of goods like wheat and gold at astonishing frequencies. They also buy and sell derivatives: bets on which way the price of the commodities will move. Yet underneath this flurry of financial activity lie clear restrictions, not least of which is that they have to trade through the exchange itself. The exchange is an organised market which is licenced and regulated in a fixed location, outside of which you cannot legally trade commodities.[13]

Even once confined to a fixed location and with clear opening hours, the exchange must be internally governed. Given the inevitable volatility of financial markets, there is the ever-present threat of crashes. For this reason, if prices drop too far then a 'circuit breaker' is activated and the exchange just ceases trading. Even outside of crashes, many trades are governed by stable prices and norms which allow planning to take place. Ensuring volatile prices do not cause massive headaches for all involved is a key issue for market governance. Breaching these kinds of rules inhibits trading itself and even when legal, is deemed a significant problem and is clamped down upon. The market is constructed by the very rules that govern it: it wouldn't work in anything like a recognisable form without these restrictions.[14]

I opened this book by discussing how formative the 2007–9 financial crisis was for me. One of the key political debates that emerged following the crisis was over banks and financial markets: how much we should tax them; how much we should regulate them; whether we should take more drastic steps like nationalising them. While I am not going to stake out a position in this debate, what I object to is the common refrain that changing or regulating the banks would inevitably lead to doom. Aside from the numerous privileges that banks receive – government bailouts, central bank support, limited liability – the commodities exchange shows that there are always rules of the game. The financial sector has adjusted to new rules in the past and it can do so in the future.

At the same time, I would not want you to go away thinking that all economic rules are arbitrary and anything goes. The emergence of capitalism and the market economy is a historically unique and curious phenomenon, and managing it is not at all easy. Out of all the ideas we can have for governing the economy, most of them probably won't work. Perhaps the future will be one that moves away from markets and capitalism entirely, but doing so requires taking things one step at a time. This doesn't mean the steps themselves have to be small, but it does mean that we have to be clear and specific about them. Notions of abolishing the system make good rallying calls, but they need to be translated into concrete proposals for a better future.

GETTING INVOLVED

There are numerous ways to get involved in *demos*. One of the first is by reading books like this so congratulations – step one is already done! You may also want to get involved in whichever causes are practical and important to you. An idea which has emerged in recent years is community wealth building, which pulls together many of the proposals discussed in this book: cooperatives, essential services, communal approaches to land and housing. Just googling it may help you find something in your area. Whether you end up doing something big or small, the fact remains that if everybody reading this became more active, it would make a huge difference. As I am writing this, I have finally resolved to get involved and volunteer at a local credit cooperative.

Building this future is not an easy or simple process. Every gain has to be fought for, from Amazon workers striking to denizens of the Amazon rainforest resisting deforestation. New policies brought forward by politicians such as the cost-of-living measures taken in Continental Europe that we saw in Chapter 7, or the 'onshoring' investments made in the USA and East Asia that we saw in Chapter 8, may be imperfect, but they will contribute to the shift in how we approach economics.

People like Andrew Haldane, who called for more democratic participation at the Bank of England when he worked there, are fighting that battle on a different front,[15] as are academics who work to decolonise and diversify their disciplines.[16] My hope is that this book will contribute in some small measure.

However, it is my feeling that writers often overestimate the importance of writing. For instance, the economist John Maynard Keynes once famously wrote that:

> The ideas of economists and political philosophers, both when they are right and when they are wrong, are more powerful than is commonly understood. Indeed, the world is ruled by little else.

Keynes was both right and wrong. Ideas are important and people need them to make change. It is a common trope for those who complain about the existing system to be asked if we have solutions; I feel this book has them in abundance thanks to the countless scholars and activists I have drawn from. Nevertheless, the history of the twentieth century shows that you need more than just a good idea. Vested interests are unlikely to surrender economic power to the people without a fight. When the people gain, these interests will wax lyrical about threats to the existing economic order. It is up to us not to listen.

ENDNOTES

INTRODUCTION: A GOOD TIME TO STUDY ECONOMICS

1 Office for National Statistics (ONS), released 31 January 2023, ONS website, statistical bulletin, UK government debt and deficit: September 2023.

2 Marmot, Michael. 'Britain's shorter children reveal a grim story about austerity, but its scars run far deeper,' *Guardian*, 25 June 2023. https://www.theguardian.com/commentisfree/2023/jun/25/britains-shorter-children-reveal-a-grim-story-about-austerity-but-its-scars-run-far-deeper.

3 Blenkov, Adam. 'Austerity is a False Economy that has Brought the Nation's Roof Crumbling Down,' *Byline Times,* 5 September 2023. https://bylinetimes.com/2023/09/05/austerity-is-a-false-economy-that-has-brought-the-nations-roof-crumbling-down/.

4 Jump, Rob Calvert, Jo Michell, James Meadway and Natassia Nascimento. 'The Macroeconomics of Austerity,' *Macroeconomics* (2023).

5 Tooze, Adam. *Crashed: How a decade of financial crises changed the world.* Penguin, 2018, 360–93.

6 'Revenge of the "PIGS": Spain and the southern countries are pulling the eurozone cart in the face of stagnation in Germany and France,' *20minutos.com,* 1 January 2024. https://www.20minutos.es/lainformacion/economia/-revancha-los-pigs-

espana-los-paises-sur-tiran-carro-eurozona-frente-estancamiento-alemania-francia-5213879/.

7   Williams, David and Henry Oks. 'The Long, Slow Death of Global Development,' *American Affairs Journal*, 20 November 2022. https://americanaffairsjournal.org/2022/11/the-long-slow-death-of-global-development/.

8   Coi, Giovanni. 'Mapped: Europe's rapidly rising right,' *Politico*, 24 May 2024. https://www.politico.eu/article/mapped-europe-far-right-government-power-politics-eu-italy-finalnd-hungary-parties-elections-polling/?

9   Beauchamp, Zach. 'Biden's America First hangover,' *Vox*, 1 May 2021. https://www.vox.com/policy-and-politics/22408089/biden-trump-america-first-policy-immigration-vaccines.

10 Malik, Shiv. 'Peter Mandelson gets nervous about people getting "filthy rich",' *Guardian*, 26 January 2012. https://www.theguardian.com/politics/2012/jan/26/mandelson-people-getting-filthy-rich.

11 The Post-Crash Economics Society. 'Economics, Education and Unlearning: Economics Education at the University of Manchester,' April 2014. http://post-crasheconomics.com/wp-content/uploads/2024/05/Economics-Unlearning-and-Education-2014.pdf.

12 Examples include:
    Smith, Yves. *ECONned: How unenlightened self interest undermined democracy and corrupted capitalism*. St Martin's Press, 2011.
    Orrell, David. *Economyths: ten ways economics gets it wrong*. John Wiley & Sons, 2010.
    Lanchester, John. *Whoops!: Why everyone owes everyone and no one can pay*. Penguin UK, 2010.
    Keen, Steve. *Debunking economics: The naked emperor dethroned?*. Zed Books Ltd, 2011.
    Aldred, Jonathan. *The skeptical economist: revealing the ethics inside economics*. Routledge, 2012.

Chang, Ha-Joon. *23 things they don't tell you about capitalism.* Bloomsbury Publishing USA, 2012.

13 Dubner, Stephen J. 'The probability that a real-estate agent is cheating you (and other riddles of modern life),' *New York Times Magazine* 23 (2003).

14 The Post-Crash Economics Society. 'Is Economics Education Fit For The 21st Century?,' May 2024. https://www.rethinkeconomics.org/wp-content/uploads/2024/05/PCES-Report-2024-3.pdf.

15 Lee, Hoesung, Katherine Calvin, Dipak Dasgupta, Gerhard Krinner, Aditi Mukherji, Peter Thorne, Christopher Trisos et al. 'IPCC, 2023: Climate Change 2023: Synthesis Report, Summary for Policymakers. Contribution of Working Groups I, II and III to the Sixth Assessment Report of the Intergovernmental Panel on Climate Change [Core Writing Team, H. Lee and J. Romero (eds.)]. IPCC, Geneva, Switzerland.' (2023): 1–34.

16 Al-Jubari, Ibrahim, Aissa Mosbah and Suha Fouad Salem. 'Employee well-being during COVID-19 pandemic: The role of adaptability, work-family conflict, and organisational response,' *Sage Open* 12, no. 3 (2022): 21582440221096142.

17 Kesar, Surbhi, Rosa Abraham, Rahul Lahoti, Paaritosh Nath and Amit Basole. 'Pandemic, informality, and vulnerability: Impact of COVID-19 on livelihoods in India.' *Canadian Journal of Development Studies/Revue canadienne d'études du développement* 42, no. 1–2 (2021): 145–64.

18 Estimates obtained from: https://pip.worldbank.org/poverty-calculator.

19 Behnassi, Mohamed, and Mahjoub El Haiba. 2022. 'Implications of the Russia–Ukraine War for Global Food Security.' *Nature Human Behaviour* 6 (754–755): 1–2. https://doi.org/10.1038/s41562-022-01391-x.'

20 Niarchos, Nicholas, 'The Dark Side of Congo's Cobalt Rush', *The New Yorker*, 24 May 2021. https://www.newyorker.com/magazine/2021/05/31/the-dark-side-of-congos-cobalt-rush'.

21 Wallace-Wells, David. *The uninhabitable earth: A story of the future.* Penguin UK, 2019, 125.

22 IPPR Environmental Justice Commission. 'Faster, further, fairer: Putting people at the heart of tackling the climate and nature emergency.' (2020).

23 Saloni Dattani, Fiona Spooner, Hannah Ritchie and Max Roser (2023) – 'Child and Infant Mortality.' Published online at OurWorldInData.org. Retrieved from: 'https://ourworldindata.org/child-mortality' [Online Resource].

24 Scanlon, Kyla. *In This Economy?: How Money & Markets Really Work.* Crown Currency, 2024.

25 'Record Numbers Not Working due to Ill Health.' *BBC Business*, 16 May 2023. https://www.bbc.co.uk/news/business-65596283.

26 'Tory MP Dismisses Disabled Woman Live on TV as She Tells Him "People Are Dying".' *Independent* 29 May 2017. https://www.independent.co.uk/news/uk/home-news/disabled-disablility-dominic-raab-dying-conservative-fiona-victoria-derbyshire-a7761291.html.

27 'Revealed: The Hidden Personal Cost of UK Long-Term Sickness That Cries out for a New National Health Mission.' *IPPR*, 27 April 2023. https://www.ippr.org/news-and-media/press-releases/revealed-the-hidden-personal-cost-of-uk-long-term-sickness-that-cries-out-for-a-new-national-health-mission.

28 'Investing in Treatment for Depression and Anxiety Leads to Fourfold Return.' www.who.int. 13 April 2016. https://www.who.int/news/item/13-04-2016-investing-in-treatment-for-depression-and-anxiety-leads-to-fourfold-return.

29 Marmot, Michael. 'Health Equity in England: The Marmot Review 10 Years On.' *The Health Foundation* 2020. https://www.health.org.uk/publications/reports/the-marmot-review-10-years-on.

30 Binagwaho, Agnes, Paul E. Farmer, Sabin Nsanzimana, Corine Karema, Michel Gasana, Jean de Dieu Ngirabega, Fidele Ngabo, et al. 2014. 'Rwanda 20 Years On: Investing in Life.'

The Lancet 384 (9940): 371–75. https://doi.org/10.1016/
s0140-6736(14)60574-2.

31 Race, Michael and Sri-Pathma. 'Bank of England economist
says people need to accept they are poorer,' *BBC News,*
26 April 2023. https://www.bbc.co.uk/news/business-
65308769.

32 A good example of the extreme view is Sowell, Thomas. *Basic
economics*. Basic Books, 2014.

CHAPTER 1: WHO IS ESSENTIAL TO THE ECONOMY?

1 Wood, Ellen Meiksins. *Democracy against capitalism;
Renewing historical materialism*. Verso, 2007, 189.

2 Wood, Ellen Meiksins. *The origin of capitalism: A longer view*.
Verso, 2002, 44–46.

3 Varoufakis, Yanis. *Talking to My Daughter about the
Economy: A Brief History of Capitalism*. The Bodley Head,
London, 2017, 19–21.

4 *ibid*, 17–20.

5 Wood, Ellen Meiksins. *The origin of capitalism: A longer view*.
Verso, 2002, 95–105.

6 *ibid*, 98–99.

7 *ibid*, 100–103.

8 *ibid*, 103–105.

9 Varoufakis, Yanis. *Talking to My Daughter about the
Economy: A Brief History of Capitalism*. The Bodley Head,
London 2017, 34–36.

10 Perelman, Michael. *The invention of capitalism: Classical
political economy and the secret history of primitive
accumulation*. Duke University Press, 2000, 43–45.

11 Findlay, Ronald and Kevin H. O'Rourke. *Power and Plenty:
Trade, War, and the World Economy in the Second Millennium*.
Princeton University Press 2007, 106–108.

12 Graeber, David. 'Games With Sex and Death'. In *Debt: The First 5000 years*. Penguin UK, 2012.

13 Polanyi, Karl. *Origins of Our Time: The Great Transformation.* Gollancz, London 1945.

14 Graeber, David. *Debt: The First 5000 years*. Penguin UK, 2012, 351.

15 Chaker, Annie. 'The New Trick to Getting Work Done: Have a Stranger Watch,' *Wall Street Journal,* July 2023. https://www.wsj.com/articles/need-to-quit-procrastinating-hire-a-body-double-ebdeefc8?mod=life_work_featured_strip_pos1.

16 Zimmermann, Christian. 'What Makes an Economy Grow? | FRED Blog.', FRED, n.d., https://fredblog.stlouisfed.org/2017/12/what-makes-an-economy-grow/.

17 Khaldun, Ibn, Franz Rosenthal, N. J. Dawood and Bruce Lawrence. *The Muqaddimah: An Introduction to History.* Princeton University Press, 2015, 273.

18 Smith, Adam. 'Of the Division of Labour.' In *The Wealth of Nations*. W. Strahan and T. Cadell, London 1776.

19 Styles, John. 2021. 'The Rise and Fall of the Spinning Jenny: Domestic Mechanisation in Eighteenth-Century Cotton Spinning.' *Textile History* 51 (2): 1–42. https://doi.org/10.1080/00404969.2020.1812472.

20 Marx, Karl. 'Chapter IV: The General Formula for Capital.' 1883. www.marxists.org. https://www.marxists.org/archive/deville/1883/peoples-marx/ch04.htm.

21 Engels, Friedrich. 2009. *The Condition of the Working Class in England*. Edited by David McLellan. Oxford World's Classics. London, England: Oxford University Press, 2.

22 Mazzucato, Mariana. *The value of everything: Making and taking in the global economy*. Hachette UK, 2018, 10, 66–68.

23 Engels, Friedrich and Karl Marx. *The communist manifesto*. Penguin UK, 2004, 222.

24 Rousseau, Jean-Jacques. *A discourse upon the origin and foundation of the inequality among Mankind*. R. and J. Dodsley, 1761, 55.

25 Smith, Adam. *The Wealth of Nations*. W. Strahan and T. Cadell, London 1776, 27.

26 Mazzucato, Mariana. *The value of everything: Making and taking in the global economy*. Hachette UK, 2018, 35-40.

27 George, Henry. Progress and Poverty: *An Inquiry into the Cause of Industrial Depressions and of Increase of Want . . . With Increase of Wealth . . . The Remedy*. Dover Publications, 1879.

28 Pistor, Katharina. *The code of capital: How the law creates wealth and inequality*. Princeton University Press, 2019.

29 *ibid*, 11. It's not that being a capitalist is always better for the individual. As a self-employed person, I've personally seen the sacrifices that you have to make in terms of stability and benefits. Pistor's point is instead about how legal coding creates capitalism itself.

30 Marglin, Stephen A. 'What do bosses do?: The origins and functions of hierarchy in capitalist production.' In *Radical Political Economy*, Routledge, 2015, 19–59.

31 Ciepley, David. 'Beyond public and private: Toward a political theory of the corporation.' *American Political Science Review* 107, no. 1 (2013): 139–58.

32 Chang, Ha-Joon. 'Spices.' In *Edible Economics: A Hungry Economist Explains the World*. Penguin Books, 2023.

33 *ibid*.

34 Davis, Mike. *Late Victorian holocausts: El Niño famines and the making of the third world*. Verso Books, 2002.

35 Varoufakis, Yanis. 'Yanis Varoufakis on the Death of Capitalism, Starmer and the Tyranny of Big Tech.' *YouTube*, 29 September 2023. https://www.youtube.com/watch?v=Q9lJQONTC7Y.

36 Naidu, Suresh. 'A political economy take on W/Y.' In *After Piketty: The agenda for economics and inequality*. Harvard University Press, 2017.

37 'England defender Harry Maguire mocked in Ghanaian parliament,' *The Independent*, 1 December 2022. https://

www.independent.co.uk/sport/football/world-cup/harry-maguire-ghana-parliament-b2237040.html.

38 'List of most expensive association football transfers,' *Wikipedia* https://en.wikipedia.org/wiki/List_of_most_expensive_association_football_transfers.

39 'Explaining the Bundesliga's 50+1 rule,' *Bundesliga.com*. https://www.bundesliga.com/en/faq/what-are-the-rules-and-regulations-of-soccer/50-1-fifty-plus-one-german-football-soccer-rule-explained-ownership-22832.

40 *ibid*.

41 Kampfner, John. *Why the Germans Do It Better: Notes from a Grown-Up Country*. Atlantic Books, 2020.

42 *ibid*, 171.

43 Jäger, Simon, Shakked Noy and Benjamin Schoefer. 'The German model of industrial relations: balancing flexibility and collective action.' *Journal of Economic Perspectives* 36, no. 4 (2022): 53–80.

44 Ryan-Collins, Josh, Laurie Macfarlane, John Muellbauer, with the New Economics Foundation. *Rethinking the Economics of Land and Housing*. Zed Books Ltd, 2017, 215–16.

45 Harju, Jarkko, Simon Jäger and Benjamin Schoefer. 'Voice at work. No. w28522.' National Bureau of Economic Research, 2021.

46 Tooze, Adam. *Crashed: How a Decade of Financial Crises Changed the World*. Penguin Books, 2018, 84–85.

47 Kampfner, John. *Why the Germans Do It Better: Notes from a Grown-Up Country*. Atlantic Books, 2020, 19.

48 Mazzucato, Mariana. 'Preface.' In *The value of everything: Making and taking in the global economy*. Hachette UK, 2018.

49 *ibid*.

50 'Review of Ipsos Veracity Index 2022.' *Ipsos*, 23 November 2022.

51 Oliphant, J. Baxter. 'Top Tax Frustrations for Americans: The Feeling That Some Corporations, Wealthy People Don't Pay

Fair Share.' Pew Research Center. 7 April 2023. https://www. pewresearch.org/short-reads/2023/04/07/top-tax-frustrations-for-americans-the-feeling-that-some-corporations-wealthy-people-dont-pay-fair-share/.

52 Blau, Francine D., Josefine Koebe and Pamela A. Meyerhofer. 2021. 'Who Are the Essential and Frontline Workers?' *Business Economics* 56 (3) 168–78. https://doi.org/10.1057/ s11369-021-00230-7.

53 Xue, Baowen and Anne McMunn. 'Working and caring during UK lockdown: who bears the brunt?' *World Economic Forum,* May 2021. https://www.weforum.org/agenda/2021/05/ women-working-caring-uk-lockdown/.

54 Guizzo, Danielle and Andrew Mearman. 'Adam Smith today: re-productive labour.' *Economics Network,* February 2024. https://economicsnetwork.ac.uk/showcase/guizzo_mearman_smith.

CHAPTER 2: WHY ARE THERE SO MANY BILLIONAIRES?

1 LaFranco, Rob, Grace Chung, Chase Peterson-Withorn. 'Forbes World's Billionaires List. The Richest In 2024.' *Forbes.* 2024. https://www.forbes.com/billionaires/.

2 Source: author's own calculations. Using the ONS website, inflation was 229% in total from February 1991 to February 2024. $582bn * 2.29 = $1.33 tn, which is less than one-tenth of $14 tn. https://www.ons.gov.uk/economy/inflationand priceindices/timeseries/l522/mm23.

3 Martin, Devin-Sean. 'The Countries With The Most Billionaires 2024.' *Forbes.* 2024. https://www.forbes.com/sites/devinsean martin/2024/04/02/the-countries-with-the-most-billionaires-2024/?sh=6158605c54f8.

4 Matza, Max. 'Jeff Bezos and the secretive world of superyachts.' *BBC News,* May 2021. https://www.bbc.co.uk/news/world-us-canada-57079327.

5   Noah, Trevor. 'Elon Musk's Billionaire Games – between the Scenes | the Daily Show.' *YouTube*, 2022. https://www.youtube.com/watch?v=Gqlbn2nPO-A.

6   Kuper, Simon. 'I'm bullish about France, but few agree,' *Financial Times*, 27 June 2024. https://www.ft.com/content/479d815d-167b-4717-a079-476f1af46e88.

7   'Master of the Brand: Bernard Arnault.' *Forbes*. 16 July 2012. https://www.forbes.com/forbes/2010/1122/fashion-bernard-arnault-lvmh-luxury-dior-master-of-brand.html?sh=664457ae62ea.

8   Vance, Ashlee. *Elon Musk: How the billionaire CEO of SpaceX and Tesla is shaping our future*. Random House, 2015, 85–90.

9   Kenton, Luke. 'Tesla's Actual Creators Speak about "Complicated" Elon Musk.' *Mail Online*. 8 February 2021. https://www.dailymail.co.uk/news/article-9238037/Teslas-actual-creators-hit-Elon-Musk-eccentric-billionaire-complicated.html.

10   Hawkins, Andrew. 'How Elon Musk took over Tesla using money, strong-arm tactics, and his own popularity,' *The Verge*. 2 August 2023. https://www.theverge.com/23815634/tesla-elon-musk-origin-founder-twitter-land-of-the-giants.

11   Vance, Ashlee. *Elon Musk: How the billionaire CEO of SpaceX and Tesla is shaping our future*. Random House, 2015, 270.

12   Solca, Luca. 'How LVMH Dominates the Luxury Business.' *The Business of Fashion*, 27 July 2022. https://www.businessoffashion.com/opinions/luxury/how-lvmh-dominates-the-luxury-business/.

13   Khan, Lina M. 'Amazon's anti-trust paradox.' *Yale Law Journal*, 2017: 710–805.

14   Buckham, David, Robyn Wilkinson and Christiaan Straeuli. 'The Industrialists.' Essay. In *Unequal: How Extreme Inequality Is Damaging Democracy, and What We Can Do about It*. Mercury, an imprint of Burnet Media, South Africa 2023, 84–88.

15 Buckham, David, Robyn Wilkinson and Christiaan Straeuli. 'Standard Oil and the Sherman Anti-Trust Act.' Essay. In *Unequal: How Extreme Inequality Is Damaging Democracy, and What We Can Do about It.* Mercury, an imprint of Burnet Media, South Africa 2023, 89–94.

16 Khan, Lina M. 'Amazon's anti-trust paradox.' *Yale Law Journal*, 2017: 710–805.

17 *ibid.*

18 Buckham, David, Robyn Wilkinson and Christiaan Straeuli. 'Amazon.com.' Essay. In *Unequal: How Extreme Inequality Is Damaging Democracy, and What We Can Do about It.* Mercury, an imprint of Burnet Media, South Africa 2023, 33–35.

19 Khan, Lina M. 'Amazon's anti-trust paradox.' *Yale Law Journal*, 2017: 710–805.

20 Clayton, James. 'Europe Agrees New Law to Curb Big Tech Dominance.' *BBC News*, 25 March 2022. https://www.bbc.co.uk/news/technology-60870287.

21 Song, Victoria. 'US v. Apple: everything you need to know.' *The Verge,* 2 May 2024. https://www.theverge.com/24107581/doj-v-apple-anti-trust-monoply-news-updates.

22 You can find the letter itself, as well as an overview of the ensuing debate, on Wikipedia: https://en.wikipedia.org/wiki/An_Open_Letter_to_Hobbyists.

23 Baker, Dean. 'Chapter 9 Is Intellectual Property The Root Of All Evil? Patents, Copyrights, And Inequality.' In *The Great Polarization: How Ideas, Power, and Policies Drive Inequality.* Columbia University Press 2022, 275–96.

24 'Ed Sheeran Wins Thinking out Loud Copyright Case.' *BBC News*, 4 May 2023. https://www.bbc.co.uk/news/entertainment-arts-65480293.

25 Baker, Dean. 'Chapter 9 Is Intellectual Property The Root Of All Evil? Patents, Copyrights, And Inequality.' In *The Great Polarization: How Ideas, Power, and Policies Drive Inequality.* Columbia University Press 2022, 275–96.

26 'Disney Refuses Grieving Father's Request to Put Spider-Man on Son's Tombstone.' *The Independent*, 5 July 2019. https://www.independent.co.uk/news/uk/home-news/spider-man-tombstone-marvel-disney-kent-ollie-jones-superhero-a8988336.html.

27 Brodkin, John. 'Bill Gates Still Helping Known Patent Trolls Obtain More Patents.' *Ars Technica*, 14 August 2013. https://arstechnica.com/tech-policy/2013/08/bill-gates-still-helping-known-patent-trolls-obtain-more-patents/.

28 Baker, Dean. *Rigged: How Globalization and the Rules of the Modern Economy Were Structured to Make the Rich Richer.* Center for Economic and Policy Research, Washington, DC, 2016, 86.

29 Baker, Dean. 'Chapter 9 Is Intellectual Property The Root Of All Evil? Patents, Copyrights, And Inequality.' In *The Great Polarization: How Ideas, Power, and Policies Drive Inequality.* Columbia University Press 2022, 275–96.

30 'Steve Jobs Pissed off by Faulty Camera.' *YouTube*, 15 January 2016. https://www.youtube.com/watch?v=1M4t14s7nSM#.

31 Guth, Robert A. 'Raising Bill Gates.' *Wall Street Journal*, 25 April 2009. https://www.wsj.com/articles/SB124061372413054653.

32 Goodin, Dan. 'Revisiting the Spectacular Failure That Was the Bill Gates Deposition.' *Ars Technica*, 10 September 2020. https://arstechnica.com/tech-policy/2020/09/revisiting-the-spectacular-failure-that-was-the-bill-gates-deposition/.

33 Battelle, John. 'Ballmer Throws A Chair At "F*ing Google",' *Searchblog.* September 2005. https://battellemedia.com/archives/2005/09/ballmer_throws_a_chair_at_fing_google.

34 'Steve Jobs Was 'Super Rude' to Elon Musk.' *YouTube*, 1 October 2018. https://www.youtube.com/watch?v=voBpeN9t7Nw&amp.

35 Mann, Mark. 'The Story of Elon Musk's First Company.' *Site Builder Report.* Accessed 9 October 2023. https://www.sitebuilderreport.com/origin-stories/elon-musk.

36 Tabahriti, Sam. 'Elon Musk Would Get 'Really Angry'
    When Employees at His First Company Zip2 Weren't Still
    Working at 9 o'clock at Night, an Ex-Colleague Told a BBC
    Documentary.' *Business Insider*, 13 October 2022. https://
    www.businessinsider.com/musk-really-angry-zip2-employees-
    not-working-after-9-pm-2022-10?op=1&r=US&
    amp;IR=T.

37 Ohnsman, Alan. 'Inside Tesla's Model 3 Factory, Where Safety
    Violations Keep Rising.' *Forbes*, 30 April 2019. https://www.
    forbes.com/sites/alanohnsman/2019/03/01/tesla-safety-
    violations-dwarf-big-us-auto-plants-in-aftermath-of-musks-
    model-3-push/?sh=c67e87d54ceb.

38 Chokshi, Niraj. 'California Sues Tesla, Saying the Company
    Permitted Racial Discrimination at Its Factory.' *New York
    Times*, 10 February 2022. https://www.nytimes.com/2022/02/
    10/technology/tesla-racial-discrimination-california-suit.html.

39 Siddiqui, Faiz. 'Six Tesla Workers File Additional Lawsuits
    Alleging Sexual Harassment.' *Washington Post*, 14 December
    2021. https://www.washingtonpost.com/technology/2021/
    12/14/tesla-sexual-harassment/.

40 McHugh, Rich. 'A SpaceX Flight Attendant Said Elon Musk
    Exposed Himself and Propositioned Her for Sex, Documents
    Show. The Company Paid $250,000 for Her Silence.' *Business
    Insider*, 19 May 2022. https://www.businessinsider.com/
    spacex-paid-250000-to-a-flight-attendant-who-accused-elon-
    musk-of-sexual-misconduct-2022-5?op=1&r=US&
    amp;IR=T.

41 Smith, Adam. *The Wealth of Nations*. W. Strahan and
    T. Cadell, London 1776, 409.

42 Bloodworth, James. 'Constantly Monitored, Searched and
    Exhausted – My Month Undercover in an Amazon Warehouse.'
    The Times, 10 February 2018. https://www.thetimes.co.uk/
    article/constantly-monitored-searched-and-exhausted-
    my-month-undercover-in-an-amazon-warehouse-
    xvgmlh39r.

43 Chan, Jenny, Greg Distelhorst, Dimitri Kessler, Joonkoo Lee, Olga Martin-Ortega, Peter Pawlicki, Mark Selden and Benjamin Selwyn. 'After the Foxconn suicides in China: a roundtable on labor, the state and civil society in global electronics.' *Critical Sociology* 48, no. 2 (2022): 211–33.

44 Sandoval, Marisol. 'Foxconned labour as the dark side of the information age: Working conditions at Apple's contract manufacturers in China.' *TripleC: Communication, Capitalism & Critique* 11, no. 2 (2013): 318–47.

45 'Conflict in the Democratic Republic of Congo', *Global Conflict Tracker,* updated 21 February 2024. https://www.cfr. org/global-conflict-tracker/conflict/violence-democratic-republic-congo.

46 Niarchos, Nicholas, 'The Dark Side of Congo's Cobalt Rush', *The New Yorker,* 24 May 2021. https://www.newyorker.com/ magazine/2021/05/31/the-dark-side-of-congos-cobalt-rush.

47 Sandoval, Marisol. 'Foxconned labour as the dark side of the information age: Working conditions at Apple's contract manufacturers in China.' *TripleC: Communication, Capitalism & Critique* 11, no. 2 (2013): 318–47.

48 Buyya, Rajkumar, Shashikant Ilager and Patricia Arroba. 'Energy-efficiency and sustainability in new generation cloud computing: A vision and directions for integrated management of data centre resources and workloads.' *Software: Practice and Experience* 54, no. 1 (2024): 24–38.

49 Smith, John. 'The GDP illusion.' *Monthly Review* 64, no. 3 (2012): 86–102.

50 O'Connor, Sarah. 'Amazon Unpacked.' *Financial Times*, 8 February 2013. https://www.ft.com/content/ed6a985c-70bd-11e2-85d0-00144feab49a.

51 Childs, Simon. 'Wrexham Fans, Decide: How Do You like Your Football – Dignified or Disneyfied?' *Guardian*, 20 September 2023. https://www.theguardian.com/commentisfree/2023/ sep/20/wrexham-football-disney-hollywood-clubs.

52 Belluz, Julia. 2015. 'The Media Loves the Gates Foundation. These Experts Are More Skeptical.' *Vox*, 10 June 2015. https://www.vox.com/2015/6/10/8760199/gates-foundation-criticism.

53 Gates, Bill. 'The next Outbreak? We're Not Ready | TED.' *YouTube*, 2015. https://www.youtube.com/watch?v=6Af6b_wyiwI.

54 Mookim, Mohit. 'The World Loses Under Bill Gates' Vaccine Colonialism,' *Wired*. 19 May 2021. https://www.wired.com/story/opinion-the-world-loses-under-bill-gates-vaccine-colonialism/.

55 Bajaj, Simar Singh, Lwando Maki and Fatima Cody Stanford. 'Vaccine Apartheid: Global Cooperation and Equity.' The Lancet 399, 10334: 1452-1453. (February 23, 2022). https://doi.org/10.1016/s0140-6736(22)00328-2.

56 Cheng, Maria, Lori Hinnant. 'Countries Urge Drug Companies to Share Vaccine Know-How.' *AP News*, 1 March 2021. https://apnews.com/article/drug-companies-called-share-vaccine-info-22d92afbc3ea9ed519be007f8887bcf6.

57 Mookim, Mohit. 'The World Loses Under Bill Gates' Vaccine Colonialism,' *Wired*. 19 May 2021. https://www.wired.com/story/opinion-the-world-loses-under-bill-gates-vaccine-colonialism/.

58 Eisinger, Jesse. 'How Mark Zuckerberg's Altruism Helps Himself.' *New York Times*, 3 December 2015. https://www.nytimes.com/2015/12/04/business/dealbook/how-mark-zuckerbergs-altruism-helps-himself.html.
Cassidy, John. 'Mark Zuckerberg and the Rise of Philanthrocapitalism,' *New Yorker,* 2 December 2015. https://www.newyorker.com/news/john-cassidy/mark-zuckerberg-and-the-rise-of-philanthrocapitalism.

59 Dorfman, Jeffrey. 'The Biggest and Best Tax Break of All Time.' *Forbes*, August 2017. https://www.forbes.com/sites/jeffreydorfman/2017/08/13/the-biggest-and-best-tax-break-of-all-time/?sh=75c303ec2b23.

60 Saez, Emmanuel and Gabriel Zucman. *How to get $1 trillion from 1000 billionaires: Tax their gains now.* University of California, Berkeley, 2021.

61 Alexander, Ella. 'Has Arnault Made Peace With Libération?,' *Vogue.* 17 September 2013. https://www.vogue.co.uk/article/bernard-arnault-drops-lawsuit-against-liberation.

62 Warrington, James. 'Bernard Arnault Tightens Grip on French Media amid Editor's "Brutal Eviction".' *Telegraph*, 24 March 2023. https://www.telegraph.co.uk/business/2023/03/24/french-journalists-uproar-claims-lvmh-founder-bernard-arnault/.

63 Lipton, Ann. 'Every Billionaire is a Policy Failure.' *Available at SSRN 4442029 (2023).*

64 Lopatto, Elizabeth. 'How the Elon Musk Biography Exposes Walter Isaacson.' *The Verge*, 1 October 2023. https://www.theverge.com/2023/10/1/23895069/walter-isaacson-biography-musk-review.

65 Grossman, Nicholas. 'The U.S. Government Can't Allow Elon Musk the Power to Intervene in Wars.' *The Daily Beast,* September 2023. https://www.thedailybeast.com/us-government-cant-allow-elon-musk-the-power-to-intervene-in-wars.

66 'Elon Musk's "Vegas Loop" Called a "Death Trap" as Traffic Piles Up.' *Independent*, 7 January 2022. https://www.independent.co.uk/tech/elon-musk-vegas-loop-traffic-b1988974.html.

67 Chafkin, Max, Sarah McBride. 'Elon Musk's Vegas Tunnel Project Has Been Racking Up Safety Violations.' *Bloomberg*, 26 February 2024. https://www.bloomberg.com/news/features/2024-02-26/elon-musk-las-vegas-loop-tunnel-has-construction-safety-issues?sref=YfHlo0rL&embedded-checkout=true.

68 Matthew, Jessica. 'There's trouble below at Elon Musk's Boring Co.,' *Fortune*, 20 November 2023. https://fortune.com/2023/11/20/elon-musk-boring-company-las-vegas-tunnels-former-employee-interviews/.

69 Hall, Dale and Nic Lutsey. 'Effects of battery manufacturing on electric vehicle life-cycle greenhouse gas emissions.' *ICCT*, February 2018.

70 Hannah Ritchie (2023) – 'Which form of transport has the smallest carbon footprint?' Published online at OurWorldInData.org. Retrieved from: 'https://ourworldindata. org/travel-carbon-footprint.

71 Holland, Stephen P., Erin T. Mansur, Nicholas Z. Muller and Andrew J. Yates. 'Distributional Effects of Air Pollution from Electric Vehicle Adoption.' *Journal of the Association of Environmental and Resource Economists,* 6 (S1): S65–94. https://doi.org/10.1086/701188.

72 Olsen, Erik. 'SpaceX Starships Keep Exploding, but It's All Part of Elon Musk's Plan.' *Popular Science*, 4 March 2021. https://www.popsci.com/story/technology/spacex-starship-explosions/.

73 Roulette, Joey. 'SpaceX Ignored Last-Minute Warnings from the FAA before December Starship Launch.' *The Verge*, 15 June 2021. https://www.theverge.com/2021/6/15/22352366/ elon-musk-spacex-faa-warnings-starship-sn8-launch-violation-texas.

74 Whittaker, Ian. 'Is SpaceX Being Environmentally Responsible?' *Smithsonian*, 7 February 2018. https://www.smithsonianmag. com/science-nature/spacex-environmentally-responsible-180968098/.

75 Wray, Dianna. 'Elon Musk's SpaceX Launch Site Threatens Wildlife, Texas Environmental Groups Say.' *Guardian.* 5 September 2021. https://www.theguardian.com/environment/ 2021/sep/05/texas-spacex-elon-musk-environment-wildlife.

76 Salazar, John. 'Coastal Texas Community Feels Pressure to Sell Homes to Elon Musk's Space X.' *Spectrum Local News,* November 2020. https://spectrumlocalnews.com/tx/austin/ news/2020/11/26/coastal-texas-community-feels-pressure-to-sell-homes-to-elon-musk-s-space-x.

77 Wolfe, Daniel. '"You Must Exit Your Home": SpaceX Launch Is Bad News for Locals.' *Quartz*. 25 August 2019. https://qz.com/1694822/spacex-starhopper-launch-prompts-blast-warnings-from-local-police.

78 Russell, Noel, Bernard Walters and David Young. *UK Economy: Microeconomics and Macroeconomics, Second Edition*. Pearson Custom Publishing, 2021, 460.

79 Bissel, Michael. 'A Public Transport Ticket that Moved a Country: Assessing the Value of the German 9-Euro-Ticket as a Socio-Technical Experiment.' *Findings*, August 2023.

80 Aydin, Eren and Kathleen Kürschner Rauck. 'Public Transport Subsidization and Air Pollution: Evidence from the 9-Euro-Ticket in Germany.' Available at SSRN 4505249, 2023.

81 'These 3 Sentences From Twitter Co-Founder Jack Dorsey Are a Masterclass in Leadership' – inc.com. 10 November, 2022. https://www.inc.com/minda-zetlin/jack-dorsey-elon-musk-twitter-layoffs-emotional-intelligence-leadership.html.

CHAPTER 3: WHO CLIMBS THE LADDER?

1 Ferriss, Timothy. *The 4-Hour Work Week: Escape The 9–5, Live Anywhere and Join the New Rich*. Random House, 2011.

2 *ibid*, 22–26.

3 *ibid*, 121.

4 *ibid*, 167.

5 Smith, Adam. *The Theory of Moral Sentiments*. United Kingdom: n.p., 1812, 103.

6 Shermer, Michael. 'Deviations: A Skeptical Investigation of Edgar Cayce's Association for Research and Enlightenment,' *Skpetic.com*, 8 November 2003. https://www.skeptic.com/eskeptic/11-08-03/#feature.

7 Wikipedia is a great place to start to understand survivorship bias: https://en.wikipedia.org/wiki/Survivorship_bias.

8 Reagle Jr, Joseph. 'Hacking Health.' In *Hacking life: Systematized living and its discontents.* MIT Press, 2019.

9 Ferriss, Timothy. *The 4-Hour Work Week: Escape The 9–5, Live Anywhere and Join the New Rich.* Random House, 2011, 16.

10 Chetty, Raj, Nathaniel Hendren, Patrick Kline, and Emmanuel Saez. 'Where is the land of opportunity? The geography of intergenerational mobility in the United States.' *The Quarterly Journal of Economics* 129, no. 4 (2014): 1553–623. Table II.

11 Source: author's own calculations, using the Longitudinal Study for Young People in England (LSYPE).

12 Azevedo, Viviane and Cesar P. Bouillon. 'Intergenerational social mobility in Latin America: a review of existing evidence.' (2010).

13 Blanden, Jo. 'Cross-country rankings in intergenerational mobility: a comparison of approaches from economics and sociology.' *Journal of Economic Surveys* 27, no. 1 (2013): 38–73.

14 Alesina, Alberto F., Marlon Seror, David Y. Yang, Yang You and Weihong Zeng. 'Persistence despite revolutions.' *NBER Working paper* w27053 (2020).

15 Mischel, Walter. *The Marshmallow Test: Understanding self-control and how to master it.* Random House, 2014.

16 Sturge-Apple, Melissa L., Jennifer H. Suor, Patrick T. Davies, Dante Cicchetti, Michael A. Skibo and Fred A. Rogosch. 'Vagal tone and children's delay of gratification: Differential sensitivity in resource-poor and resource-rich environments.' *Psychological Science* 27, no. 6 (2016): 885–93.

17 Kidd, Celeste, Holly Palmeri and Richard N. Aslin. 'Rational snacking: Young children's decision-making on the marshmallow task is moderated by beliefs about environmental reliability.' *Cognition* 126, no. 1 (2013): 109–114.

18 Sheehy-Skeffington, Jennifer, and Jessica Rea. 'How poverty affects people's decision-making processes.' 2017.

19 Shah, Anuj K., Sendhil Mullainathan, and Eldar Shafir. 'Some consequences of having too little.' *Science* 338, no. 6107 (2012): 682–85.

20 Pratchett, Terry. *Men at arms*. Vol. 15. Random House, 2013, 29.

21 Parmar, Sheetal. 'I'm Sick of Influencers Asking for Free Cake.' *BBC News*, 16 October 2020. https://www.bbc.co.uk/news/business-54543279.

22 Mani, Anandi, Sendhil Mullainathan, Eldar Shafir, and Jiaying Zhao. 'Poverty impedes cognitive function.' *Science* 341, no. 6149 (2013): 976–80.

23 Shah, Anuj K., Eldar Shafir, and Sendhil Mullainathan. 'Scarcity frames value.' *Psychological Science* 26, no. 4 (2015): 402–12.

24 Bramley, Glen, Donald Hirsch, Mandy Littlewood, and David Watkins. 'Counting the cost of UK poverty.' Joseph Rowntree Foundation, York, 2016.

25 Lindert, Peter H. *Making Social Spending Work*. Cambridge University Press, 2021, 18.

26 Heckman, James J. 'Invest in early childhood development: Reduce deficits, strengthen the economy.' *The Heckman Equation* 7, no. 1–2 (2012).

27 Hendren, Nathaniel and Ben Sprung-Keyser. 'A unified welfare analysis of government policies.' *Quarterly Journal of Economics* 135, no. 3 (2020): 1209–1318.

28 'Jordan Peterson Debate on the Gender Pay Gap, Campus Protests and Postmodernism.' *YouTube*, 16 January 2018. https://www.youtube.com/watch?v=aMcjxSThD54&amp.

29 Blau, Francine D., and Lawrence M. Kahn. 'The gender wage gap: Extent, trends, and explanations.' *Journal of Economic Literature* 55, no. 3 (2017): 789–865.

30 Bruenig, Matt. 'The Gender Pay Gap Is Bigger Than You Thought,' *Jacobin*. April 2018. https://jacobin.com/2018/04/gender-pay-gap-statistics-national-womens-law-center.

31 'Jordan Peterson – Successful Men Are Insane And Work All The Time,' *YouTube*, 25 November 2019. https://www.youtube.com/watch?v=oteAPGPB6Uw.

32 Charmes, Jacques. *The Unpaid Care Work and the Labour Market: An analysis of time use data based on the latest World Compilation of Time-use Surveys.* Geneva: ILO, 2019.

33 Neumark, David. 'Experimental research on labor market discrimination.' *Journal of Economic Literature* 56, no. 3 (2018): 799–866.

34 Moss-Racusin, Corinne A., John F. Dovidio, Victoria L. Brescoll, Mark J. Graham and Jo Handelsman. 'Science faculty's subtle gender biases favor male students.' *Proceedings of the National Academy of Sciences* 109, no. 41 (2012): 16474-479.

35 Steinpreis, Rhea E., Katie A. Anders and Dawn Ritzke. 'The impact of gender on the review of the curricula vitae of job applicants and tenure candidates: A national empirical study.' *Sex Roles* 41, no. 7–8 (1999): 509–28.

36 MacNell, Lillian, Adam Driscoll and Andrea N. Hunt. 'What's in a name: Exposing gender bias in student ratings of teaching.' *Innovative Higher Education* 40 (2015): 291–303.

37 All studies can and should be critiqued and it's not the case that the men in the study are definitely wrong about the findings – but the asymmetry is itself interesting. See Handley, Ian M., Elizabeth R. Brown, Corinne A. Moss-Racusin, and Jessi L. Smith. 'Quality of evidence revealing subtle gender biases in science is in the eye of the beholder.' *Proceedings of the National Academy of Sciences* 112, no. 43 (2015): 13201–206.

38 Rich, Judith, 'What Do Field Experiments of Discrimination in Markets Tell Us? A Meta Analysis of Studies Conducted Since 2000.' *IZA Discussion Paper No. 8584*, Available at SSRN: https://ssrn.com/abstract=2517887 or http://dx.doi.org/10.2139/ssrn.2517887.

39 Bertrand, Marianne and Sendhil Mullainathan. 'Are Emily and Greg more employable than Lakisha and Jamal? A field

experiment on labor market discrimination.' *American Economic Review* 94, no. 4 (2004): 991–1013.

40   Harford, Tim. *The logic of life: Uncovering the new economics of everything*. Hachette UK, 2010, 134–36.

41   Mueller, Gerrit and Erik Plug. 'Estimating the effect of personality on male and female earnings.' *ILR Review* 60, no. 1 (2006): 3–22.

42   Babcock, Linda, Maria P. Recalde, Lise Vesterlund and Laurie Weingart. 'Gender differences in accepting and receiving requests for tasks with low promotability.' *American Economic Review* 107, no. 3 (2017): 714–47.

43   Heilman, Madeline E. and Julie J. Chen. 'Same behavior, different consequences: reactions to men's and women's altruistic citizenship behavior.' *Journal of Applied Psychology* 90, no. 3 (2005): 431.

44   Arrow, Kenneth J. 'What has economics to say about racial discrimination?' *Journal of Economic Perspectives* 12, no. 2 (1998): 91–100.

45   'Who Are "The New Puritans"? | Andrew Doyle', *YouTube*, 18 August 2023. https://www.youtube.com/watch?v=ybSYxrninxc.

46   Singal, Jesse. 'Social Science Is Hard: Resume Audit Studies Edition.' *Singal-Minded*, 11 April 2021. https://jessesingal. substack.com/p/social-science-is-hard-resume-audit.

47   On the influence of teachers, see Campbell, Tammy. 'Stereotyped at seven? Biases in teacher judgement of pupils' ability and attainment.' *Journal of Social Policy* 44, no. 3 (2015): 517–47.
On the influence of peers, see Raabe, Isabel J., Zsófia Boda and Christoph Stadtfeld. 'The social pipeline: How friend influence and peer exposure widen the STEM gender gap.' *Sociology of Education* 92, no. 2 (2019): 105–23.
On the influence of parents, see Parsons, Jacquelynne Eccles, Terry F. Adler and Caroline M. Kaczala. 'Socialization of achievement attitudes and beliefs: Parental influences.' *Child Development* (1982): 310–21.

48 Patrick, Carlianne, Heather Stephens and Amanda Weinstein. 'Born to care (or not): How gender role attitudes affect occupational sorting.' *Labour,* 2023.

49 'More women to be supported back into STEM jobs in Government-backed training.' *News, Gov.uk*, 11 February 2023, https://www.gov.uk/government/news/more-women-to-be-supported-back-into-stem-jobs-in-government-backed-training.

50 Ghodsee, Kristen. 'What the US can learn from women in the Soviet workforce,' *Quartz,* 13 November 2019. https://qz.com/1746284/socialist-countries-employ-more-women-in-math-and-science/.

51 Weingarten, Elizabeth. 'The Stem Paradox: Why Are Muslim-Majority Countries Producing so Many Female Engineers?' *Slate*, 9 November 2017. https://slate.com/human-interest/2017/11/the-stem-paradox-why-are-muslim-majority-countries-producing-so-many-female-engineers.html.

52 Lippmann, Quentin and Claudia Senik. 'Math, Girls and Socialism.' *Journal of Comparative Economics* 46, no. 3 (2018): 874–88.

53 Maria, Charles. 'What Gender Is Science?' *Contexts*, May 2011. https://contexts.org/articles/what-gender-is-science/.

54 Stout, Jane G., Nilanjana Dasgupta, Matthew Hunsinger and Melissa A. McManus. 'STEMing the tide: using ingroup experts to inoculate women's self-concept in science, technology, engineering, and mathematics (STEM).' *Journal of Personality and Social Psychology* 100, no. 2 (2011): 255.

55 Hicks, Marie. 'Women's work: how Britain discarded its female computer programmers', *New Statesman*, 1 February 2019. https://www.newstatesman.com/politics/2019/02/womens-work-how-britain-discarded-its-female-computer-programmers.

56 Chang, Emily. 'Oh My God, This Is So F---ed Up': Inside Silicon Valley's Secretive, Orgiastic Dark Side', *Vanity Fair,* 2 January 2018. https://www.vanityfair.com/news/2018/01/brotopia-silicon-valley-secretive-orgiastic-inner-sanctum.

57 Reeves, Aaron, Sam Friedman, Charles Rahal, and Magne Flemmen. 'The decline and persistence of the old boy: Private schools and elite recruitment 1897 to 2016.' *American Sociological Review* 82, no. 6 (2017): 1139–66.

58 Savage, Mike. *Social class in the 21st century*. Penguin UK, 2015.

59 This was an observation at Dalkey book festival by Simon Kuper, a *Financial Times* journalist and the author of *Chums: How a Tiny Caste of Oxford Tories Took Over the UK*.

60 Bhattacharya, Snehashish and Surbhi Kesar. 'Precarity and development: Production and labor processes in the informal economy in India.' *Review of Radical Political Economics* 52, no. 3 (2020): 387–408.

61 Banerjee, Abhijit, Marianne Bertrand, Saugato Datta and Sendhil Mullainathan. 'Labor market discrimination in Delhi: Evidence from a field experiment.' *Journal of Comparative Economics* 37, no. 1 (2009): 14–27.

62 Stansbury, Anna and Robert Schultz. 'The economics profession's socioeconomic diversity problem.' *Journal of Economic Perspectives* 37, no. 4 (2023): 207–30.

63 Savage, Mike. *Social class in the 21st century*. Penguin UK, 2015, 189–201.

64 Rivera, Lauren A. and András Tilcsik. 'Class advantage, commitment penalty: The gendered effect of social class signals in an elite labor market.' *American Sociological Review* 81, no. 6 (2016): 1097–131.

65 Barr, Nicholas Adrian. *The welfare state as piggy bank: information, risk, uncertainty, and the role of the state*. Oxford University Press, 2001.

66 Sowell, Thomas. 'Productivity And Pay.' In *Basic Economics*. Basic Books, 2014.

67 *ibid*.

68 Savage, Mike. *Social class in the 21st century*. Penguin UK, 2015, 69–72.

69 Blumenstock, Joshua, Michael Callen and Tarek Ghani. 'Why do defaults affect behavior? Experimental evidence from Afghanistan.' *American Economic Review* 108, no. 10 (2018): 2868–901.

70 Barr, Nicholas Adrian. 'Pension Design: the Options.' In *The welfare state as piggy bank: information, risk, uncertainty, and the role of the state.* Oxford University Press, 2001.

71 Barr, Nicholas Adrian. 'The Mirage of Private Unemployment Insurance.' In *The welfare state as piggy bank: information, risk, uncertainty, and the role of the state.* Oxford University Press, 2001.

72 Admittedly I have simplified the nuanced theory of adverse selection here. See 'Hackmann, Martin B., Jonathan T. Kolstad and Amanda E. Kowalski. 'Adverse selection and an individual mandate: When theory meets practice.' *American Economic Review* 105, no. 3 (2015): 1030–66.' For a more detailed discussion of health insurance in the USA, see Handel, Benjamin, and Jonathan Kolstad. 'The Affordable Care Act After a Decade: Industrial Organization of the Insurance Exchanges.' *Annual Review of Economics* 14 (2022): 287–312. For a more general view on healthcare economics check out Cookson, Richard Andrew, Karl Philip Claxton and Tony Culyer. *The humble economist: Tony Culyer on health, health care and social decision making.* University of York and Office of Health Economics, 2012.

73 Bruenig, Matt. 'Why We Need the Welfare State', *People's Policy Project,* 18 February 2022. https://www.peoples policyproject.org/2022/02/18/why-we-need-the-welfare-state/.

74 Folbre, Nancy. 'Care Provision and the Boundaries of Production.' *Journal of Economic Perspectives* 38, no. 1 (2024): 201–20.

75 Savage, Mike. *Social class in the 21st century.* Penguin UK, 2015, 184–88.

CHAPTER 4: IS POVERTY GETTING BETTER?

1 Rosling, Hans. *Factfulness: Ten Reasons We're Wrong about the World – and Why Things Are Better than You Think.* Flatiron Books, 2018.

2 Pinker, Steven. *Enlightenment Now: The Case for Reason, Science, Humanism and Progress.* Penguin, 2019.

3 World Bank Poverty and Inequality Platform (2024) – with major processing by Our World in Data. '$2.15 a day – Number in poverty – World Bank' [dataset]. World Bank Poverty and Inequality Platform, 'World Bank Poverty and Inequality Platform (PIP) 20240326_2017, 20240326_2011' [original data]. Retrieved 20 May 2024 from https://ourworldindata.org/grapher/total-population-in-extreme-poverty.

4 Fischer, Andrew Martin. *Poverty as Ideology: Rescuing Social Justice from Global Development Agendas.* Zed Books, 2018, 76.

5 Stevenson, Tom. 'The Prosperity Hoax.' *The Baffler.* 8 November 2020. https://thebaffler.com/outbursts/the-prosperity-hoax-stevenson.

6 Drèze, Jean and Anmol Somanchi. 'Weighty Evidence? Poverty Estimation with Missing Data.' *Ideas for India*, 10 April 2023. https://www.ideasforindia.in/topics/poverty-inequality/weighty-evidence-poverty-estimation-with-missing-data.html.

7 World Bank (2023); Bolt and van Zanden – Maddison Project Database 2023 (2024); Maddison Database 2010 – with major processing by Our World in Data. 'Global GDP over the long run – World Bank, Maddison Project Database, Maddison Database – Historical data' [dataset]. World Bank, 'World Bank World Development Indicators'; Bolt and van Zanden, 'Maddison Project Database 2023'; Angus Maddison, 'Maddison Database 2010' [original data]. Retrieved 20 May 2024 from https://ourworldindata.org/grapher/global-gdp-over-the-long-run.

8   Fagan, G. *Bathing in Public in the Roman World*. University of Michigan Press, 2002, 181–189.

9   Source: the Shakespeare Bus Tour in Stratford-Upon-Avon.

10 Skoski, Joseph Richard. *Public baths and washhouses in Victorian Britain, 1842–1914*. Indiana University, 2000.

11 *Guardian*. 'More than half of British homes don't have a bathroom – archive, 1950', 29 November 2018. https://www. theguardian.com/global-development/2018/nov/29/ five-million-families-in-britain-living-in-houses-without-baths- archive-1960

12 Hickel, Jason. 'Progress and Its Discontents.' *New Internationalist*, August 7th, 2019. https://newint.org/ features/2019/07/01/long-read-progress-and-its-discontents.

13 Davis, Mike. *Late Victorian holocausts: El Niño famines and the making of the third world*. Verso Books, 2002.

14 Allen, Robert C. 'Poverty and the labor market: today and yesterday.' *Annual Review of Economics* 12 (2020): 107–34.

15 Jerven, Morten. 'Development by Numbers–A primer.' *Development Research Institute Working Paper* (2016).

16 *ibid.*

17 *ibid.*

18 Hannah Ritchie, Pablo Rosado and Max Roser (2023). 'Hunger and Undernourishment'. Published online at OurWorldInData.org. Retrieved from: 'https://ourworldindata. org/hunger-and-undernourishment' [Online Resource].

19 Studwell, Joe. *How Asia Works: Success and Failure in the World's Most Dynamic Region*. Profile Books, London, 2014.

20 Stevenson, Tom. 'The Prosperity Hoax.' *The Baffler*. 28 November 2020. https://thebaffler.com/outbursts/ the-prosperity-hoax-stevenson.

21 Pritchett, Lant. 'Who is not poor? Proposing a higher international standard for poverty.' *Center for Global Development Working Paper* 33 (2003).

22 Poverty estimates obtained from: https://pip.worldbank.org/poverty-calculator.

23 Williams, David and Henry Oks. 'The Long, Slow Death of Global Development.' *American Affairs Journal*. 20 November 2022. https://americanaffairsjournal.org/2022/11/the-long-slow-death-of-global-development/.

24 Thirlwall, Anthony P. and Penélope Pacheco-López. *Economics of development: theory and evidence*. Bloomsbury Publishing, 2017, 88–91.

25 Hochuli, Alex. 'The Brazilianization of the World.' *American Affairs Journal*, 20 May 2021. https://americanaffairsjournal.org/2021/05/the-brazilianization-of-the-world/.

26 Williams, David, and Henry Oks. 'The Long, Slow Death of Global Development.' *American Affairs Journal*. 20 November 2022. https://americanaffairsjournal.org/2022/11/the-long-slow-death-of-global-development/.

27 Bhattacharya, Snehashish and Surbhi Kesar. 'Precarity and development: Production and labor processes in the informal economy in India.' *Review of Radical Political Economics* 52, no. 3 (2020): 387–408.

28 O'Connor, Sarah and John Burn-Murdoch. 'Left Behind: Can Anyone Save the Towns the UK Economy Forgot?' *Financial Times*. 16 November 2017. https://www.ft.com/blackpool.

29 Sandoval, Marisol. 'Foxconned labour as the dark side of the information age: Working conditions at Apple's contract manufacturers in China.' In *Marx in the Age of Digital Capitalism*. Brill, 2016, 350–95.

30 Pinker, Steven. *Enlightenment Now: The Case for Reason, Science, Humanism and Progress*. Penguin, 2019, 129–130.

31 Clark, Andrew E., Paul Frijters and Michael A. Shields. 'Relative income, happiness, and utility: An explanation for the Easterlin paradox and other puzzles.' *Journal of Economic Literature* 46, no. 1 (2008): 95–144.

32 Sapolsky, Robert. *Behave: the Biology of Humans at Our Best and Worst*. Penguin Press, 2017, 291–296.

33 Wilkinson, Richard and Kate Pickett. *The Inner Level: How more equal societies reduce stress, restore sanity and improve everyone's well-being.* Penguin, 2019, 41–43.

34 Stewart, Neil, Nick Chater and Gordon D.A. Brown. 'Decision by Sampling.' *Cognitive Psychology* 53, no. 1 (2006): 1–26.

35 Smith, Adam. *The Wealth of Nations.* W. Strahan and T. Cadell, London 1776, 939.

36 Engels, Friedrich. 2009. *The Condition of the Working Class in England.* Edited by David McLellan. Oxford World's Classics. London, England: Oxford University Press, 151.

37 Gobetti, Sérgio Wulff and Rodrigo Octávio Orair. 'Taxation and distribution of income in Brazil: new evidence from personal income tax data.' *Brazilian Journal of Political Economy* 37 (2017): 267–86.

38 Pinheiro-Machado, Rosana, and Lucia Mury Scalco. 'The right to shine: Poverty, consumption and (de) politicization in neoliberal Brazil.' Journal of Consumer Culture 23, no. 2 (2023): 312–330.

39 Frank, Robert, Adam Levine and Oege Dijk. 'Expenditure cascades.' *Review of Behavioral Economics* 1 (2004): 55–73.

40 Andrews, Christina W. 'Anti-poverty policies in Brazil: reviewing the past ten years.' *International Review of Administrative Sciences* 70, no. 3 (2004): 477–88.

41 Gobetti, Sérgio Wulff and Rodrigo Octávio Orair. 'Taxation and distribution of income in Brazil: new evidence from personal income tax data.' *Brazilian Journal of Political Economy* 37 (2017): 267–86.

42 Skoski, Joseph Richard. *Public baths and washhouses in Victorian Britain, 1842–1914.* Indiana University, 2000.

43 Lindert, Peter H. *Making Social Spending Work.* Cambridge University Press, 2021, 141–42, 169, 212–15.

44 'Global Gender Gap Report 2023', *World Economic Forum*, 20 June 2023, https://www.weforum.org/publications/global-gender-gap-report-2023/.

45 See two reviews of multiple trials of UBI and its null effect on working hours: de Paz-Báñez, Manuela A., María José

Asensio-Coto, Celia Sánchez-López and María-Teresa Aceytuno. 'Is there empirical evidence on how the implementation of a universal basic income (UBI) affects labour supply? A systematic review.' *Sustainability* 12, no. 22 (2020): 9459.

Gilbert, Richard, Nora A. Murphy, Allison Stepka, Mark Barrett and Dianne Worku. 'Would a basic income guarantee reduce the motivation to work? An analysis of labor responses in 16 trial programs.' *Basic Income Studies* 13, no. 2 (2018): 20180011.

46 Egger, Dennis, Johannes Haushofer, Edward Miguel, Paul Niehaus and Michael Walker. 'General equilibrium effects of cash transfers: experimental evidence from Kenya.' *Econometrica* 90, no. 6 (2022): 2603–643.

47 Ferdosi, Mohammad, Tom McDowell, Wayne Lewchuk and Stephanie Ross. 'Southern Ontario's Basic Income Experience.' Hamilton Community Foundation, 2020.

48 Lakner, Christoph and Branko Milanovic. 'Global income distribution: From the fall of the Berlin Wall to the Great Recession.' World Bank policy research working paper 6719 (2013).

49 Hickel, Jason. 'We Can't Grow Our Way Out Of Poverty,' *New Internationalist,* April 2020. https://newint.org/features/2020/02/10/we-cannot-grow-our-way-out-poverty.

50 Singer, Peter. 'The drowning child and the expanding circle.' 1997.

51 Aguilera, Rodrigo. 'Built For The Future.' In *The glass half-empty: Debunking the myth of progress in the twenty-first century*. Repeater, 2020.

52 Baker, Dean. 'Introduction: Trading in Myths,' in *Rigged: How Globalization and the Rules of the Modern Economy Were Structured to Make the Rich Richer,* Center for Economic and Policy Research, Washington, DC, 2016, 9–20.

53 Shaxson, Nicholas. 'Tackling Tax Havens' *IMF*, September 2019. https://www.imf.org/en/Publications/fandd/issues/2019/09/tackling-global-tax-havens-shaxon.

54 Picciotto, Sol. *Towards unitary taxation of transnational corporations*. Tax Justice Network, London, 2012.

CHAPTER 5: WHAT ON EARTH HAS HAPPENED TO HOUSING?

1 'Established Titles | Become a Lord Today.' *Established Titles,* n.d. https://establishedtitles.com/.
2 Stone, Devin. 'Yes, Established Titles Is A Scam* | Legal Eagle' *YouTube,* 2022. https://www.youtube.com/watch?v= NG4Ws74RV04.
3 Cox, Wendell. 'Demographia International Housing Affordability – 2023 Edition', *Urban Reform Institute,* 14 March 2023. https://policycommons.net/artifacts/3527078/ demographia-international-housing-affordability/4327867/.
4 Perlman, Janice E. 'The Myth of Marginality Revisited: The Case Of Favelas In Rio De Janeiro, 1969–2003.' In *Becoming Global and the New Poverty of Cities.* Washington, DC: Woodrow Wilson International Center for Scholars, 2005, 15.
5 Quoted in 'Carvalho, Camila, and Diogo de Carvalho Cabral. 'Beyond the Favelas: An Analysis of Intraurban Poverty Patterns in Brazil.' *Professional Geographer* 1–13 (2021). https://doi.org/10.1080/00330124.2020.1844571.'
6 *ibid.*
7 Perlman, Janice E. 'The Myth of Marginality Revisited: The Case Of Favelas In Rio De Janeiro, 1969–2003.' In *Becoming Global and the New Poverty of Cities.* Washington, DC: Woodrow Wilson International Center for Scholars, 2005, 9–55.
8 *ibid.*
9 *ibid.*
10 *ibid.*
11 Hardin, Garrett. 'The tragedy of the commons: the population problem has no technical solution; it requires a fundamental extension in morality.' *Science* 162, no. 3859 (1968): 1243–48.
12 Sen, Amartya K. 'Rational fools: A critique of the behavioral foundations of economic theory.' *Philosophy & Public Affairs* (1977): 317–44.
13 Wood, Ellen Meiksins. *The origin of capitalism: A longer view.* Verso, 2002, 105–15.

14 Ostrom, Elinor. 'Beyond markets and states: polycentric
    governance of complex economic systems.' *American Economic
    Review* 100, no. 3 (2010): 641–72.

15 Foster, Sheila R., and Christian Iaione. 'Ostrom in the city:
    Design principles and practices for the urban commons.'
    In *Routledge Handbook of the Study of the Commons*,
    Routledge, 2019, 235–55.

16 'Full Documentary. The Men of Fifth World – Planet Doc Full
    Documentaries,' *YouTube*, 2 August 2014. https://www.
    youtube.com/watch?v=-1Td8VUcKk0.

17 Rikap, Cecilia. 'Capitalism as usual? Implications of digital
    intellectual monopolies.' *New Left Review* 139 (2023): 145–60.

18 Smith, Adam. *The Wealth of Nations*. W. Strahan and
    T. Cadell, London 1776, 27.

19 *ibid*.

20 Lent, George E. 'The Taxation of Land Value.' *IMF Staff
    Papers 14 (1967)* 89–123. https://link.springer.com/article/
    10.2307/3866385.

21 Quoted in Ryan-Collins, Josh, Tolloyd, and Laurie Macfarlane.
    Rethinking the Economics of Land and Housing. Zed, 2017, 74.

22 Kwak, Sally and James Mak. 'Political Economy of Property
    Tax Reform: Hawaii's Experiment with Split-Rate Property
    Taxation.' *American Journal of Economics and Sociology* 70,
    no. 1 (2011): 4–29.

23 Oates, Wallace E. and Robert M. Schwab. 'The impact of
    urban land taxation: The Pittsburgh experience.' *National Tax
    Journal* 50, no. 1 (1997): 1–21.

24 Murray, Cameron K. and Jesse Hermans. 'Land value is a
    progressive and efficient property tax base: Evidence from
    Victoria.' *Austl. Tax F.* 36 (2021): 243.

25 'Moving House Stress Signals.' *Legal and General*. 26 April
    2022. https://www.legalandgeneral.com/insurance/life-
    insurance/moving-house-stress-signs.

26 Clarke, Stephen, Adam Corlett and Lindsay Judge. 'The Housing
    Headwind: The Impact of Rising Housing Costs on UK Living

Standards.' *Resolution Foundation,* 28 June 2016. https://www.resolutionfoundation.org/publications/the-housing-headwind-the-impact-of-rising-housing-costs-on-uk-living-standards/.

27 Ryan-Collins, Josh, Tolloyd and Laurie Macfarlane. *Rethinking the Economics of Land and Housing.* Zed, 2017, 24.

28 *ibid,* 105–107.

29 'English Housing Survey, 2019 to 2020: Home Ownership.' *Gov.uk,* 8 July 2021 https://www.gov.uk/government/statistics/english-housing-survey-2019-to-2020-home-ownership.

30 Clarke, Stephen, Adam Corlett and Lindsay Judge. 'The Housing Headwind: The Impact of Rising Housing Costs on UK Living Standards.' *Resolution Foundation,* 28 June 2016. https://www.resolutionfoundation.org/publications/the-housing-headwind-the-impact-of-rising-housing-costs-on-uk-living-standards/.

31 Wheeler, Zak. 'Horror Graph Finally Settles the Boomers vs Millennials Housing Debate.' *Mail Online.* 9 September 2023. https://www.dailymail.co.uk/news/article-12499059/Horror-graph-finally-settles-boomers-vs-millennials-housing-struggle-argument.html.

32 Clarke, Stephen, Adam Corlett and Lindsay Judge. 'The Housing Headwind: The Impact of Rising Housing Costs on UK Living Standards.' *Resolution Foundation,* 28 June 2016. https://www.resolutionfoundation.org/publications/the-housing-headwind-the-impact-of-rising-housing-costs-on-uk-living-standards/.

33 Pettifor, Ann. *The production of money: how to break the power of bankers.* Verso Books, 2017, 52.

34 Ryan-Collins, Josh, Tolloyd and Laurie Macfarlane. *Rethinking the Economics of Land and Housing.* Zed, 2017, 122–169.

35 Ryan-Collins, Josh. 'Breaking the housing–finance cycle: Macroeconomic policy reforms for more affordable homes.' *Environment and Planning A: Economy and Space* 53, no. 3 (2021): 480–502.

36 Cheshire, Paul and Stephen Sheppard. 'Estimating the demand for housing, land, and neighbourhood characteristics.' *Oxford Bulletin of Economics and Statistics* 60, no. 3 (1998): 357–82 (Table 1).

37 Adler, Moshe. *Economics for the Rest of Us: Debunking the Science That Makes Life Dismal.* The New Press, New York, 209, 82.

38 Ryan-Collins, Josh. 'Breaking the housing–finance cycle: Macroeconomic policy reforms for more affordable homes.' *Environment and Planning A: Economy and Space* 53, no. 3 (2021): 126.

39 Kampfner, John. *Why the Germans Do It Better: Notes from a Grown-Up Country.* Atlantic Books, 2020, 228–32.

40 Mason, Josh. 'Wealth Distribution and the Puzzle of Germany.' *Jwmason.org*, 7 April 2014. https://jwmason.org/slackwire/ wealth-distribution-and-puzzle-of/.

41 Sagner, Pekka, and Michael Voigtländer. "Supply side effects of the Berlin rent freeze." *International Journal of Housing Policy* 23, no. 4 (2023): 692–711.

    Hahn, Anja M., Konstantin A. Kholodilin, Sofie R. Waltl, and Marco Fongoni. "Forward to the past: Short-term effects of the rent freeze in Berlin." *Management Science* 70, no. 3 (2024): 1901–1923.

42 Mason, Josh. 'Considerations on Rent Control.' *Jwmason.org*, November 2019. https://jwmason.org/slackwire/considerations- on-rent-control/

    Kholodilin, Konstantin A., and Sebastian Kohl. "Do rent controls and other tenancy regulations affect new construction? Some answers from long-run historical evidence." *International Journal of Housing Policy* 23, no. 4 (2023): 671–691.

43 Murray, Cameron. *The Great Housing Hijack: The hoaxes and myths keeping prices high for renters and buyers in Australia.* Allen & Unwin, 2024, 199–200

44 Sims, David P. "Out of control: What can we learn from the end of Massachusetts rent control?." *Journal of Urban Economics* 61, no. 1 (2007): 129–151.

45 Diamond, Rebecca, Tim McQuade, and Franklin Qian. "Who Benefits from Rent Control? The Equilibrium Consequences of San Francisco's Rent Control Expansion." *Standford University Mimeo* (2018): 1–6.

46 Sagner, Pekka, and Michael Voigtländer. "Supply side effects of the Berlin rent freeze." *International Journal of Housing Policy* 23, no. 4 (2023): 692–711.

    Hahn, Anja M., Konstantin A. Kholodilin, Sofie R. Waltl, and Marco Fongoni. "Forward to the past: Short-term effects of the rent freeze in Berlin." *Management Science* 70, no. 3 (2024): 1901–1923.

47 Gardner, Max. "The effect of rent control status on eviction filing rates: Causal evidence from San Francisco." *Housing Policy Debate* (2022): 1–24.

48 Sims, David P. "Out of control: What can we learn from the end of Massachusetts rent control?." *Journal of Urban Economics* 61, no. 1 (2007): 129–151.

49 Freemark, Yonah. Mandating Access to Affordable Housing, City by City: Is France's Fair-Share SRU Law a Model for US Metropolitan Areas. Lincoln Institute of Land Policy, Cambridge MA, 2021.

50 Fuller, Thomas. 'How Does Paris Stay Paris? By Pouring Billions Into Public Housing' New York Times, 17 March 2024 https://www.nytimes.com/2024/03/17/realestate/paris-france-housing-costs.html?smid=url-share&unlocked_article_code=1.dU0.Ld75.FZyG2gtqcsts

51 Bruenig, Matt. 'Why we need social housing in the US.' *Guardian*, 5 April 2018. https://www.theguardian.com/society/2018/apr/05/why-we-need-social-housing-in-the-us.

52 Kontrast.at. 'Finland Ends Homelessness and Provides Shelter for All in Need.' *The Better*. 29 January 2020. https://scoop.me/housing-first-finland-homelessness/.

53 Kontrast.at. 'Finland is successfully fighting homelessness – despite new political developments' *The Better*. 4 February 2024. https://thebetter.news/interview-juha-kahila-housing-first-finland/.

54 Murray, Cameron. *The Great Housing Hijack: The hoaxes and myths keeping prices high for renters and buyers in Australia.* Allen & Unwin, 2024, 264–267.

55   Ryan-Collins, Josh. 'Breaking the housing–finance cycle: Macroeconomic policy reforms for more affordable homes.' *Environment and Planning A: Economy and Space* 53, no. 3 (2021): 202–4.

56   Murray, Cameron. *The Great Housing Hijack: The hoaxes and myths keeping prices high for renters and buyers in Australia*. Allen & Unwin, 2024, 267–269.

57   Davis, Jenna and Joseph Weil Huennekens. 'YIMBY divided: A qualitative content analysis of YIMBY subreddit data.' *Journal of Urban Affairs* (2022): 1–27.

58   Coates, Ta-Nehisi. 'The Case for Reparations.' *The Atlantic*. 22 May 2014. https://www.theatlantic.com/magazine/archive/2014/06/the-case-for-reparations/361631/.

59   Britschgi, Christian. 'Eliminating Single-Family Zoning Isn't the Reason Minneapolis Is a YIMBY Success Story.' *Reason.com*. 11 May 2022. https://reason.com/2022/05/11/eliminating-single-family-zoning-isnt-the-reason-minneapolis-is-a-yimby-success-story/.

60   Note that I do not agree with the assessment that they should have been stopped, as environmental reasons are specious in this case. See Britschgi, Christian. 'Environmentalists' Lawsuit Brings Minneapolis', YIMBY Success Story to a Screeching Halt.' *Reason.com*. 17 June 2022. https://reason.com/2022/06/17/environmentalists-lawsuit-brings-minneapolis-yimby-success-story-to-a-screeching-halt/.

61   Cowgill, Matt. 'When You Buy a House, You Shouldn't Buy the Neighbourhood with It.' *Guardian*, 25 December 2013. https://www.theguardian.com/commentisfree/2013/dec/26/when-you-buy-a-house-you-shouldnt-buy-the-neighbourhood-with-it.

62   Sisson, Alistair. 'Yes to the City: Millenials and the Fight for Affordable Housing.' *Urban Policy and Research*. 1–4 February. https://doi.org/10.1080/08111146.2023.2179882.

63   Niquette, mark, Augusta Saraiva, Bloomberg. 'Minneapolis Has a YIMBY Message for America: Build More Houses and Get Rid of Suburban-Style Zoning and Inflation Will Disappear.' *Fortune*,

9August2023.https://fortune.com/2023/08/09/minneapolis-housing-zoning-real-estate-inflation-yimby-nimby-minnesota/.

64 Murray, Cameron. *The Great Housing Hijack: The hoaxes and myths keeping prices high for renters and buyers in Australia.* Allen & Unwin, 2024, 141–144.

65 Smith, Nicholas Boys and Kieran Toms. 'From NIMBY to YIMBY: How to win votes by building more homes.' Create Streets Research Report. https://www.createstreets.com/wp-content/uploads/2018/04/Nimby-to-Yimby-280418.pdf.

66 Roos, David. 'Kowloon Walled City Once Was the Most Densely Packed Place on Earth,' 7 December 2021. https://history.howstuffworks.com/world-history/kowloon-walled-city.htm.

67 Holleran, Max. *Yes to the City: Millennials and the Fight for Affordable Housing.* Princeton University Press, 2022, 46.

68 BritMonkey. 'BRITAIN IS A DUMP!!!!!!!!!!!!,' *YouTube,* 3 June 2024. https://www.youtube.com/watch?v=b5aJ-57_YsQ&list=WL.

69 Pennington, Mark. *Property rights, public choice and urban containment: A study of the British planning system.* PhD diss., London School of Economics and Political Science, 1998.

70 Moran, Cahal and Ganga Shreedhar. 'HS2 reveals the pervasiveness of optimism bias in government decision making.' British Politics and Policy at LSE, 2024.

71 Smith, Nicholas Boys and Kieran Toms. 'From NIMBY to YIMBY: How to win votes by building more homes.' Create Streets Research Report https://www.createstreets.com/wp-content/uploads/2018/04/Nimby-to-Yimby-280418.pdf.

72 Balmer, Ivo and Jean-David Gerber. 'Why are housing cooperatives successful? Insights from Swiss affordable housing policy.' *Housing Studies* 33, no. 3 (2018): 361–85.

73 Fruet, Genoveva Maya. 'The low-income housing cooperatives in Porto Alegre, Brazil: a state/community partnership.' *Habitat International* 29, no. 2 (2005): 303–24.

74 Kelleher, Ellen. 'Call for UK national investment bank,' *Financial Times.* 13 March 2011. https://www.ft.com/content/dce8a17c-4c20-11e0-82df-00144feab49a.

75   Makortoff, Kalyeena and Julia Kollewe. 'Rachel Reeves launches £7.3bn national wealth fund,' *The Guardian*, 9 July 2024. https://www.theguardian.com/business/article/2024/jul/09/rachel-reeves-national-wealth-fund-labour?

CHAPTER 6: WHERE DOES MONEY COME FROM?

1   Graeber, David. *Debt: The First 5,000 Years*. Melville House Publishing, New York, 2011, 61.

2   *ibid*, 34–38.

3   *ibid*, 29.

4   *ibid*, 23.

5   Mining, Genesis. 2019. 'New Genesis Mining Study Finds 29% of Americans Believe the US Dollar Is Still Backed by Gold.' *Prnewswire.com*. 30 October 2019. https://www.prnewswire.com/news-releases/new-genesis-mining-study-finds-29-of-americans-believe-the-us-dollar-is-still-backed-by-gold-300947883.html.

6   'Boost Productivity with a New National Investment Bank.' *Civitas: Institute for the Study of Civil Society*. n.d. https://www.civitas.org.uk/press/.
boost-productivity-with-a-new-national-investment-bank/.

7   Keen, Steve. 'Reducing Debt via a Modern Debt Jubilee.' *Brave New Europe*. 8 May 2021. https://braveneweurope.com/steve-keen-reducing-debt-via-a-modern-debt-jubilee.

8   Sheffield, Hazel. 'Younger Generation Priced out of Property Market.' *Independent*. 2 March 2015. https://www.independent.co.uk/incoming/younger-generation-priced-out-of-property-market-a150126.html.

9   Izoulet, Maxime. 'The Invention of Double-Entry Bookkeeping.' Available at SSRN 3853815, 2021.

10 Eichengreen, Barry. 'Understanding the Great Depression.' *Canadian Journal of Economics/Revue Canadienne d'Economique* 37, no. 1 (2004): 1–27.

11 Galbraith, John Kenneth. *Money: Whence it Came, Where it Went*. Princeton University Press, 2017, 22.

12 Paraphrased from Minsky, Hyman P. and Henry Kaufman. *Stabilizing an unstable economy*. Vol. 1. New York: McGraw-Hill, 2008, 78–79.

13 Wang, Joseph. 'Two Tiered Monetary System.' *Fed Guy*. 29 August 2020. https://fedguy.com/two-tiered-monetary-system/.

14 Tankus, Nathan. 'What If the Federal Reserve Just . . . Spent Money?' *Notes on the Crises*. 24 March 2020. https://www. crisesnotes.com/what-if-the-federal-reserve-just/.

15 Tankus, Nathan. 'The Federal Government Always Money-Finances Its Spending: A Restatement.' *Notes on the Crisis,* 30 June 2020. https://nathantankus.substack.com/p/ the-federal-government-always-money.
    Tymoigne, Eric. 'Money and Banking – Part 6: Treasury and Central Bank Interactions', *New Economic Perspectives,* 14 February 2016. https://neweconomicperspectives.org/2016/02/ money-banking-part-6.html.

16 Kelton, Stephanie. *The deficit myth: modern monetary theory and the birth of the people's economy*. Public Affairs, New York, 2020, 74.

17 Roche, Cullen O. 'Hyperinflation-It's More than Just a Monetary Phenomenon.' Available at SSRN 1799102, 2011.

18 Eichengreen, Barry. 'Understanding the Great Depression.' *Canadian Journal of Economics/Revue Canadienne d'Economique* 37, no. 1 (2004): 1–27.

19 White, Lawrence H. *Free Banking in Britain: Theory, Experience and Debate, 1800–1845*. Institute Of Economic Affairs, London, 2009.

20 Bordo, Michael D. 'A brief history of central banks.' *Economic Commentary* 12/1/2007.

21 'Keynes celebrates the end of the Gold Standard,' *YouTube*, 4 September 2010. https://www.youtube.com/watch?v= U1S9F3agsUA.

22 Eichengreen, Barry. 'Understanding the Great Depression.' *Canadian Journal of Economics/Revue Canadienne d'Economique* 37, no. 1 (2004): 1–27.

23 Kaldor, Nicholas. 1985. 'How Monetarism Failed.' *Challenge* 28 (2): 4–13. https://doi.org/10.1080/05775132.01.11470996.

24 McLeay, Michael, Amar Radia and Ryland Thomas. 'Money in the modern economy: an introduction.' Bank of England Quarterly Bulletin (2014): Q1.

25 'Inflation targeting', Wikipedia, https://en.wikipedia.org/wiki/Inflation_targeting.

26 Patel, Rupal and Jack Meaning. *Can't We Just Print More Money?: Economics in Ten Simple Questions*. Random House, 2022, 242–245.

27 Frankel, Jeffrey. 'The Death of Inflation Targeting,' *Project Syndicate,* 16 May 2012. https://www.project-syndicate.org/commentary/the-death-of-inflation-targeting.

28 Yu, Edison. 'Did quantitative easing work?' *Economic Insights* 1, no. 1 (2016): 5–13.

29 Coy, Peter. 'Economics Textbooks Are Finally Getting a Vital Update.' *New York Times,* 17 January 2024. https://www.nytimes.com/2024/01/17/opinion/economics-textbooks-monetary-policy.html.

30 Blanchard, Olivier. 'It is time to revisit the 2% inflation target.' *Financial Times,* 28 November 2022. https://www.ft.com/content/02c8a9ac-b71d-4cef-a6ff-cac120d25588.

31 Boait, Fran. 'The Bank of England's Monetary Policy Has Made Inequality Worse – This Is How to Solve It.' *Independent*. 10 April 2018. https://www.independent.co.uk/voices/quantative-easing-bank-of-england-inequality-financial-crisis-how-to-solve-it-a8297926.html.

32 Vestergaard, Jakob. 2022. 'What a Green Monetary Policy Could Look Like.' Institute for New Economic Thinking. Accessed 22 June 2023. https://www.ineteconomics.org/perspectives/blog/what-a-green-monetary-policy-could-look-like.

33 Coppola, Frances. *The Case for People's Quantitative Easing.* Polity, London, 2019.

34 Pigeaud, Fanny, Ndongo Samba Sylla and Thomas Fazi. *Africa's Last Colonial Currency: The CFA Franc Story.* Pluto Press, 2021.

35 *Ibid*, 64–66.

36 Williams, David and Henry Oks. 'The Long, Slow Death of Global Development.' *American Affairs Journal.* 20 November 2022. https://americanaffairsjournal.org/2022/11/the-long-slow-death-of-global-development/.

37 Patel, Palak. *The Tyranny of Nations.* Bifocal Press, New York, 2021, 2.

38 *Ibid*, 1–24.

39 Tooze, Adam. *Shutdown: How Covid Shook the World's Economy.* Penguin Books, 2021, 125–26.

40 Bradlow, Daniel D. and Stephen Kim Park. 'A global leviathan emerges: The Federal Reserve, COVID-19, and international law.' *American Journal of International Law* 114, no. 4 (2020): 657–65.

41 Tooze, Adam. 'Chartbook 216: Heroic Periodization: Histories Of Bretton Woods & The "New Washington Consensus",' *Chartbook,* 29 March 2023. https://adamtooze.com/2023/05/29/chartbook-216-heroic-periodization-histories-of-bretton-woods-the-new-washington-consensus/.

42 Graeber, David. *Debt: The First 5,000 Years.* Melville House Publishing, New York, 2011, 46.

CHAPTER 7: WHY DOES INFLATION HIT US SO HARD?

1 'Inflation and Price Indices', *ONS*, https://www.ons.gov.uk/economy/inflationandpriceindices.

2 'Viral Twitter Thread Says Inflation Figures "Ignore the Reality of Cost of Living".' *Independent.* 21 January 2022. https://

www.independent.co.uk/life-style/jack-monroe-cost-of-living-viral-twitter-b1997795.html.

3   Harford, Tim. 'Why real inflation is so hard to measure.' *Financial Times*, 4 February 2022. https://www.ft.com/content/a3c1fd89-bfd5-4a41-aa21-e0886e621f2a.

4   'How public sector services are incorporated in the Retail Price Index (RPI) and other inflation data,' *Office for National Statistics*, 17 June 2024. https://www.ons.gov.uk/aboutus/transparencyandgovernance/freedomofinformationfoi/howpublicsectorservicesareincorporatedintheretailpriceindexrpiandotherinflationdata.

5   'Consumer price inflation basket of goods and services: 2022.' Office for National Statistics, 14 March 2022. https://www.ons.gov.uk/economy/inflationandpriceindices/articles/ukconsumerpriceinflationbasketofgoodsandservices/2022

6   Harford, Tim. 'Why real inflation is so hard to measure.' *Financial Times*, 4 February 2022. https://www.ft.com/content/a3c1fd89-bfd5-4a41-aa21-e0886e621f2a.

7   'The use of democratic weighting | Household Costs Indices: methodology.' Office for National Statistics, 19 December 2017. https://www.ons.gov.uk/economy/inflationandpriceindices/methodologies/householdcostsindicesmethodology#the-use-of-democratic-weighting.

8   Harford, Tim. 'Why real inflation is so hard to measure.' *Financial Times*, 4 February 2022. https://www.ft.com/content/a3c1fd89-bfd5-4a41-aa21-e0886e621f2a.

9   'Consumer price inflation basket of goods and services: 2021.' Office for National Statistics, 15 March 2021. https://www.ons.gov.uk/economy/inflationandpriceindices/articles/ukconsumerpriceinflationbasketofgoodsandservices/2021.

10 'Research into the use of scanner data for constructing UK consumer price statistics,' *ONS*, 6 April 2021. https://www.ons.gov.uk/economy/inflationandpriceindices/articles/researchintotheuseofscannerdataforconstructingukconsumerpricestatistics/2021-04-06.

11 Jaravel, Xavier. 'Inflation inequality: Measurement, Causes, and Policy Implications.' *Annual Review of Economics* 13 (2021): 599–629.

12 Kaplan, Greg and Sam Schulhofer-Wohl. 'Inflation at the Household Level.' *Journal of Monetary Economics* 91 (2017): 19–38.

13 Handbury, Jessie. 'Are poor cities cheap for everyone? Non-homotheticity and the cost of living across US cities.' *Econometrica* 89, no. 6 (2021): 2679–715.

14 Kaplan, Greg and Sam Schulhofer-Wohl. 'Inflation at the Household Level.' *Journal of Monetary Economics* 91 (2017): 19–38.

15 Borio, Claudio, Piti Disyatat, Dora Xia and Egon Zakrajšek. 'Looking under the Hood: The Two Faces of Inflation.' *VoxEU*, 25 January 2022. https://voxeu.org/article/looking-under-hood-two-faces-inflation.

16 Walker, Andrew. 'Inflation targeting is 25 years old, but has it worked?' *BBC News,* 11 March 2015. https://www.bbc.co.uk/news/31559074.

17 Barker, Tim. 'A Socialist Primer on Monetary Policy and Inflation.' *Jacobin,* September 2021, https://jacobin.com/2021/09/socialist-primer-monetary-policy-inflation-federal-reserve-volcker-shock-class-tim-barker-interview.

18 Mason, Josh. 'The Fed Doesn't Work for You.' *Jacobin*, January 2016. https://jacobin.com/2016/01/federal-reserve-interest-rate-increase-janet-yellen-inflation-unemployment/.
Mason, Josh. 'Inflation, Interest Rates and the Fed: A Dissent.' *Jwmason.org,* 25 March, 2022. https://jwmason.org/slackwire/inflation-interest-rates-and-the-fed-a-dissent/.

19 Garibaldi, Pietro. 'The asymmetric effects of monetary policy on job creation and destruction.' *Staff Papers* 44, no. 4 (1997): 557–84.
Karras, Georgios. 'Asymmetric effects of monetary policy with or without Quantitative Easing: Empirical evidence for the US.' *Journal of Economic Asymmetries* 10, no. 1 (2013): 1–9.

Tenreyro, Silvana and Gregory Thwaites. 'Pushing on a string: US monetary policy is less powerful in recessions.' *American Economic Journal: Macroeconomics* 8, no. 4 (2016): 43–74.

Barnichon, Regis, Christian Matthes and Timothy Sablik. 'Are the effects of monetary policy asymmetric?' *Richmond Fed Economic Brief* (2017).

Angrist, Joshua D., Òscar Jordà and Guido M. Kuersteiner. 'Semiparametric estimates of monetary policy effects: string theory revisited.' *Journal of Business & Economic Statistics* 36, no. 3 (2018): 371–87.

Debortoli, Davide and Forni, Mario and Gambetti, Luca and Sala, Luca, 'Asymmetric Effects of Monetary Policy Easing and Tightening' (July 2020). CEPR Discussion Paper No. DP15005, Available at SSRN: https://ssrn.com/abstract=3650120

Aastveit, Knut Are and André K. Anundsen. 'Asymmetric effects of monetary policy in regional housing markets.' *American Economic Journal: Macroeconomics* 14, no. 4 (2022): 499–529.

Barnichon, Regis and Christian Matthes. 'Functional approximation of impulse responses.' *Journal of Monetary Economics* 99 (2018): 41–55.

20 Storm, Servaas. 'Collateral Damage From Higher Interest Rates.' *INET*, 5 November 2022, https://www.ineteconomics.org/perspectives/blog/collateral-damage-from-higher-interest-rates.

21 Wearden, Graeme. 'Britons 'Need to Accept' They're Poorer, Says Bank of England Economist.' *Guardian*, 25 April 2023. https://www.theguardian.com/business/2023/apr/25/britons-need-to-accept-theyre-poorer-says-bank-of-england-economist.

22 Gonzalez, Sarah, Greg Rosalsky, Jess Jiang and Sam Yellowhorse Kesler. 'What has been driving inflation? Economists' thinking may have changed,' *NPR Planet Money*, 12 May 2023. https://www.npr.org/2023/05/11/1175487806/corporate-profit-price-spiral-wage-debate.

23 Calmfors, Lars and John Driffill. 'Bargaining structure, corporatism and macroeconomic performance.' *Economic Policy* 3, no. 6 (1988): 13–61.

24 Olivier Blanchard @olivierblanchard, Twitter, 30 December 2022. https://twitter.com/ojblanchard1/status/1608967176232525824. Olivier Blanchard @olivierblanchard, Twitter, 31 December 2022. https://twitter.com/ojblanchard1/status/1609283037568 679938.

25 Monetary Policy Committee 'Monetary Policy Report,' *Bank of England,* May 2023. https://www.bankofengland.co.uk/monetary-policy-report/2023/may-2023.

26 MSE Team. 'Cost of living help guide,' *MoneySavingExpert,* 24 August 2022. https://www.moneysavingexpert.com/family/cost-of-living-survival-kit/.

27 Monetary Policy Committee 'Monetary Policy Report,' *Bank of England,* May 2023. https://www.bankofengland.co.uk/monetary-policy-report/2023/may-2023.

28 Baines, Joseph and Sandy Brian Hager. 'Profiting amid the energy crisis: the distribution networks at the heart of the UK's gas and electricity system.' *Common Wealth*, March 2022.

29 Stiglitz, Joseph E. and Ira Regmi. 'The Causes of and Responses to Today's Inflation.' *Roosevelt Institute*, 6 December 2022.

30 Jump, Rob Calvert, Jo Michell, James Meadway, and Natassia Nascimento. 'The Macroeconomics of Austerity', *Macroeconomics* (2023).

31 Cribb, Jonathan and Laurence O' Brien. 'Recent trends in public sector pay,' *The IFS*, 26 March 2024. https://ifs.org.uk/publications/recent-trends-public-sector-pay.

32 Jones, Russell. *Decade in Tory: An Inventory of Idiocy from the Coalition to Covid.* Unbound, London, 2022, 31, 95, 136, 162.

33 Evans, S. 'Cutting the 'green crap' has added £2.5bn to UK energy bills' *Carbon Brief*, 20 January 2022. https://www.carbonbrief.org/analysis-cutting-the-green-crap-has-added-2-5bn-to-uk-energy-bills/.

34 Savage, Michael. 'Cameron's Decision to Cut "Green Crap"
    Now Costs Each Household in England £150 a Year.'
    Guardian, 19 March 2022. https://www.theguardian.com/
    money/2022/mar/19/david-cameron-green-crap-energy-
    prices.

35 Uxó González, Jorge. 'Inflation and counter-inflationary policy
    measures: The case of Spain.' No. 83-5. IMK Study, 2022.

36 Bolhuis, Marijn A., Judd NL Cramer, Karl Oskar Schulz and
    Lawrence H. Summers. *The Cost of Money is Part of the
    Cost of Living: New Evidence on the Consumer Sentiment
    Anomaly*. No. w32163. National Bureau of Economic
    Research, 2024.

37 Stock, James H. and Mark W. Watson. 'Slack and cyclically
    sensitive inflation.' *Journal of Money, Credit and Banking* 52,
    no. S2 (2020): 393–428.

38 Source: 'ASPUS' and 'FEDFUNDS' on https://fred.stlouisfed.org/.

39 'Bank of England raises interest rates to 4%.' *BBC News*,
    https://www.bbc.co.uk/news/live/business-64457377.

40 Weber, Isabella M., Jesus Lara Jauregui, Lucas Teixeira and
    Luiza Nassif Pires. 'Inflation in times of overlapping
    emergencies: Systemically significant prices from an input–
    output perspective.' *Industrial and Corporate Change* 33, no. 2
    (2024): 297–341.

41 Mason, J. W. and Arjun Jayadev. 'Rethinking supply constraints.'
    Review of Keynesian Economics 11, no. 2 (2023): 232–51.

42 Lynch, David J. 'Falling Inflation, Rising Growth Give U.S. The
    World's Best Recovery.' *Washington Post*, 29 January 2024.
    https://www.washingtonpost.com/business/2024/01/28/
    global-economy-gdp-inflation/.

CHAPTER 8: WHY DID THE GLOBAL ECONOMY BREAK?

1 Quoted in 'Building resilient supply chains, revitalizing American manufacturing, and fostering broad-based growth: 100-day reviews under Executive Order 14017.' *A Report by The White House* (2021).'

2 Friedman, Milton. 'I, Pencil.' 2012. *YouTube*. https://www.youtube.com/watch?v=67tHtpac5ws.

3 Smith, Adam. *Of the Division of Labour. In The Wealth of Nations*. W. Strahan and T. Cadell, London, 1776.

4 Peaucelle, Jean-Louis and Cameron Guthrie. 'How Adam Smith Found Inspiration In French Texts On Pin Making In The Eighteenth Century.' *History of Economic Ideas* 19, no. 3 (2011): 41–67. http://www.jstor.org/stable/23723615.

5 Lynn, Barry C. 'Why Economists Can't See the Economy.' *American Prospect*, 10 March 2020. https://prospect.org/features/economists-see-economy/.

6 Sheffi, Yossi and Barry C. Lynn. 'Systemic supply chain risk.' *The Bridge (Fall)* 22 (2014): 29.

7 Dayen, David. 'Re-Engineering Our Supply Chains.' *American Prospect*, 11 February 2022. https://prospect.org/economy/re-engineering-our-supply chains/.

8 'Building resilient supply chains, revitalizing American manufacturing, and fostering broad-based growth: 100-day reviews under Executive Order 14017.' *A Report by The White House* (2021), 26.

9 *Economist, The*. 'Taiwan's dominance of the chip industry makes it more important,' *The Economist*, 6 March 2023. https://www.economist.com/special-report/2023/03/06/taiwans-dominance-of-the-chip-industry-makes-it-more-important.

10 Studwell, Joe. *How Asia Works: Success and Failure in the World's Most Dynamic Region*. Profile Books, London, 2014.

11 Sheffi, Yossi and Barry C. Lynn. 'Systemic supply chain risk.' *The Bridge (Fall)* 22 (2014): 29.

12 Kuttner, Robert. 'China: Epicenter of the Supply Chain Crisis.' *American Prospect*, 7 February 2022. https://prospect.org/economy/china-epicenter-of-the-supply chain-crisis/.

13 *ibid.*

14 Behnassi, Mohamed and Mahjoub El Haiba. 2022. 'Implications of the Russia–Ukraine War for Global Food Security.' *Nature Human Behaviour* 6 (754–755): 1–2. https://doi.org/10.1038/s41562-022-01391-x.

15 Lynn, Barry C. 'Why Economists Can't See the Economy.' *American Prospect*, 10 March 2020. https://prospect.org/features/economists-see-economy/.

16 *ibid.*

17 Alfaro, Laura and Davin Chor. *Global supply chains: The looming 'great reallocation'*. No. w31661. National Bureau of Economic Research, 2023.

18 Dayen, David. 'Re-Engineering Our Supply Chains.' *American Prospect,* 11 February 2022. https://prospect.org/economy/re-engineering-our-supply chains/.

19 Ting-Fang, Cheng, Lauly Li. 'The Resilience Myth: Fatal Flaws in the Push to Secure Chip Supply Chains.' *Nikkei Asia.* 27 July 2022. https://asia.nikkei.com/Spotlight/The-Big-Story/The-resilience-myth-Fatal-flaws-in-the-push-to-secure-chip-supply chains.

20 Alvarez, Omar. 'Real 'Supply Chain Crisis' Is Shortage of Companies Treating Truck Drivers with Respect.' *USA Today*, 12 January 2022. https://eu.usatoday.com/story/opinion/voices/2022/01/12/blame-truck-driver-shortage-shipping-companies/9080637002/.

21 Meyerson, Harold. 'Why Trucking Can't Deliver the Goods.' *American Prospect*, 14 February 2022. https://prospect.org/economy/why-trucking-cant-deliver-the-goods/.

22 Wiungrove, Josh, Jill R Shah and Brendan Case. 'Biden Races Clock and Holds Few Tools in Supply-Chain Crisis,' *Bloomberg,* 21 October 2021. https://www.bloomberg.com/news/articles/2021-10-21/biden-tackles-supply-chain-crisis-with-few-tools-clock-ticking?srnd=premium&sref=vuYGislZ.

23 Alvarez, Omar. 'Real 'Supply Chain Crisis' Is Shortage of
    Companies Treating Truck Drivers with Respect.' *USA Today*,
    12 January 2022. https://eu.usatoday.com/story/opinion/
    voices/2022/01/12/blame-truck-driver-shortage-shipping-
    companies/9080637002/.

24 Meyerson, Harold. 'Why Trucking Can't Deliver the Goods.'
    American Prospect, 14 February 2022. https://prospect.org/
    economy/why-trucking-cant-deliver-the-goods/.

25 *ibid*.

26 *ibid*.

27 Woody, Katherine. 'Brazil: Economic Impact of the Brazilian
    Trucker Strike.' *USDA Foreign Agricultural Service*, 6 July
    2018. https://www.fas.usda.gov/data/brazil-economic-impact-
    brazilian-trucker-strike.

28 'State of Indian Trucking Industry: From Bad to Worse?'
    Logistics Insider, 16 May 2020. https://www.logisticsinsider.in/
    indian-trucking-industry-from-bad-to-worse/.

29 Alloway, Tracey and Joe Weisenthal. 'Transcript: Craig Fuller
    on Why the Trucking Industry Is Such a Mess Right Now.'
    Bloomberg: Odd Lots, 22 June 2021. https://www.bloomberg.
    com/news/articles/2021-06-22/transcript-craig-fuller-on-why-
    the-trucking-industry-is-such-a-mess-right-now?embedded-
    checkout=true.

30 Russon, Mary-Ann. 'The Cost of the Suez Canal Blockage.'
    BBC News, 29 March 2021. https://www.bbc.co.uk/news/
    business-56559073.

31 'Container Ship Crashes in Suez Canal.' *Telegraph*, 6 December
    2023. https://www.telegraph.co.uk/business/2023/12/06/
    ftse-100-markets-latest-news-boe-sustainability-report-live/.

32 Dyane, David. 'The Inflation-Fighting Bill You Don't Know
    About.' *American Prospect*, 13 December 2021. https://
    prospect.org/economy/inflation-fighting-bill-you-dont-
    know-about/.

33 Stoller, Matt. 'Too Big to Sail: How a Legal Revolution Clogged
    Our Ports.' *The Big Newsletter*. Accessed 4 October 2023.

https://www.thebignewsletter.com/p/too-big-to-sail-how-a-legal-revolution.

34   Kay, Grace. 'The Supply chain Crisis Propelled the World's Largest Shipping Company to Its Most Profitable Quarter in 117 Years.' *Business Insider*, 2 November 2021. https://www.businessinsider.com/largest-shipping-company-maersk-most-profitable-quarter-supply chain-crisis-2021-11?op=1&r=US&IR=T.

35   Merk, Olaf, Jan Hoffmann, and Hercules Haralambides. 'Post-Covid-19 Scenarios for the Governance of Maritime Transport and Ports.' *Maritime Economics & Logistics*, March. https://doi.org/10.1057/s41278-022-00228-8.

36   Tankus, Nathan. '[PREMIUM TRANSCRIPT] Notes on the Crises Podcast #1: Joe Weisenthal on Supply Chains.' *Notes on the Crises*, 29 November 2021. https://www.crisesnotes.com/premium-transcript-notes-on-the-crises-podcast-1-joe-weisenthal-on-supply-chains/.

37   *ibid*.

38   Federal Maritime Commission. 'US container port congestion and related international supply chain issues: Cases, consequences and challenges.' (2015).

39   Lind, Mikael, Wolfgang Lechmacher, Jan Hoffmann et al 'Synchronisation across Maritime Value Chains Can Ease Inflation.' *Port Economics*, 20 March 2022. https://www.porteconomics.eu/synchronisation-across-maritime-value-chains-can-ease-inflation/.

40   Galer, Susan. 'SAP Brand Voice: How to De-Risk Supply Chains in an Unpredictable World.' *Forbes*. 23 May 2023. https://www.forbes.com/sites/sap/2023/05/23/how-to-de-risk-supply-chains-in-an-unpredictable-world/?sh=e79d4e152d5b.

41   'About Us.' *FlexPort*, accessed 8 April 2024, https://www.flexport.com/company/about-us/.

42   Alloway, Tracey and Joe Weisenthal. 'Transcript: Ryan Petersen on How Global Supply Chains Have Gotten Even Worse.' *Bloomberg: Odd Lots*, 14 Oct 2021. https://www.bloomberg.

com/news/articles/2021-10-14/transcript-ryan-petersen-on-how-global-supply-chains-have-gotten-even-worse.

43 Kuttner, Robert. 'Flying Blind.' *American Prospect*, 21 December 2021. https://prospect.org/economy/flying-blind-fragmentation-information-global-supply-chain/.

44 Chua, Charmaine. 'Docking: Maritime ports in the making of the global economy.' In *The Routledge Handbook of Ocean Space*. Routledge, 2022, 126–37.

45 Sammon, Alexander. 'We Were Warned about the Ports.' *American Prospect*. 3 February 2022. https://prospect.org/economy/we-were-warned-about-the-ports/.

46 'Building resilient supply chains, revitalizing American manufacturing, and fostering broad-based growth: 100-day reviews under Executive Order 14017.' *A Report by The White House* (2021), 11.

47 *ibid*, 7.

48 Julien, Garphil and Garphil Julien. 'To Fix the Supply Chain Mess, Take on Wall Street.' *Washington Monthly*, 18 January 2022. https://washingtonmonthly.com/2022/01/17/to-fix-the-supply-chain-mess-take-on-wall-street/.

49 Davies, Christian, Song Jung-A, Kathrin Hille and Qianer Liu. 'The race between Intel, Samsung, and TSMC to ship the first 2 nm chip', *Ars Technica*, 11 December 2023, https://arstechnica.com/gadgets/2023/12/the-race-between-intel-samsung-and-tsmc-to-ship-the-first-2nm-chip/.

50 Studwell, Joe. *How Asia Works: Success and Failure in the World's Most Dynamic Region*. Profile Books, London, 2014.

51 'Building resilient supply chains, revitalizing American manufacturing, and fostering broad-based growth: 100-day reviews under Executive Order 14017.' *A Report by The White House* (2021), 11.

52 'Maersk Receives Subpoena in DOJ Anti-trust Investigation of Carriers.' *The Maritime Executive*. 16 March 2022. https://maritime-executive.com/article/maersk-receives-subpoena-in-doj-anti-trust-investigation-of-carriers.

53   Curtis, Laura. 'The Backbone of Global Trade Faces Anti-trust
     Questions in US Congress.' *Bloomberg,* 28 March 2023.
     https://www.bloomberg.com/news/newsletters/2023-03-28/
     supply-chain-latest-container-lines-and-us-anti-trust-
     exemption?embedded-checkout=true.
     'European Commission makes dramatic change in anti-trust
     rules for container shipping.' *MDS Transmodal,* 12 October
     2023. https://www.mdst.co.uk/european-commission-makes-
     dramatic-change-in-anti-trust-rules-for-container-shipping.
54   Ghosh, Jayati. 'The Myth of Global Grain Shortages.' *Project
     Syndicate*, August 2023. https://www.project-syndicate.org/
     commentary/there-is-no-global-grain-shortage-by-jayati-
     ghosh-2023-08.
55   Bailey, Andrew. 'Supply matters – speech by Andrew Bailey,'
     Bank of England, 27 March 2023. https://www.bankofengland.
     co.uk/speech/2023/march/andrew-bailey-speech-at-london-
     school-of-economics.

CONCLUSION: THE POLITICS OF ECONOMICS

1   Bisset, Victoria and Ellen Francis. 'CEO calls for more
    unemployment to give companies upper hand over workers.'
    The Washington Post, 13 September 2023. https://www.
    washingtonpost.com/world/2023/09/13/
    tim-gurner-unemployment/
2   Qiu, Linda and Daniel Victor. 'Fact-Checking a Mogul's
    Claims about Avocado Toast, Millennials and Home Buying.'
    New York Times, 16 May 2017. https://www.nytimes.
    com/2017/05/15/business/avocado-toast-millennials.html.
3   Kalecki, Michal. 'Political aspects of full employment.' In *The
    Political Economy: Readings in the Politics and Economics of
    American Public Policy*. Routledge, 2021, 27–31.

4   Wood, Ellen Meiksins. *Democracy against capitalism; Renewing historical materialism.* Verso, 2007, 181–203.

5   Turnbull, Tiffanie, and Natalie Sherman. 'Tim Gurner apologises over call for more unemployment to fix worker attitudes.' BBC News, 14 September 2023. https://www.bbc.co.uk/news/business-66803279.

6   *ibid*, 189.

7   *ibid*, 204–37.

8   Tankus, Nathan and Luke Herrine. 'Competition Law as Collective Bargaining Law.' In *Cambridge Handbook of Labou in Competition Law,* Cambridge University Press, 2022.

9   Chang, Ha-Joon. *Economics: the user's guide.* Bloomsbury Publishing USA, 2015, 185.

10 Logue, John and Jacquelyn Yates. 'Productivity in cooperatives and worker-owned enterprises: Ownership and participation make a difference!' Geneva: International Labour Office, 2005.

11 Moran, Cahal. 'Worker Democracy | Unlearning Economics', December 2024 https://www.youtube.com/watch?v=yZHYiz60R5Q.

12 Blasi, Joseph, Richard Freeman and Douglas Kruse. 'Do broad-based employee ownership, profit sharing and stock options help the best firms do even better?' *British Journal of Industrial Relations* 54, no. 1 (2016): 55–82.

13 Tankus, Nathan and Luke Herrine. 'Competition Law as Collective Bargaining Law.' In *Cambridge Handbook of Labou in Competition Law,* Cambridge University Press, 2022.

14 *ibid.*

15 Haldane, Andrew G. 'Climbing the public engagement ladder.' Speech at the Royal Society, 2018.

16 Dutt, Devika, Carolina Alves, Surbhi Kesar, Ingrid Harvold Kvangraven. *Decolonizing Economics: An Introduction.* Polity Press, London, 2024.

ACKNOWLEDGEMENTS

There are many people who have supported me over the course of writing this book, as well as in the years beforehand when the idea was building up. Writing a book full-time is not an easy or profitable task, and during writing I often wondered if I should title this book *Why I'm Getting Poorer*. I therefore needed intellectual, moral and financial support throughout. Thank you to Carolina Alves for providing all three of these. Thank you to my various families for moral and financial support, especially Richard, Rachel, Sim, Rich, Dee, Tracey, Graeme and Judith. Thank you to my friends Frank, Sam, Emily, Beth, Naomi, Hobbie, Niall, Tristan, Lydia, Rosie, Henry, Chris, Alex, Kane, Emma and Josie for being there when I needed them. I have even more friends than that, but I won't list them all.

Thank you to Danielle Guizzo, Joeri Schasfoort, Tom Gander, Amy Loyst, David Dungworth, Aric Wright, Sam Kane, Charlie Silva, William Brown and Alexander Bray for giving me feedback on my ideas and drafts. Naturally, any remaining mistakes are entirely their fault. Thank you to Amberley, Jamie, Shoaib, Jo, Tom and Charlie for editing and for helping with the whole process.

Thank you, too, to absent yet inspirational friends. To Nikky, who would have loved the pedantry and corrective nature of this book. To James, who would have loved the downbeat tone. And to Missy, who probably just would have eaten the book.

Finally, thank you to my enemies. You are not infrequently the only thing that gives me the energy to keep going.

LIST OF ILLUSTRATIONS

P. 168: Redrawn from Lakner, Christoph, and Branko Milanovic, 'Global income distribution: From the fall of the Berlin Wall to the Great Recession', World Bank policy research working paper 6719 (2013), p.30/Figure 1.

P. 170: Redrawn from Lakner, Christoph, and Branko Milanovic, 'Global income distribution: From the fall of the Berlin Wall to the Great Recession', World Bank policy research working paper 6719 (2013), p.30/Figure 1.

p. 214: Apartment building, Kowloon, Hans Georg Roth, Getty Images.

p. 224: King Charles III bank note. https://www.flickr.com/photos/bankofengland/52573683419/in/album-72157662787666013.

p. 253: Cadbury Freddo bar, Carolyn Jenkins / Alamy Stock Photo.

p. 300: Indian trucks, Prisma by Dukas Presseagentur GmbH / Alamy Stock Photo.

INDEX